ELEMENTARY

HISTORY OF ENGLAND,

BY

THOMAS KEIGHTLEY,

AUTHOR OF MYTHOLOGY OF GREECE AND ITALY,
HISTORY OF GREECE, HISTORY OF ROME, HISTORY OF THE ROMAN
EMPIRE, ETC. ETC.

LONDON:
LONGMAN, ORME, BROWN, GREEN, AND LONGMANS,
PATERNOSTER-ROW.

DUBLIN: MILLIKEN AND SON; AND J. CUMMING.

1841.

PREFACE.

I HAVE written the HISTORY OF ENGLAND in three volumes in octavo, from original authorities. Conciseness, accuracy, and impartiality are the qualities by which I have sought to distinguish it. It is designed for those who, though anxious to be acquainted with the history of their country, have not at their disposal the time required for reading and digesting voluminous works. Such are most private families, men engaged in business or in public employments, officers of the army and navy, and others whom I need not enumerate. The only complete history is that of Hume and his continuators, which usually forms about twenty volumes; and independently of Hume's inaccuracies and prejudices, I am inclined to think that the person who has carefully read and digested my *concise* History, will really know more of the history of England than he who has waded through those twenty volumes.

There is also an edition of my History in two volumes, in duodecimo, for the use of schools. Though the narrative is in the main the same in both, the former, beside its great superiority in form and appearance, contains much which will be vainly sought for in the latter. Such are the copious appendixes, in which there is much curious matter, the more full and complete views of the progress of the constitution and state of manners, numerous notes, and many parts of the narrative itself.

PREFACE.

I term the present an Elementary history, and not an abridgement, as it is only a selection of such parts of the history of England as I think likely to prove interesting and intelligible to children. I have been induced to compile it in consequence of the complaints made to me by persons engaged in education, of the dryness, want of interest, and in some cases the too great length of the ordinary abridgements. This, with the similar Histories of Greece and Rome, which will be shortly published, and my small Mythology, will, I think, form a sufficient course of reading till the pupils are old enough to commence my regular histories.

Minute accuracy will, of course, not be required in a work of this kind. I have also given very few dates in the text, for I doubt if children should be teased with chronology. I have, however, at the end, given a chronological table for the use of those who may think differently. In proper names, whose accentuation might be doubtful, the accent is marked when they first occur. The style will, I hope, be found to be simple and clear; but I have not scrupled to use such terms as will be met with in almost every book the pupils will read.

The use of these elementary works will, I expect, lessen the labour in reading my histories; and young students will probably experience pleasure in perusing in detail what they had learned only in outline, and in becoming acquainted with the causes and consequences of events which they had read merely as stories. T. K.

London, January 1, 1841.

CONTENTS.

ANGLO-SAXON PERIOD.

CHAPTER I.
BRITAIN UNDER THE ROMANS.

The Ancient Britons.—Invasions of the Romans.—Carácatacus.—Conquest of the Isle of Mona.—Boadicea.—Agricola.—State of Roman Britain. 1

CHAPTER II.
ANGLO-SAXON KINGDOMS.

Hengist and Horsa.—Kingdoms founded by the Invaders.—Conversion of the Anglo-Saxons.—Offa of Mercia.—Edburga. . . 5

CHAPTER III.
ANGLO-SAXON KINGS.

The Danes.—Alfred the Great.—Athelstan.—Edmund the Magnificent.—St. Dunstan.—Elgiva.—Edgar the Peaceful.—Elfrida.—Edward the Martyr.—Ethelred the Unready.—Edmund Ironside. 11

CHAPTER IV.
DANISH KINGS, AND SAXON LINE RESTORED.

Canute and his Sons.—Edward the Confessor.—Godwin.—Harold.—Battle of Hastings. 21

ANGLO-NORMAN PERIOD.

CHAPTER I.
WILLIAM I. (THE CONQUEROR).

Conquest of England.—Hereward.—Fate of the English Nobles.—William and his Sons.—Death of William.—The Feudal System. 29

CHAPTER II.
WILLIAM II. (RUFUS).

Attack on Prince Henry.—The Crusade.—Death of William. . 35

CHAPTER III.
HENRY I. (BEAUCLERC).

Fate of Duke Robert.—Death of Prince William.—Death of the King. 37

CONTENTS.

CHAPTER IV.
STEPHEN (OF BLOIS)

Civil War between Stephen and Matilda. 39

HOUSE OF PLANTAGENET.

CHAPTER I.
HENRY II. (PLANTAGENET).

Power of Henry.—Thomas à Becket.—Becket made Archbishop.—Quarrel between the King and Becket.—Murder of Becket.—Canonization of Becket.—Conquest of Ireland.—Henry and his Sons.—Fair Rosamond. 41

CHAPTER II.
RICHARD I. (CŒUR DE LION).

King Richard's Crusade.—Imprisonment of Richard.—Death of King Richard. 49

CHAPTER III.
JOHN (LACKLAND).

Fate of Prince Arthur.—John's Contest with the Pope.—Magna Charta.—War with the Barons. 52

CHAPTER IV.
HENRY III. (OF WINCHESTER).

Character of Henry.—Confirmation of the Great Charter.—Barons' War.—Origin of House of Commons.—Prince Edward's Escape.—Defeat and Death of Leicester.—Prince Edward's Crusade. 57

CHAPTER V.
EDWARD I. (LONGSHANKS).

Conquest of Wales.—Conquest of Scotland.—William Wallace.—Robert Bruce. 60

CHAPTER VI.
EDWARD II. (OF CARNARVON).

Piers Gaveston.—Battle of Bannockburn.—Hugh Spenser.—Deposition and Death of Edward. 66

CHAPTER VII.
EDWARD III. (OF WINDSOR).

Fall of Mortimer.—Edward's Claim of the Crown of France.—Battle of Cressy.—Siege of Calais.—Battle of Poitiers.—Last Days of the Black Prince and of the King. 69

CHAPTER VIII.
RICHARD II. (OF BORDEAUX).

Rising of the Peasantry.—Limitation of the King's Authority.—Murder of Gloucester.—Quarrel between Norfolk and Hereford.—Lancaster in arms against the King.—Capture of the King.—Death of King Richard. 78

CHAPTER IX.
HENRY IV. (OF BOLINGBROKE).

Rebellion of Northumberland.—Stories of the Prince of Wales.—Death of the King. 85

CHAPTER X.
HENRY V. (OF MONMOUTH).

Renewal of the Claim to the Crown of France.—Battle of Agincourt.—Final Success of Henry. 88

CHAPTER XI.
HENRY VI. (OF WINDSOR).

Siege of Orleans.—The Maid of Orleans.—Deaths of Gloucester and Suffolk.—Jack Cade.—Duke of York's Claim of the Crown.—War of the Roses.—Battle of Wakefield.—Duke of York made King. 92

CHAPTER XII.
EDWARD IV.

Battle of Towton.—Adventures of Queen Margaret.—Marriage of King Edward.—Quarrel between the King and Warwick.—Flight and Return of Edward.—Battle of Barnet.—Battle of Tewkesbury.—Fate of Clarence. 100

CHAPTER XIII.
EDWARD V.—RICHARD III.

Seizure of the King's Relations.—Death of Lord Hastings.—The young Duke of York.—Jane Shore.—Gloucester's Usurpation of the Crown.—Murder of the Princes.—Fate of Buckingham.—Battle of Bosworth. 106

HOUSE OF TUDOR.

CHAPTER I.
HENRY VII.

Title of Henry.—Lambert Simnel.—Perkin Warbeck.—Fate of Warwick.—Prince Arthur.—Henry's Avarice. 113

CHAPTER II.
HENRY VIII.

Commencement of Henry's Reign.—Battle of Spurs.—Battle of Flodden-Field.—Marriage of Henry's Sister.—Cardinal Wolsey.—Field of the Cloth of Gold.—The Reformation.—Origin of Henry's Divorce.—Anne Boleyn.—Proceedings in the Divorce.—Fall of Wolsey.—Henry's Divorce and Breach with Rome.—Execution of Bishop Fisher and Sir Thomas More.—Fall of Anne Boleyn.—Execution of Anne Boleyn.—Suppression of Monasteries.—Anne of Cleves.—Fall of Cromwell.—Catherine Howard.—Attempt to ruin Cranmer.—Attack on the Queen.—Last Days of Henry. . . 119

CHAPTER III.
EDWARD VI.

Fate of Lord Seymour.—Fall of Somerset.—Last Days of King Edward. 139

CHAPTER IV.
MARY.

Lady Jane Grey.—Execution of Lady Jane Grey.—Danger of Elizabeth.—The Queen's Marriage.—Change of Religion.—Burning of Rogers and Hooper.—Burning of Ridley and Latimer.—Death of Cranmer.—Last Days of the Queen. 142

CHAPTER V.
ELIZABETH.

Accession of Elizabeth.—First Years of Elizabeth.—The Queen of Scots.—Return of Mary to Scotland.—First Years of Mary's Reign.—Lord Darnley.—Murder of Rizzio.—Bothwell.—Murder of Darnley.—Marriage of Mary and Bothwell.—Deposition of Mary.—Flight of Mary into England.—Detention of Queen Mary.—Fate of the Duke of Norfolk.—Massacre of St. Bartholomew.—Revolt of the Dutch.—Sir Philip Sidney.—Babington's Conspiracy.—Trial of the Queen of Scots.—Execution of the Queen of Scots.—Sir Francis Drake.—The Spanish Armada.—Taking of Cadiz.—The Earl of Essex.—Essex in Ireland.—Fall of Essex.—Death of Elizabeth. 152

HOUSE OF STUART.—PART I.

CHAPTER I.
JAMES I.

The Gunpowder Plot.—The Favourites.—Somerset.—Buckingham.—Fate of Sir Walter Raleigh.—The Prince's Expedition to Spain.—Breaking off the Match with Spain.—Anecdote of King James. 183

CONTENTS. xi

CHAPTER II.
CHARLES I.

Charles' First Parliament.—Buckingham's Insolence.—War with France.—Murder of Buckingham.—Despotism of Charles.—Ship-Money.—Affairs of Scotland.—The Short Parliament.—The Long Parliament.—Strafford.—Trial of Strafford.—Execution of Strafford.—The Irish Rebellion.—The Five Members.—Commencement of the Civil War.—Battle of Edgehill.—Progress of the War.—Death of Hampden.—Siege of Gloucester.—Battle of Newbury.—Battle of Marston-Moor.—Second Battle of Newbury.—Trial and Execution of Laud.—The New Model.—Battle of Naseby.—End of the War.—Charles and the Scots.—Seizure of the King by the Army.—The King with the Army.—The King's Flight.—Second Civil War.—Pride's Purge.—Seizure of the King. —Trial of the King.—Execution of the King. 194

CHAPTER III.
THE COMMONWEALTH.

Abolition of the Monarchy.—The Marquess of Montrose.—Charles in Scotland.—Battle of Dunbar.—The Start.—Battle of Worcester.—Escape of Charles.—Parliament dissolved by Cromwell. 238

CHAPTER IV.
THE PROTECTORATE.

Barebone's Parliament.—Cromwell made Protector.—Pomp of Cromwell.—Cromwell's vigorous Government.—Capture of Jamaica. —Victories and Death of Blake.—Last Days of Cromwell . . . 248

CHAPTER V.
THE COMMONWEALTH RESTORED.

Cromwell's Funeral.—General Monk.—Restoration of the King. 256

CHAPTER VI.
CHARLES II.

Execution of the Regicides.—Trial and Execution of Sir Henry Vane.—Conduct of the King.—First Dutch War.—The Great Plague. —Fire of London.—Attack on Sir John Coventry.—Attempt on the Duke of Ormond.—Blood's attempt to steal the Regalia.—Second Dutch War.—The Prince of Orange.—The Popish Plot.—Sir Edmundbury Godfrey.—William Bedloe.—Executions on account of the Plot.—The Meal-tub Plot.—The Rye-house Plot.—Trial of Lord Russell.—Last Days of Lord Russell.—Death of Lord Essex. —Trial and Execution of Sidney.—Illness and Death of the King. 260

CHAPTER VII.
JAMES II.

Religion of King James.—Monmouth's Invasion.—Execution of Monmouth.—Jeffreys' Campaign.—Efforts of James in favour of

Popery.—Trial of the Bishops.—Landing of the Prince of Orange.
—Flight of James. 281

HOUSE OF STUART.—PART II.

CHAPTER I.

WILLIAM III. AND MARY II.

Battle of Killicrankie.—Siege of Derry.—James' Parliament.—
Battle of the Boyne.—Siege of Athlone, and Battle of Aghrim.—
Massacre of Glenco.—Battle of La Hogue.—Last Days of King
William. 295

CHAPTER II.

ANNE.

The Duke of Marlborough.—Victories of Marlborough.—War in
Spain.—Admiral Benbow.—Dr. Sacheverell.—Change of Ministry.
—Death of the Queen.—Union with Scotland. 303

HOUSE OF BRUNSWICK.

CHAPTER I.

GEORGE I.

Accession of George I.—Mar's Rebellion.—The Quadruple
Alliance. 311

CHAPTER II.

GEORGE II.

King's Accession.—War with Spain.—Admiral Vernon.—Anson's Voyage.—Battle of Dettingen.—Battle of Fontenoy.—Scottish Rebellion.—Admiral Byng.—Hostilities in America.—Taking
of Quebec.—Successes of Clive.—Taking of Calcutta.—The Black
Hole.—Victories of Clive. 314

CHAPTER III.

GEORGE III.

Termination of the War.—Voyages of Discovery.—American
War.—Victories of Rodney.—Major André.—Siege of Gibraltar.—
The French War.—Naval Victories.—Mutiny of the Fleet.—The
Irish Rebellion.—French in Egypt.—Battle of the Nile.—Battle
of the Baltic.—Battle of Trafalgar.—Peninsular War.—Victories
of Wellington.—Conclusion. 327

AN ELEMENTARY HISTORY OF ENGLAND.

ANGLO-SAXON PERIOD.

CHAPTER I.

BRITAIN UNDER THE ROMANS.

The Ancient Britons.

WHEN the Romans about nineteen hundred years ago first became acquainted with the island of Britain, it was in a condition widely different from that which it exhibits at the present day. The country was covered with forests and marshes; the people dwelt in wicker cabins; what were called their towns were mere inclosures in the woods; they lived on the flesh and milk of their cattle, (for they had hardly any agriculture,) and clad themselves with their skins: the only vessel with which they navigated their seas and rivers was the *coracle*, or boat of framework covered with hides. In war they used chariots drawn by two horses, from which they fought, like the heroes of Homer; and to appear the more terrible to their enemies they painted their bodies of various colours, like the North-American Indians.

The religion of the Britons was of a gloomy sanguinary character. The altars of their gods were frequently smeared with the blood of human victims slain in their honour.

Their priests, named Druids, enjoyed great power and consideration, being free from all taxes and other burdens, and not required to serve in war. They are said to have possessed a good deal of knowledge in natural science; but they confined it to their own order, and kept the people in general in the grossest ignorance. One of their principal religious doctrines was that of the transmigration of souls, or their passage at death from one body into another.

Invasions of the Romans.—Caráctacus.

The first Roman general who invaded Britain was the celebrated Julius Cæsar. He landed twice in the island; the first time he did little more than debark his troops near Deal, in Kent, and drive off the natives who came to oppose his landing; but the second time he advanced into the country, passed the Thames near Hampton-Court, took the chief town of a prince named Cassivelaunus, to whom the Britons had given the command of their army, and made them promise to pay tribute to the Romans. But when Cæsar was gone, the Britons never thought more of their promise.

Nearly a century elapsed before the Romans renewed their efforts for the conquest of Britain. A general named Plautius then invaded it by command of the emperor Claudius, and conquered the country south of the Thames. Another general, named Ostorius, carried his army beyond the Severn. He was valiantly opposed by Caráctacus, the prince of the Silurians, as the people of a part of South Wales were called; but Ostorius at length defeated him in a great battle, and took the whole of his family captive. Caractacus himself fled, and sought refuge with Cartismándua, queen of the Brigantians, or people of Yorkshire; but the unworthy queen basely surrendered him to the Romans, and he and his whole family were led to Rome in bonds. As the fame of Caractacus had been widely spread on account of his gallant resistance to the Roman arms, the emperor caused all the troops at Rome to be drawn out, and all the people to be assembled to witness the ceremony of his reception of the illustrious captive. Caractacus, undismayed by the display of pomp and power, addressed the emperor in dignified and manly terms, and Claudius had the magnanimity to grant life and liberty to himself and his family.

Conquest of the Isle of Mona.

The Romans were now the masters of a great part of the island, but still the unsubdued portion of the natives, especially those who possessed the mountains of Wales, gave them a great deal of trouble. As the island of Mona, or Anglesea, which was the chief seat of the Druids, seemed to be the great point of union to the Britons, and the place where their plans of resistance were concerted, Suetonius Paulínus, the Roman commander in Britain, resolved to invade and conquer it. He therefore led his army to the Ménai, or strait which divides it from the main land. As the soldiers looked across they beheld the opposite shore covered with armed Britons, among whom were running to and fro women, who, with streaming hair and wild and frantic gestures, and brandishing flaming torches, excited them to courage, while the venerable Druids, standing apart, with uplifted hands, were uttering imprecations on the godless invaders of their sacred isle. The superstitious feelings of the Romans were excited, and they hesitated to advance; but they soon yielded their wonted obedience to the voice of their leader, and planted their standards on the hallowed isle. The resistance of the Britons was brief and feeble ; the Romans became masters of the island, where they raised a fort, and they cut down the groves which so often had witnessed the human sacrifices of the Druids.

Boadicea.

While Suetonius was thus occupied he received alarming intelligence from the Roman part of the island. The king of the Icenians had lately died, and the Roman officers had taken possession of his kingdom, where they acted with the greatest insolence and cruelty. The persons of the princesses, his daughters, were violated; their mother Boadicea was actually beaten and scourged, and the nobles were robbed of their property and reduced to slavery. The Brigantians flew to arms; they were joined by the southern tribes; the Roman colony of Maldon was destroyed; the same was the fate of St. Alban's, and of the even then great and wealthy city of London; and not less, it is said, than seventy thousand persons were slaughtered by the enraged Britons. At length Suetonius, who had returned from Mona, gave battle to the British confederates in a position where his army was secured by hills on the left and right, and by a wood in the rear. Boadicea, carrying her insulted daughters in her chariot, drove along the British line, calling on the warriors to avenge their injuries. The Britons displayed in the battle their wonted courage; but courage is of little avail against skill and discipline, and they were defeated with a loss of eighty thousand men. Boadicea, to escape captivity and insult, terminated her life by poison. The Romans spread their ravages all through the island, and the unhappy natives endured the greatest miseries.

Agricola.— State of Roman Britain.

The northern parts of the island had been as yet unmolested by the Romans; but at length a general, named Agricola, crossed the Tweed, and subdued the country as far as the modern cities of Edinburgh and Glasgow. To secure his conquests from the Caledonians, as the people of Scotland were named, he built a line of forts from the frith of Forth to the frith of Clyde, and when the Caledonians made an attack on this line, he invaded their own wild country in return. At the foot of the Grampian hills a Caledonian army of thirty thousand men, commanded by a chief named Gálgacus, gave him battle. But as usual victory was on the side of the Romans, and when night came on, ten thousand of the brave Caledonian warriors lay dead on the plain. After this great victory Agricola met with no opposition; but he did not seek to retain any of the country north of the friths. His fleet, however, sailed round the whole island, visiting the Orkney and other isles, and exhibiting the Roman power to their rude inhabitants.

The whole of Britain south of the friths now obeyed the Roman emperors. The Roman language and manners were gradually diffused among the Britons, and numerous towns and cities were founded. The Christian religion, by the zeal of pious missionaries, was spread over the island, and it produced its usual good fruits of piety and holiness. Britain was in general tranquil, but it suffered like most of the other parts of the empire from the incursions of the barbarians. Its enemies were the Scots and Picts (as the people of Caledonia were now called), and the Saxons and other tribes of German freebooters who occasionally landed and ravaged its coasts.

CHAPTER II.

ANGLO-SAXON KINGDOMS.

Hengist and Horsa.

THE Roman dominion in Britain had lasted nearly four centuries, when the difficulties of the Empire, assailed on all sides by the barbarians, became so great that it was found necessary to withdraw the troops from the more distant parts to employ them in the defence of France and Italy. The Roman legions therefore quitted Britain never to return; and the Britons had only their own valour to depend on for their protection against the Saxon pirates and the savage clans of the north. It might have been expected that they would heartily unite for the common defence; but on the contrary the Romans were hardly gone when they fell into dissensions among themselves; and the Scots and Picts, taking advantage of their mutual enmities, ravaged the island in a fearful manner. A British prince named Vórtigern at length adopted the desperate expedient of committing the defence of the country against them to a body of the Saxon freebooters, and he formed a contract with two of their leaders, named Hengist and Horsa, agreeing to give them in return for their services the fertile Isle of Thanet, at the mouth of the Thames.

Hengist and Horsa were speedily joined by great numbers of their countrymen. In compliance with their engagement they turned their arms against the Scots and Picts, and soon relieved the Britons from apprehension on that side: but they at the same time viewed their fruitful plains and valleys and their wealthy towns with a covetous eye; they soon, therefore, contrived to pick a quarrel with them, and the contest terminated in their remaining masters of all Kent, which Hengist and his son Æsk (for Horsa had fallen in battle) formed into a kingdom.

The British historians relate that Hengist had a beautiful daughter, named Rowéna, whom he employed as the means of obtaining influence over the mind of Vortigern. At a banquet which he gave to the British prince, the fair Rowena advanced, bearing a golden goblet filled with wine, and presented it to Vortigern. The monarch, struck with her extreme beauty, became suddenly enamoured. He proffered love; his suit was successful, and she became his queen. But the advantages which Hengist counted on did not result; for the Britons deposed Vortigern and gave the throne to his son Vórtimer. It is also said that after the first war between the Saxons and Britons a banquet was held, for the ratification of the peace, at the ancient monument of Stonehenge on Salisbury plain. Hengist made his companions conceal their *seaxes*, or short swords, beneath their garments, and on his giving the appointed signal they drew them and slew three hundred of the British nobles, and made Vortigern a prisoner.

Kingdoms founded by the Invaders.

Though we call Hengist and his people Saxons, they were, properly speaking, Jutes from the peninsula of Jutland. Their neighbours and confederate tribes in Germany were the Saxons and Angles, who soon hastened to follow their example and make conquests in Britain. A Saxon chief named Ella conquered the country west of Kent, and the kingdom which he founded there was named Sussex, or South Saxony. Another Saxon chief, named Cerdic, landed to the west of Sussex and formed the kingdom of Wessex, or West Saxony. Other Saxons formed the kingdoms of Essex, or East Saxony, and of Middlesex, or Middle Saxony. The Angles followed and settled more to the north: their first kingdom was East Anglia, comprising the South-folk or Suffolk, and the North-folk or Norfolk; they also established themselves north of the Humber. Their possessions there were called by the general name of Northumbria, or North-Humber-land, but they formed two separate kingdoms, called Déira and Bernícia, divided by the river Tyne. The present midland counties of England were called Mercia, that is, the *march-* or border-land, as lying next to the territories of the independent Britons. It was chiefly settled by the Angles. As the Angles and Saxons were much more numerous than the Jutes, the people in general were named Anglo-Saxons, which name may also signify the Saxons of England as distinguished from those of Germany.

As for the unfortunate Britons, they gradually lost the whole of the plain country; and all that remained to them was Cornwall, Wales, and the coast thence northward to the river Clyde, named Cumbria.

Conversion of the Anglo-Saxons.

The Anglo-Saxons, as the conquerors of Britain are

usually named, were heathens at the time when they invaded it, and more than a century elapsed before the Christian faith was preached to them. The following was the occasion of their conversion. The Christian religion had not as yet succeeded in abolishing the odious custom of slavery; and as a pious ecclesiastic named Gregory was one day passing through the slave-market at Rome, his attention was caught by some boys with fair long hair and blooming complexions who were offered for sale. He asked the slave-dealer what was their country? Being told that they were Angles from Britain, he said in Latin, the language then spoken at Rome, "With reason are they so called, for they are fair as *angels*, and would that they might be cherubim in heaven! But from what province of Britain are they?" "From Deïra." "Deïra," said he, "that is good; they must be delivered from the wrath (*de ira*) of God. But what is the name of their king?" "Ella." "Ella! then Allelujah should be sung in his dominions." He forthwith resolved to go to Britain as a missionary, and he obtained the pope's permission; but the people of Rome valued him too highly to permit his departure.

Some years after Gregory himself became pope, and he then resolved to put his project for the conversion of the Anglo-Saxons into execution. He selected a monk, named Augustine, and sent him with forty companions to Britain. Augustine landed in the Isle of Thanet, and he sent to Éthelbert king of Kent, who was married to a Christian princess, to solicit an interview. The king granted his request; but fearful of magic arts of the strangers, against which his priests cautioned him, he required that the meeting should take place in the open air. The missionaries advanced, chanting litanies, and bearing aloft a silver cross and a banner wrought with the image of Christ. They addressed the king, and explained to him the articles of their faith: Ethelbert gave them permission to preach to his subjects, and assured them of his protection. They proceeded with their pious work, and in a short time the king and all his court were among the converts, and so eagerly did the people follow the example of their sovereign that no less than ten thousand persons were baptized on one Christmas. Ethelbert gave up his own palace to the missionaries, and the present cathedral of Canterbury stands, it is said, on the site of the church which they built.

Christianity spread rapidly among the Anglo-Saxons. Its mode of introduction into Northumbria was curious and interesting. Edwin, king of that country, was married to a daughter of Ethelbert of Kent, and he permitted a missionary named Paulínus to preach in his dominions. The safety of the queen one time in childbirth, and a great victory which Edwin gained over his enemy the king of Wessex, being ascribed to the prayers of the missionary, Edwin held several private conferences with him on the subject of Christianity, and at length summoned his council to take the subject into consideration.

Coifi, the heathen high-priest, was the first to speak: "If our gods," said he, "had the power to bestow blessings, I who have always served them should have been most highly favoured, whereas the contrary is the case." He thence inferred the nothingness of his gods, and declared for a change of faith. One of the nobles likened the soul to a sparrow, which in the mid-winter, when the king is enjoying himself with his lords by the fire, flies into the warm hall where they are sitting, and having flitted about it for some time goes out again into the storm by another door. "Thus," said he, "we know nothing of the origin or end of the soul, and, if the new doctrine can give us any certainty, we should embrace it." All assented to this opinion; and Coifi proposed that they should commence by the destruction of the temple at which he himself officiated. It was the custom among the Anglo-Saxons that the priests should only ride on mares, and should never carry arms; but Coifi now, to show his change of faith and his contempt for the old superstition, mounted a stately war-horse, and, brandishing a lance, galloped on to the temple. The people thought him mad, and when they saw him hurl his lance against the fane, they fully expected that he would be destroyed by the power of the gods. No such result however having followed, they gazed in silence at the demolition of the temple, and such numbers of them became converts, that for the space of six-and-thirty days Paulinus was from morning to night engaged in baptizing them.

Offa of Mercia.

Among the Anglo-Saxon princes of these early times, the most celebrated was Offa king of Mercia. He drove the remains of the Britons entirely out of the plain-country, and forced them to retire into the mountains of Wales; and to secure his dominions against their incursions he made a great embankment, called Offa's Dyke, a part of which still remains, which extended from the mouth of the Dee near Chester to that of the Wye in South Wales. Offa was a warlike prince, but he also was treacherous. He had long been at enmity with Ethelbert king of East Anglia: at length it was proposed to terminate their differences by a marriage, and Ethelbert went to Offa's palace at Tamworth to espouse one of his daughters. But Offa's queen, who perhaps was worse than himself, counselled him not to let slip the opportunity of vengeance now that he had his old enemy in his power; and the unsuspecting Ethelbert was assassinated by the order of Offa. It was intended that all his followers should share his fate; but the princess, who detested the conduct of her parents, gave them timely warning, and they effected their escape. Offa, however, added East Anglia to his dominions.

Edburga.

Offa had another daughter, named Edburga, who was more worthy of him than the princess of whom we have just spoken. She was married to the king of Wessex, whom she continually stimulated to deeds of cruelty. She made him put several of his nobles to death, and was even herself frequently the agent of the murder. But one time when she had mixed a bowl of poison for one of the nobles, the king himself partook of it by mistake, and died. The people rose and drove Edburga out of the country; she sought refuge at the court of the great emperor Chárlemagne; but her conduct was so bad that she was obliged to leave it, and she died at last a common beggar in the city of Pavía in Italy.

Another refugee at the court of Charlemagne was a young prince named Egbert, of the royal house of Wessex, who had sought protection there from the cruelty of the husband of Edburga. After the death of him and Offa Egbert returned; and gradually, by his valour and prudence, he made himself sole ruler of the whole island, which was henceforth named Angle-land, or England—the name by which it has since become so glorious in the annals of the world, and which, we trust, will if possible be rendered still more illustrious by deeds of valour, justice, and magnanimity.

CHAPTER III.

ANGLO-SAXON KINGS.

The Danes.

It was fortunate that England was thus united under one sceptre; for just at this very time a formidable enemy began to make descents on her coasts, and to renew the ravages of the Saxons in the time of the Romans.

This enemy was called the Danes, from the name of the principal people who formed their hosts. But Swedes and Norwegians, and all the people of the north, sent their hardy sons to man the fleets which, under the command of their Víkingar, or sea-kings, spread devastation along the shores of France and England, pillaging the cities, towns, and open country, burning the churches and monasteries, torturing the priests and monks, and dragging away the wretched people into captivity.

The latter years of king Egbert and the entire reigns of his four immediate successors were spent in incessant conflicts with the pirates of the North, who every year became more powerful and more daring.

Alfred the Great.

At length the sceptre came to Alfred, the grandson of Egbert and younger brother of the last three kings. He was only two-and-twenty years of age; yet in the very first year of his reign he fought no less than nine battles beside several skirmishes with the invaders. He was mostly victorious, and he more than once compelled them to swear to quit his kingdom: but they set oaths at nought, and by breaking their treaties and invading Alfred's dominions at a time when no danger was apprehended, they at length reduced him to the very brink of ruin.

It is related that king Alfred was brought so low at this time that he found it necessary to lay aside his royal habit and all the ensigns of his dignity, and, assuming a humble garb, to conceal himself in the cottage of one of his own cowherds, to whom his person was unknown. As he was one day sitting by the fireside, adjusting his bow, arrows, and other arms, the good woman of the house set some cakes on the hearth to bake, naturally expecting that her guest would have an eye to them. She then went about her household concerns, and the king, whose thoughts were occupied with the affairs of his kingdom and the misfortunes of his poor subjects, probably forgot that there were such things as cakes in existence. The consequence was that when the good woman turned about by accident, she saw her cakes all burnt and spoilt. She rated the king well, it is said, telling him that he was ready enough at eating them, and so might have minded them. Alfred bore her reproaches with great good humour, and he remained undiscovered.

At length Alfred was able to collect a small band of devoted followers, with whom he retired to a bog or morass, formed by the waters of the rivers Thone and Parret, in Somerset. There was in the midst of it a piece of firm land about two acres in extent, on which they raised a habitation, where they led the life of outlaws, hunting the deer, and catching the fish, and making plundering excursions against the Danes or those English who had submitted to them. At length, however, they received tidings which raised their spirits and inspired them with thoughts of more extensive warfare. A Danish chief, named Hubba, having landed on the coast of Devon, the people took to arms, and, led by their sheriff, defeated and slew the invader. They also captured the Raven, the standard of the Danes, which the pirates believed to have magic power, it having been woven, as they said, in one afternoon by the three daughters of their great chief Ragnar Lodbrok, and that it would announce victory by appearing like a live raven flying, and defeat by hanging down and drooping.

Alfred now resolved to commence operations against the Danes; but previously, in order to ascertain their strength and their designs, he entered their camp himself disguised as a minstrel. The rude warriors received him with boisterous joy, and he was brought to make melody before Guthrum their leader. The Danish chief was gratified with his music and songs, and allowed him to go where he would through the camp. He stayed a few days, and having learned all he wanted retired without having been discovered. He then summoned the men of the adjoining counties, and gave the Danes battle and a total defeat. They retired to their fortified camp, but he forced them to surrender; and Guthrum and most of his men consented to become Christians and be baptized.

Alfred carried on war with success against other bodies of the Danes, and he employed himself in improving the military condition of his kingdom, rebuilding and fortifying the towns, forming a navy, and training the people to the use of arms. But he was still more anxious to diffuse sound knowledge among his subjects, and in particular to have the clergy well-instructed, who had hitherto been grossly ignorant, as he informs us himself. "When I took the kingdom," says he, "very few on this side of the Humber, very few beyond, not one that I recollect south of the Thames, could understand their prayers in English or could translate a letter from Latin into English." By inviting over eminent scholars from the continent, and by setting a good example himself, (for he was a great writer,) he removed this evil, and left after him a sufficient number of well-educated clergymen.

It is remarkable that Alfred himself, though the son of a king, was twelve years old before he learned even to read. When he was of that age his mother one day showed him and his brothers a volume of Anglo-Saxon poems, saying that he who first could read it should be its owner. Alfred, who had always been fond of listening to the lays of the minstrels, and who greatly admired the beautiful illuminations or coloured letters of the book, eagerly inquired if she was in earnest. On her assuring him that she was, he looked out for a teacher, and he was speedily the proprietor of the book. He afterwards studied Latin, and became one of the most learned men of the age.

After a glorious reign of thirty years king Alfred died in peace. He is called the Great, and the title was well-merited; but he was more than great—he was good. He possessed every virtue; and his regard for truth in particular was such, that he was commonly called the Truth-teller.

A'thelstan.

King Áthelstan the grandson of Alfred was monarch of all England and a great and powerful prince. The king of Scotland and the Britons of Wales and Cumbria, made one time a great effort to shake off his yoke. They were joined by one Anlaf a Danish prince, who having rebelled against Athelstan and being forced to fly had become a leader of pirates. The hostile powers met at a place named Brûnanburgh in Yorkshire; but before they engaged, Anlaf, imitating the stratagem of Alfred, entered the English camp disguised as a minstrel. He was brought to play before the king and his nobles, and was then dismissed with a suitable reward. His pride however would not let him keep the money, and he buried it when he thought himself unobserved; but a soldier saw and recognised him, and when Anlaf was gone he went and informed the king. Athelstan asked him why he had not told him sooner, so that he might have seized his enemy. The man replied that he had once served and sworn fidelity to Anlaf, and if he had betrayed him, the king might justly suspect that he would prove a traitor to himself. Athelstan praised him, and suspecting Anlaf's design, removed his tent to another part of the camp. The vacant place was occupied by the bishop of Sherborne, who arrived that evening with his troops; for bishops were warriors in those days. In the middle of the night Anlaf and his men burst into the English camp, and making for what they thought was the royal tent, slaughtered the bishop and his companions. At sunrise a regular battle commenced, and a glorious victory crowned the arms of Athelstan, who passed the remainder of his reign in peace and tranquillity, beloved by his subjects and respected by all the kings of the continent.

Edmund the Magnificent.

The son and successor of Athelstan was named Edmund the Magnificent. He was a warlike and fortunate prince, but he did not long enjoy his power. As he was sitting with his nobles at a banquet on a festival-day, he saw a notorious outlaw named Leof taking his seat at the table. The king was enraged at his audacity, and starting up caught him by his long hair, and dragged him to the ground; but in the struggle Leof drew a dagger and gave the king a mortal wound.

St. Dunstan.

In the reigns of kings Athelstan, Edmund, and their successors, lived St. Dunstan, the most distinguished churchman of the age. Dunstan, who was a man of great talents and accomplishments, was early introduced at the court of king Athelstan, but the envy and jealousy of the courtiers soon drove him from it. His uncle, who was archbishop of Canterbury, wished him to become a monk; but Dunstan, who was in love with a beautiful maiden, could not bring himself to renounce matrimony. At length, viewing a fever which he had as a judgement from heaven, he complied with his uncle's wishes. Being well skilled in the art of working the metals, and desirous of mortifying himself, he built a cell so short that he could not lie at his full length in it, and he there set up a forge at which he wrought when not engaged in prayer. It was said that one evening as he was working at his forge the devil came to the little window of the cell, and thrusting in his head, began to tempt him with wanton language. Dunstan took no notice, but putting the tongs into the fire made them red-hot, and seizing the demon by the nose held him till his yells were heard all over the country. The fame of this exploit added greatly to the reputation of Dunstan for sanctity.

Elgíva.

When Edwy the grandson of king Edmund came to the crown, the power and reputation of Dunstan were at their height. This king, who was only seventeen years of age, married a young lady named Elgíva, who was related to him in a degree prohibited by the church. Nothing however seems to have occurred till the day of the coronation, when while the nobles were carousing in the royal halls after the Saxon fashion Edwy stole away to the apartments of his wife.

The nobles, highly offended at this conduct of the king, deputed Dunstan and one of the bishops to go and fetch him back. Dunstan finding him sitting with his wife and her mother, abused the two ladies in the grossest terms, and seizing the king dragged him away and made him resume his seat at the festive board. To punish this insolence Edwy banished Dunstan the kingdom; but the people, excited by Odo archbishop of Canterbury, rose in rebellion, and Edwy was forced to surrender his wife to that prelate, who caused her face to be scarred with a red-hot iron and banished her to Ireland. As soon however as her wounds were healed, she returned and was on her way to join her husband, when by Odo's orders she was seized and hamstringed, and she died in great torture. The unfortunate Edwy did not long survive her; his brother Edgar was made king, and Dunstan became archbishop of Canterbury.

Edgar the Peaceful.—Elfrida.

Edgar was named the Peaceful on account of the peace and tranquillity that prevailed during his reign. He was a very powerful monarch; and all the princes of the Scots and Britons submitted to his authority. One time when he was at Chester, where they had waited on him to perform their homage, he entered with them a barge on the river Dee. Each prince took an oar, the king held the rudder, and they rowed down to a monastery on the banks of the river, and having there heard mass, returned in the same state.

Edgar, who was a great admirer of female beauty, hearing that of Elfrida daughter of the earl of Devon greatly extolled, became very anxious to know if fame spake true. He therefore directed one of his favourites named Áthelwold to visit the earl, and see if the charms of his daughter justified their reputation. But at the sight of the fair Elfrida Athelwold became violently enamoured, and on his return to court he told the king that the report of her beauty was greatly exaggerated, for in reality she was no ways different from other maidens. The king ceased to think of her, and some time after Athelwold saying that homely as she was her fortune would make her an advantageous match for himself, obtained the king's consent to a marriage and a strong recommendation to the parents of Elfrida, who in consequence became his wife. But ere long his treachery was made known to the king, who dissembling his resentment told him one day that he intended to visit him and be introduced to his wife. Athelwold in great consternation craved permission to go before and make preparations to receive him. When he reached his home, he told Elfrida the whole truth, excusing his conduct by the violence of his love, and praying her to use every art to conceal her beauty. Elfrida promised compliance, but secretly incensed at him for having caused her to miss a crown, she appeared at the banquet in the full blaze of her charms. The king's heart was instantly subdued; a few days after he slew Athelwold with his own hand at a hunting party, and he then made Elfrida his queen.

In the reign of Edgar the whole race of wolves was extirpated in England. They had already been driven out of the plain-country, but they still harboured in the mountains of Wales, whence they descended to commit their ravages. The king therefore by way of tribute required of the Welsh princes three hundred wolves' heads a year; and in consequence within a very short time no more wolves were to be found.

Edward the Martyr.

After the death of Edgar there was a dispute for the throne, one party setting up Edward his son by his first wife, another Éthelred the son of Elfrida. As Dunstan supported Edward he obtained the crown; but the revengeful Elfrida soon managed to deprive him of it and his life together. For as he was one day hunting in Dorsetshire he happened to come near Corfe Castle, where she and her son were residing, and he went unattended to pay them a visit.

Elfrida received him with much apparent kindness; but when he had mounted and was taking a draught of mead on horseback, one of her servants stabbed him in the back. Finding himself wounded, he gave spurs to his horse; but he soon fell, and was dragged along till he expired. This prince was named the Martyr.

Ethelred the Unready.

Ethelred though innocent, for he bitterly wept the death of his brother, thus gained the crown by the guilt of his mother; but at the coronation Dunstan pronounced a curse on his reign, and the malediction was terribly fulfilled. The savage Danes now recommenced their ravages, and the king's council instead of raising troops and boldly meeting them in the field, like Alfred or Athelstan, adopted the cowardly expedient of buying them off with large sums of money. This course had the effect which might easily have been foreseen; the Danish inroads became more formidable every year. Another mode of getting rid of them was then devised. As there were a great number of Danes residing in England, who were apt to join their countrymen and give them information, secret orders were sent all through the kingdom to fall on and slay them on a certain day. These orders were punctually obeyed, and the Danes, men, women and children, without distinction of age or rank, were ruthlessly slaughtered.

But this barbarous and treacherous deed did not go long unpunished. Sweyn king of Denmark appeared with a numerous fleet, and spread his ravages along all the coasts. All attempts at resistance proved unavailing: the Danes sailed up the Thames; London repelled them, but they obtained possession of Canterbury by the treachery of a priest. They dragged the archbishop, a venerable old man, to their ships, in the hope of extorting a large ransom from him; but he declared that he had no goods of his own, and he would not waste those of the church, which belonged to the poor, nor, as he expressed it, "provide Christian flesh for pagan teeth by robbing his countrymen for them." They hauled him before their chiefs at a rude banquet; their cry was, "Gold, bishop, gold!" and when he still refused they pelted him with bones and cow-horns. At length one of them struck him with an axe and killed him.

Ethelred and his family were at length obliged to fly and seek a refuge at the court of the duke of Normandy, and Sweyn became the master of all England. He died soon after, leaving his power to his son Canute; and the English, grown weary of the Danish yoke, recalled king Ethelred. The war was resumed and carried on with various success, the English troops being led by the king's eldest son Edmund, who was named Ironside on account of his great size, strength, and valour.

Edmund Ironside.

Ethelred died soon after, and the contest for the throne was continued by Edmund and Canute, and four great battles were fought within a very short space of time. There was at this time an English traitor named Edric, a man of great influence, who sometimes was on one side and sometimes on the other. In one of these battles, when he was fighting for Canute, he saw that the brave Edmund had cleft the shield of Canute with his battle-axe, and that the Danes, who hastened to the relief of their king, had surrounded him. He instantly cut off the head of a slain nobleman, and holding it up cried out, "The head of Edmund!" The English were beginning to give way, when Edmund ascending a bank took off his helmet and made himself known. In another battle Edric was on the side of Edmund, and just as the action commenced he cried out, "Flee, English! flee, English! dead is Edmund!" and himself set the example of flight, and thus gave the victory to Canute. On another occasion, when the opposite armies were in array of battle, Edmund proposed that they should decide their claims by single combat; but

Canute saying that he, who was a man of small stature, would have little chance against the tall athletic Edmund, suggested that it would be better for them to divide the kingdom. This was agreed to; Edmund had the south and Canute the north of England; but before the end of the year Edmund died, murdered it was said by Edric, and Canute remained sole monarch of England.

CHAPTER IV.

DANISH KINGS, AND SAXON LINE RESTORED.

Canute and his Sons.

BESIDE England, Canute reigned over Denmark and Norway, and he was superior lord of Sweden and Scotland. He was thus the most powerful monarch of the age. His rule in England was at first very rigorous and oppressive; he put several of the nobles to death, and gave their properties to his Danes. It is gratifying to observe that one of the first to suffer was the traitor Edric. Canute had given him the government of the whole kingdom of Mercia; but not content with it, he demanded more, pleading his treason to Edmund as a merit. Canute told him that he who had been a traitor to one master would hardly be faithful to another, and a Dane named Eric, raising his battle-axe, struck him dead. His head was cut off and fixed on the highest gate of London, and his body was flung into the Thames.

Age mitigated the harshness of Canute's character, and he gradually gained the affections of his English subjects. He also turned his thoughts to the subject of religion, and, as was the practice at the time, made a pilgrimage to Rome. After his return as he was residing at Southampton his courtiers one day began to extol his power and authority as if nothing were able to resist him. He directed his chair to be placed on the strand where the tide was coming in, and as lord of the ocean commanded it not to approach, but heedless of his mandate the waves rolled on and soon flowed round his chair. The king then turning toward his flatterers bade them confess the weakness of all human power compared with that of Him who had said to the ocean "Thus far shalt thou go and no further." After this he deposited his crown in the cathedral of the adjacent city of Winchester, and never wore it again.

Canute divided his dominions at his death among his three sons Sweyn, Harold and Hárdacnute. Harold, who was named Harefoot from his swiftness, obtained England; but he died shortly after, and was succeeded by his brother Hardacnute. This king's reign was also brief; for having drunk too much wine at the wedding-feast of one of his nobles he fell down speechless and shortly after died. As he was the last of Canute's family, and the English were heartily weary of the Danish yoke, they gladly returned to the line of their ancient princes and gave the crown to Edward the only remaining son of Ethelred, whom we find honoured with the religious title of the Confessor on account of his superstitious practices, which in those days were regarded as true piety.

Edward the Confessor.—Godwin.—Harold.

There was at this time in England a very powerful nobleman named Godwin, to whose influence Edward was chiefly indebted for his crown. In return he married Edith the Fair, Godwin's daughter, and he gave the government of large districts of the kingdom to Godwin and his two sons Sweyn and Harold. Concord did not however long exist between them and the king; they took up arms against him, but they were finally obliged to quit the kingdom. They returned soon after with a great force, and their troops and those of the king were drawn out for battle in the

Strand, outside of the walls of London. An accommodation however was effected, and Godwin and his sons were restored to their honours. But on the following Easter as Godwin was sitting at the king's table he fell suddenly dead. The story went that the king having charged him with the murder of his brother Alfred, who was cruelly put to death in the reign of Harold, he cried, "May this morsel be my last if I did it!" and the piece of bread which he attempted to swallow stuck in his throat and choked him. His son Harold succeeded to his power and honours.

The great province of Northumbria was governed by a powerful nobleman named earl Siward. In the reign of Edward, Duncan king of Scotland was treacherously murdered by one of his subjects named Macbeth, who then usurped the crown and tyrannised over the country. The rightful heir Malcolm implored the aid of king Edward, who gave orders to earl Siward to restore him. Siward marched his troops into Scotland, and at a place named Dunsináne defeated and slew the usurper and restored Malcolm to the throne of his ancestors. In the battle Siward's eldest son was slain; the earl asked how he had fallen, and on being told that all his wounds were in front, he said he was satisfied and desired no better death for himself. When some time after he felt his own death approaching, he declared that he would meet it like a warrior, and causing himself to be arrayed in his armour, and a spear to be placed in his hand, he breathed his last with composure.

As king Edward had no children and was now advanced in years, Harold began to aspire to the kingdom; but the king, who did not like him, made a will appointing his cousin William, the young duke of Normandy, his successor. Some time after Harold happened to be shipwrecked on the coast of Ponthieu in the north of France, and, according to the barbarous usage of the times, he was made a prisoner by count Guy, the lord of that country, who hoped to obtain for him a large ransom. Harold sent to inform the duke of Normandy, whose vassal the count was, and the duke forthwith caused him to be sent to Rouen, where he resided. He there treated Harold with the utmost courtesy, and informing him of king Edward's intentions in his favour, offered him the hand of his daughter Ádela if he would give him his interest. Harold, knowing himself to be in the duke's power, promised everything. William required his oath. A book of devotion called the Missal was produced, and Harold, laying his hand on it, swore in the presence of the duke and his court. The missal was then removed, and under it appeared a vessel filled with the bones of saints and other relics as they are named, by which he was now held to have sworn, and which rendered his oath still more solemn.

Harold.

Harold however on his return to England thought little of this compulsory oath, and on the death of king Edward he at once assumed the crown. When William sent to remind him of his solemn engagement, he set him at nought and defied his power. William then began to assemble troops to assert his claim by arms; the pope sent him a consecrated banner and a ring, in which was what was said to be a hair of St. Peter, and he also condemned the perjury of Harold.

While the duke of Normandy was making his preparations Harold had to encounter another formidable foe. After the death of earl Siward he had caused his earldom to be given to his own brother Tosti; but the new earl proved such a tyrant that the people rose and expelled him. As Harold had given his sanction to this act, Tosti now applied to William, who furnished him with money to procure ships for the recovery of his earldom; he also declared himself a vassal of Harold Hárdrada king of Norway, and the Norwegian monarch entered the Humber with a large fleet, where he was joined by Tosti; and they landed their forces and advanced toward York. The two great northern earls (two brothers named Edwin and Morcar,) gave them battle, but were defeated, and York was besieged. Harold hastened to the north with the army which he had collected to oppose the duke of Normandy. Tosti advised the king of Norway to fall back to his ships; but the Norwegian, though he had only a part of his forces with him, was too proud to retire before a foe. At Stamford-bridge on the river Derwent he drew up his troops in order of battle. Their array was a hollow circle, in the centre of which waved the Land-waster, as the royal banner was named; the outer rank fixed their spears in the ground, and those of the second rank were advanced beyond them. As Hardrada was riding round the circle his horse stumbled and he fell. "Who is that warrior in the blue mantle with a glittering helmet that has fallen?" inquired Harold. Being told that it was the king of Norway, "He is a large and stately person," said he, "but his fall shows that his end is at hand." Before the battle Harold sent to Tosti offering him his earldom and other honours. "That offer should have been made last winter," said Tosti; "but if I accept it what will be given to the king of Norway?" "Seven feet of ground, or as he is a very tall man perhaps a little more," replied the envoy. "Go back," cried he, "and tell king Harold to make him ready for the fight, for never shall it be said that earl Tosti left Harold son of Sigurd, and went over to his foes."

In the battle which ensued, the English troops, who were mostly cavalry, by charging and then retreating, caused the enemy to break their firm array, and they then rushed in at the opening which had been made and slaughtered them. The king of Norway and Tosti were both slain, and most of the Norwegian nobles shared their fate. Harold dismissed in safety Olave the son of Hardrada.

Battle of Hastings.

Harold led his victorious army to York, and while he was there holding a royal banquet tidings came of the landing of the duke of Normandy in Sussex: for William, after he had assembled his army, had been detained an entire month by contrary winds, and a storm had afterwards shattered his fleet; circumstances which, though he thought otherwise at the time, had been greatly in his favour, for the month's delay gave Hardrada time to land and thus draw Harold and his troops away to the north, and the storm had prevented the English fleet from keeping the sea. He therefore landed without opposition at Pevensey in Sussex. In jumping out of his galley it is said he stumbled and fell. As this might be regarded as an ill omen, the soldier who raised him, seeing his hands full of mud, cried out with great presence of mind, "Fortunate leader! you have already taken England; its earth is in your hands!"

William advanced to Hastings. Harold, who had returned to London, was busily engaged in collecting troops, for those he had led to the north had left him. He sent spies to ascertain the strength of the enemy, and when they were discovered, William, instead of putting them to death according to the laws of war, caused them to be led through his camp and then dismissed. He also proposed to Harold to decide their quarrel by a single combat; but Harold though a brave man refused the challenge, saying that God should judge between them.

The two armies met at a place then named Senlac, now called Battle from the event, about eight miles on the London side from Hastings. The night before the battle was spent by the Normans in devotion, by the English in feasting and revelry. At dawn next morning king Harold drew up his troops on the side of a hill in a solid mass; each man bore a shield to cover him, and grasped a battle-axe, the ancient English weapon. In the centre waved the royal banner, which displayed the figure of a fighting warrior woven in gold, and the king and his brothers Gurth and Leofwin took their station beneath it. On an opposite eminence the duke disposed his troops in three lines, the first of archers, the second of heavy infantry, the third of cavalry. The banner sent by the pope was borne in the front by a knight named Toustaine the Fair, and round the neck of the duke were hung the relics on which Harold had sworn.

The war-cry of the Normans was "God! help us!"; that of the English "Holy rood [*i. e.* cross]! God's rood!" A knight named Taillefer preceded the Norman army mounted on a stately war-horse, tossing up his sword with one hand and catching it with the other, while he sang the deeds of an ancient hero named Roland. He slew two English warriors, but fell by the hand of a third. The Normans then began to ascend the hill; their archers having discharged their arrows fell back on the infantry, who then advanced to the charge, but could make no impression on the solid mass of the English. The cavalry then charged, but were cut down by the formidable battle-axes. The whole of the left wing of the Normans turned and fled; a report was spread that the duke had fallen, but he took off his helmet and rode along the line to reassure his men. At length by feigning flight the Normans induced the English to break their ranks and pursue, and then turned on them and cut them to pieces. The main body however still stood firm and unbroken, till William directed his archers to shoot their arrows up into the air so as to fall on the enemies. One of these arrows wounded Harold in the eye; twenty Norman knights rushed to seize the royal banner; the king was slain, and the English then broke and fled. It was now night, but the Normans continued the pursuit by the light of the moon; the fugitives however turned and took a severe vengeance for their defeat.

William caused a spot near where Harold had fallen to be cleared, and pitched a tent there, in which he and his nobles supped that night. He afterwards founded an abbey on that very spot, which was named Battle Abbey, that prayers might be continually offered up for the souls of those who had fallen. It is said that two monks of the abbey of Waltham, which Harold had founded, who had followed him to the field, craved permission of William to search for the body of their benefactor. Having obtained it they went over the field, but were unable to recognise it. They then fetched Harold's mistress, Edith, named the Swan's Neck, for her beauty; and her affectionate eye speedily discerned the royal corpse, which the monks then conveyed to Waltham. Others said that when Harold's mother applied to William for the body of her son, offering its weight in gold, he refused it, and caused it to be buried on the sea-shore, saying, "He guarded the coast when living, let him guard it still now that he is dead."

Such was the great battle of Hastings, fought on the 15th of October 1066, and thus was England conquered by the Duke of Normandy!

ANGLO-NORMAN PERIOD.

CHAPTER I.

WILLIAM I. (THE CONQUEROR.)

Conquest of England.

AFTER his victory at Hastings William marched along the coast to Dover, and thence to the neighbourhood of London. No opposition was offered anywhere; the English prelates and nobles crowded to his camp, and swore allegiance to him. On the following Christmas-day he was crowned in Westminster abbey. In the spring he returned to Normandy, leaving the government of England in the hands of his half-brother Odo bishop of Bayeux, and of a baron named William Fitz-Osborn.

William had seized the estates of a great number of the English and given them to his Norman followers, who proved very tyrannical and oppressive to the people, and the regents gave no heed to the complaints which were made to them. The consequence was that the English took arms and rose in various parts. William returned immediately from Normandy: he led his troops against the insurgents, and defeated them in all parts; and so highly offended was he with the people of the north for their standing up in defence of their liberty and property, that from the Humber to the Tyne he did not leave a town, hardly even a house, standing; the whole country was turned into a desert, and more than one hundred thousand persons perished of famine.

Of the Saxon nobility and gentry a part had perished in the field, or had been executed as traitors and rebels; some fled to Scotland or the North of Europe, while a daring band, headed by Siward, earl of Gloucester, sailed to Constantinople, and became the guards of the emperors of the East. The properties of all were confiscated and bestowed on the Normans, who thus became possessed of nearly all the land of England.

Hereward.

But there were many of the English who would neither abandon their country nor submit to the Normans. They harboured in the woods and morasses, whence they issued and attacked the Normans when they found an opportunity. The principal retreats of these Outlaws, as they came to be named, were the isles of Ely and Thorney, in the fens of Cambridgeshire. Here they formed their Camp, or Fort of Refuge as it was termed, and secured it strongly with defences of wood and earth. Morcar, and several other nobles and prelates, repaired to the Camp; but the person who had the chief command was a brave warrior named Héreward.

This Hereward had been living on the continent; when, hearing from some of the exiles that his father was dead, and that his estate had been given to one of the Normans, and his mother was in great distress, he resolved to return to England, and right himself by the strong hand. He soon collected a gallant body of his relations and dependents, and drove the intruder from the house of his fathers. He was in consequence engaged in continual conflicts with the Normans; and as he was usually victorious his fame spread far and wide, and his deeds became the themes of the popular ballads. Those who were in the Camp of Refuge sent to him, requesting him to come and be their commander, and he accepted the invitation.

The power of this brave band of outlaws soon became so formidable that the king found it necessary to take the field in person against them. In order to reach their retreat he commenced forming a causeway, three miles in length, across the marshes: but Hereward, by his sallies, impeded the work so much, that the Normans, fancying he must be aided by the Evil One, brought a sorceress, and placed her in a wooden tower, in advance of the works, to perform her incantations. Hereward, however, making a sudden sally, set fire to the reeds of the marsh and burnt the sorceress and most of the soldiers who were at work. At length the treachery of the monks of Ely frustrated the valour of Hereward. These men, fonder of themselves than of their country, when they found themselves deprived of their customary indulgences, sent secretly to inform the king that if he would secure them in their property they would put him in possession of the isle. William accepted their offer: by their means his troops got into the isle and assailed the Camp. Most of its defenders were slain or forced to surrender: Hereward, with a few brave men, made his escape across the marshes, and he continued to be the terror of the Normans. At length a rich Saxon lady, charmed with his valour, gave him her hand, and he made his peace with the king; but some time after he was treacherously slain by a party of the Normans as he was sleeping out in the open air after his dinner. It is pleasing to be able to add that the monks of Ely gained little by their treachery. A party of Norman soldiers was quartered on them; they were obliged to pay a large sum of money; their plate and ornaments were seized, and their lands were divided among the Normans.

Fate of the English Nobles.

We will here relate the fate of some of the principal English nobles. Earl Morcar was among those taken in the Camp of Refuge, and he was sent a prisoner to Normandy, where he was kept for the remainder of William's reign. When his brother Edwin, who was in the north, heard of his fate, he attempted to raise a force for his rescue; but he was betrayed by some of his followers, and his flight being impeded by a stream which was swollen by the tide, he was slain after a gallant resistance. The traitors brought his head to William; but their reward was a sentence of perpetual banishment. Another English earl was Waltheof, the son of the brave old earl Siward. The Conqueror had been extremely favourable to him, and had given him his own niece Judith in marriage. But Waltheof having happened to be present at a banquet where some of the Norman nobles had concerted a rebellion, and not having given information, his wife, who was in love with another, and some of the Normans, who coveted his lands, took advantage of the circumstance to ruin him. He was brought to trial on a charge of treason, and after having been kept in prison for an entire year at Winchester, he was taken early one morning, before the townspeople (who might have attempted his rescue) were out of their beds, to an eminence without the town, and there beheaded. Waltheof was regarded as a martyr by the English, and they believed that miracles were wrought at his tomb. Judith, like the monks of Ely, gained nothing by her treachery. The king ordered her to marry a knight who was lame and deformed. She refused; and William then gave the knight Waltheof's eldest daughter by a former marriage and his estates, and Judith passed the rest of her days in poverty and contempt.

Another Englishman of high rank was Edgar Átheling, the nephew of Edward the Confessor. But though he was very brave, he was a man of so little talent or capacity that no one ever thought of asserting his claim to the crown, and the Conqueror, who did not fear him, always treated him with kindness.

It was a part of William's policy to displace all the English bishops and abbots and give their dignities to Normans and other foreigners. The last English prelate was Wulfstan bishop of Worcester; and he was called on to resign for no other reason than that he could not speak

French, the language of the Normans. Wulfstan, it is said, stood up and walked over to the tomb of king Edward, in Westminster abbey, where the council was held, and where the tomb may yet be seen, and said, " Edward, thou gavest me this pastoral staff: to thee then I commit it." Then, turning round to the king, he said, "A better than thou gave it me; pluck it away if thou canst." He struck it into the solid tomb, whence no one could pull it till the sentence was revoked. He then drew it out himself with ease.

William and his Sons.

William had three sons; Robert, named Curthose from the shortness of his legs; William, called Rufus from his ruddy complexion and the colour of his hair; and Henry, styled Beauclerc, or Fine-scholar, from his love of learning. Robert was a hot-headed turbulent prince, and when one day his two brothers came to the house in which he resided and made a great noise in it, and even rudely poured water down on him as he was walking before the door, he drew his sword and ran up, and was only prevented by the presence of his father from slaying them. He then went away and seized one of the royal castles. The king came himself and besieged it. One day Robert fought with and unhorsed a knight, who proved to be his father. Robert, when he heard his voice, alighted and helped him to his horse, and a reconciliation took place. But soon after Robert went away again and did not return any more.

Death of William.

William's death occurred in the following manner. He had become extremely corpulent, and by his physician's directions he took medicines and remained in bed. The king of France one day said joking, " By my faith, the king of England is a long time lying-in! There will be great doings at his churching." When William heard of these words he swore that when he got up he would light a thousand tapers * in France. He soon after invaded that country, and in his rage he set the town of Mantes on fire; but as he was galloping through it, his horse chancing to tread on some hot embers threw him on the pummel of the saddle, and the injury he sustained caused his death shortly afterwards.

The scenes which ensued on the death of William present a curious picture of the state of the times. As soon as he had breathed his last all who were about him mounted their horses and rode home to secure their property; the servants then pillaged the royal abode, carrying off everything of value, and the corpse was left nearly naked on the floor. When it was removed for interment at Caen, there was no one to take charge of it, and a private knight transported it thither at his own expense. At the funeral, when mass had been said and they were about to lower the corpse into the grave before the altar, a voice from the crowd cried, "Clerks and bishops, this ground is mine; it is the site of my father's house: the man you are praying for took it from me to build his church. On the part of God I forbid the body of the despoiler to be covered with my mould." It being found that he spoke the truth, the bishops paid him on the spot for the grave, and promised him payment for the rest of the ground, and the remains of the Conqueror were then consigned to the earth.

The Feudal System.

The feudal system was, if not first introduced into England by the Normans, brought to perfection by them in that country. By this system the king was regarded as the owner of all the lands in the kingdom. Those to whom he granted them were obliged to swear *fealty* or fidelity to him, and to perform *homage*, that is kneeling before him with their hands in his to declare themselves to be

* It was the custom at that time for women to bear lighted tapers at their churching.

his *men*, in Latin *homo*, whence *homagium*. He was called their *lord*, they were his *vassals*. They were obliged to attend him in war for limited periods of time (the longest being forty days) at their own expense, to help to pay his ransom if he was taken captive, and to give him sums of money on various occasions, such, for example, as the marriage of his eldest daughter, to whose portion they were bound to contribute.

Those who were tenants *in chief*, as it was called, or who held their lands directly of the crown, might grant their lands in a similar way and have vassals of their own. But these inferior vassals were bound by allegiance to the crown; and though it was their duty to aid their lord in his private quarrels, if they bore arms for him against the king they were regarded and treated as traitors.

CHAPTER II.

WILLIAM II. (RUFUS.)

Attack on Prince Henry.

THE late king, by his will, left England to his second son; but Robert, who inherited the dukedom of Normandy, claimed the whole of his father's dominions, and a war was on the point of breaking out between the brothers when an accommodation was effected by their barons. They then joined their forces to attack their brother Henry, and they besieged him in a strong fortress in Normandy. Want of water had nearly reduced him to a surrender, when Robert hearing of his distress gave him permission to supply himself, and even sent him wine for his table. When William upbraided him for this ill-timed generosity, the duke replied, " What! should I let my own brother die of thirst? Where shall we find another when he is gone?" As the king himself was riding out to view the castle he was fallen on by two soldiers and unhorsed. One was about to slay him, when he cried, "Hold, knave! I am the king of England." The soldier raised him from the ground, and William took him into his service. Shortly after Henry was obliged to surrender, and go seek a refuge among strangers.

The Crusade.

It was in the reign of William Rufus that those romantic expeditions to the East, for the recovery of the Holy Land out of the hands of the Turks and Saracens, commenced. They were named Crusades, from the *cross* which those who went on them, and who thence were called Crusaders, wore on the right shoulder of their garment. Most of the princes of the West of Europe took part in this first and greatest crusade, and Robert of Normandy, who in valour yielded to none, was of the number. But his wasteful extravagant temper left him always without money; and in order to be able to equip himself suitably to his rank, he found it necessary to give his duchy for a term of five years to the king of England, who was extremely rich. Robert, having thus obtained the requisite funds, set out in gallant array for the East, and William took possession of Normandy.

Death of William.

Some time after, the great duke of Guienne, in France, being about to set out for the Holy Land, entered into treaty with the king of England for money; and William was in hopes of getting possession of that duke's dominions also. But while he was staying at Winchester, apparently with the intention of embarking at Southampton, he went one day to hunt in the adjoining New Forest, for the formation of which his father had laid waste a large tract of Hampshire. His attendants dispersed in pursuit of the game; and in the evening some colliers, in passing through the forest, found the king lying dead with an arrow stuck in his breast, and placing the body on their cart, they conveyed it to Winchester.

It is doubtful how the king came by his death; the account most generally received is that a French knight named Walter Tyrrell having shot at a stag, his arrow glanced from a tree and hit the king, and Tyrrell, fearing for the consequences of this accident, put spurs to his horse, and getting over to France joined a body of Crusaders who were setting out for the Holy Land. Tyrrell, however, it is said, afterwards denied this; and William was such an oppressive tyrant that he may have fallen by the hand of some secret enemy.

CHAPTER III.

HENRY I. (BEAUCLERC.)

Fate of Duke Robert.

PRINCE Henry was hunting in another part of the forest when he heard of his brother's death. He immediately rode to Winchester, and secured the royal treasure, and then hastening to London, caused himself to be crowned without delay. As by an agreement between Robert and William, if either died without children, the other was to inherit his dominions, and William had never married, the crown now of right belonged to Robert; but he was far away in the Holy Land, and Henry, who was on the spot, seized it in the manner we have seen. Robert on his return prepared to assert his right, and he assembled an army and landed at Portsmouth. Henry advanced to oppose him, but the bishops and barons interfered, and an accommodation similar to that between Robert and William was effected.

Some time after, Robert's bad government having disgusted a great number of his subjects, his brother Henry took advantage of it; and passing over to Normandy gave Robert a great defeat at a place named Ténchebrai, and took him prisoner. He removed him to England, and for the long term of thirty years the unhappy prince was transferred from castle to castle, and he breathed his last in that of Cardiff, in Wales, in the eightieth year of his age. It is said, but it does not appear to be true, that his eyes had been put out by the command of his unnatural and cruel brother.

Death of Prince William.

If Henry, regardless of the rights of nature and kindred, treated his own generous but imprudent brother in this barbarous manner, he was punished for it in his own family. When his eldest son, named William, had attained the age of eighteen years, he took him over to Normandy to have him recognised as his successor. As they were on their return the ship which carried the prince struck on a rock and foundered, in consequence of the captain and crew having got drunk. The prince entered the boat and was quite out of danger, when hearing the cries of his sister, the countess of Perche, he put back to save her; but when the boat approached the ship such numbers crowded into it that it went down, and all in it perished. Of all who had been on board one man alone, a butcher, escaped by clinging to the mast. The captain also grasped the mast, but when he learned that the prince was drowned he said he would not survive him, and let go his hold. The king when he heard of the calamity fainted away, and never again was seen to smile.

Death of the King.

Henry's only remaining child was a daughter named Matilda, or Maud, who had been married to the emperor of Germany. As she was now a widow, he gave her in marriage to Geoffrey Plantágenet, son of the count of Anjou, and caused her to be recognised as the heiress of all his dominions. Matilda became the mother of three sons, and the king made his nobility renew their oath of allegiance to her and her eldest son prince Henry. Some time after, having eaten too heartily of lampreys, a dish of which he was very fond, he got a surfeit, and died in the sixty-fourth year of his age.

CHAPTER IV.
STEPHEN (OF BLOIS.)

Civil War between Stephen and Matilda.

It will be remembered how king Henry defrauded his brother Robert of the crown of England. His own daughter was defrauded in a similar manner by her cousin Stephen count of Blois. Like his uncle, Stephen made himself master of the royal treasure and caused himself to be crowned immediately, and it was some time before Matilda was in a condition to assert her rights. At length she landed in England, and a civil war commenced, which lasted nearly twenty years, and inflicted such dreadful calamities on the country, that, as the old chronicle expresses it, " men said openly that Christ and his saints slept."

One severe winter during this war Matilda was closely besieged by Stephen in the castle of Oxford. When her stock of provisions was exhausted she dressed herself and three of her knights in white, as the ground was covered with snow; a sentinel who had been bribed conducted them through the enemy's posts; they crossed the Thames on the ice, proceeded to Abingdon on foot, and having procured horses rode thence to Wallingford. This escape of the empress was looked upon by her friends as being little less than miraculous.

Matilda shortly after left England, but the contest for the crown was soon renewed by her son prince Henry. It was at length terminated by a compromise, Stephen being permitted to retain the crown for his life, and the succession being secured to Henry. Stephen died in the following year, and Henry mounted the throne without opposition.

HOUSE OF PLANTAGENET.

CHAPTER I.

HENRY II. (PLANTAGENET*.)

Power of Henry.

HENRY Plantagenet was only in the twenty-first year of his age when he mounted the throne of England. He was the most powerful monarch of his time; for he inherited by his mother England, and Normandy and Maine in France; from his father, Anjou and Tourraine in the same country; and by marrying Eleanor, the divorced queen of Louis king of France, he obtained Guienne and several other provinces in the west and south of France, so that in fact he possessed an entire third of that kingdom.

The first years of the reign of king Henry were prosperous and happy. At length his ill fortune engaged him in a contest with the church, which was so powerful in those days.

Thomas à Becket.

There was at this time in England a clergyman named Thomas à Becket, the son of a citizen of London named Gilbert à Becket. A romantic tradition told that Gilbert, being one time on a pilgrimage to Jerusalem, was made captive by a Saracen emir or chief, by whom, however, he

---

* So the dukes of Anjou were named, from their device, a sprig of broom—in French *plante de genêt*.

was treated with much kindness, and the emir's daughter saw and fell in love with him. She told him that she longed to become a Christian, and she learned from him his name, and that of his country. Some time after Gilbert contrived to make his escape, and he thought no more, as it would seem, of the emir's daughter. But *her* love was of a more enduring character. She quitted her father's abode in disguise, and went down to the coast. She knew but two English words, Gilbert and London; by means of the latter she contrived to get her passage to England, and when she arrived in London, she went about the streets calling Gilbert. Her strange manner and her foreign dress drew a crowd about her; and as she happened to go through the very street in which Gilbert dwelt, his servant Richard, who had been with him in the East, recognised her. He immediately informed his master, who took and placed her for the present in a nunnery, and soon after made her his wife, and she bore him a son, who was named Thomas.

As the young Becket showed considerable symptoms of talent, he was carefully educated. When he grew up, Theobald archbishop of Canterbury took him into his family, and bestowed various benefices on him. He also introduced him to king Henry, who made him his chancellor, and lived with him on terms of the greatest familiarity, and on the death of archbishop Theobald, he resolved to bestow the vacant see on his favourite.

Becket made Archbishop.

Becket, who, though a churchman, had hitherto led a gay and dissipated life, remonstrated against the appointment, alleging his utter unfitness for such a situation; but Henry would not be diverted from his purpose, and Becket became the primate of England. An immediate change took place in his mode of life. Throwing aside his splendid raiment, he wore sackcloth next his skin; his food was

of the meanest kind, and his drink made unpalatable by
an infusion of bitter herbs. He frequently applied the
scourge to his naked back, and he every day washed on
his knees the feet of thirteen poor persons. He devoted
his hours to prayer and to the reading of the Scrip-
tures.

By this change of life Becket seems to have been preparing himself for the contest which he foresaw he would
have to wage with the king. The church, of which he now
regarded himself as the champion, had of late been making
great efforts to free itself from the control of the courts of
law, pretending that when an ecclesiastic committed any
offence, he should be amenable only to the ecclesiastical
courts. As these inflicted no higher punishment than penance, and as the bishops conferred orders on all sorts of
people indiscriminately, the number of crimes committed
by churchmen was considerable, and they are charged with
no less than one hundred homicides in the first six years
of the king's reign. It was in the hope that he should
find in Becket a ready assistant in suppressing this nui-
sance, that Henry made him primate. But never was
monarch doomed to a more thorough disappointment.

Quarrel between the King and Becket.

The quarrel between the king and the primate broke
out on the following occasion. A clergyman having se-
duced a young lady in Worcestershire, murdered her father,
that their guilty commerce might not be interrupted. The
public indignation at this act was great, and the king required that the criminal should be surrendered to justice;
but Becket, to save him, caused him to be placed in the
bishop's prison of the diocese. Henry then required that
clerks, if found guilty of a crime in the bishop's court,
should be degraded and handed over to the civil power
To this reasonable demand the bishops seemed willing to
agree, till Becket dissuaded them. He, however, afterwards gave way, and promised compliance, and even set

his seal to the laws that were made to regulate the relations of the church and state. But he soon after treated them as of no effect; and after a vain effort had been made to induce him to submit to the royal will, he stole privately out of the kingdom, and sought refuge in France.

The pope and the king of France both took part with Becket, and the quarrel between the king of England and the primate continued for some years. On one occasion, when king Louis tried to effect a reconciliation between them, Henry said, "There have been many kings of England before me, some who had greater some who had less power than I. There have been many archbishops of Canterbury before him, great and holy men. What the greatest and holiest of his predecessors did for the least of mine, let him do for me, and I shall be content." Yet even this just and reasonable demand was rejected by the haughty prelate, and Louis, who was a superstitious man, and secretly hostile to Henry, still protected him, saying, "If the king of England will thus cling to what he calls the customs of his fathers respecting the church, he must let me adhere to those of *mine*, which ever were to protect the exile and the fugitive."

Murder of Becket.

At length a reconciliation was effected, and Becket returned to England, where he soon began to act with the greatest insolence, and seemed resolved to renew the war with the king. The archbishop of York and others whom he excommunicated repaired to the king, who was in Normandy, and Henry, on hearing from them how he was acting, exclaimed, before his whole court, "To what a miserable state am I reduced, when I cannot be at rest in my own realm by reason of one single priest! Is there no one to deliver me out of my troubles?"

Four knights, who heard him, bound themselves by a secret oath to make the primate alter his conduct, or to put him to death. They passed over to England, and reached Canterbury a few days after Christmas. They went in to the primate, and required him to quit the kingdom or absolve the bishops whom he had excommunicated. Words grew high; he told them that he despised their threats. "We will do more than threaten," said they, and went out of the apartment, and began to arm themselves. When the time of the evening service was come, the primate, preceded by his silver cross, entered the cathedral, and he was ascending the steps of the choir when the four knights rushed in, crying, "Where is Thomas à Becket? Where is that traitor to the king and kingdom?" No reply being made, they cried, "Where is the archbishop?" Becket then advanced, saying, "Here am I, no traitor, but a priest ready to suffer in the name of Him who redeemed me." They required him to absolve the prelates, but he refused; they then bade him fly thence, or they would slay him. He declared his willingness to die for the sake of the church. One of them struck him with the flat of his sword; the others attempted to drag him away, but he clung to one of the pillars, and flung them off. He called one of them a pimp; and the knight, stung with the reproach, made a blow of his sword at him, which nearly cut off the arm of his cross-bearer, and wounded Becket himself in the crown of the head. "To God," said he, "to St. Mary, and the saints the patrons of this church, and to St. Denis, I commend myself and the church's cause." A second blow brought him to the ground; he drew his robe about him, folded his hands in prayer, and expired beneath repeated blows.

Canonization of Becket.

Nothing could exceed the consternation of king Henry when he heard of the murder of the archbishop. He saw the advantage which it would give the church against him, and he therefore made every effort in his power to convince the pope of his innocence. As he was really guiltless, and it might not be safe to drive him to desperation, the pontiff, after he had made all the submissions required of him, consented to forgive him and receive him again to favour. The murdered prelate was pronounced by the court of Rome to be a martyr, or one who had perished in the cause of religion, and he was canonized, or made a saint, under the title of St. Thomas of Canterbury. Numerous miracles, it was said, took place at his tomb, which became a favourite object of pilgrimage for nearly four centuries*. The murderers retired at first to a strong castle belonging to one of them in Yorkshire. As the church had refused to submit to the law of the land, the law in return would not punish any offence against a churchman, and they thus remained unmolested. Finding themselves however generally shunned, they at length went to Rome and implored the pontiff's forgiveness. He enjoined, by way of penance, a pilgrimage to the Holy Land, and they died at Jerusalem.

Some years after, when Henry was engaged in a war with the king of Scotland, he resolved to make a pilgrimage to the tomb of the new saint, in order to obtain his intercession with Heaven in his favour, or with perhaps a view of policy. When he came within sight of the church, he alighted from his horse, and walked to it barefoot. Having prostrated himself at the shrine of the martyr, he passed the entire night alone in the church, and in the morning he assembled the monks, and placing a scourge in the hand of each, stripped his back and submitted to the discipline which they inflicted. He then received absolution, and set out for London, where soon after tidings arrived of the defeat and capture of the king of Scots; and as this had occurred on the very day of his absolution, the people now

---

* Thus the fine old poet Chaucer says,—
    And chiefely from every shire's end
    Of Engleland to Canterbury they wend (*go*),
    The holy blissful martyr for to seek,
    Who them hath holpen when that they were sick.

regarded him as perfectly reconciled with Heaven and the blessed martyr.

Conquest of Ireland.

It was in the reign of Henry II. that the English first invaded Ireland. One of the kings of that island, named Dermot MacMorrough, having carried off the wife of a chieftain named O'Ruark, the latter applied to Roderic O'Connor, the supreme king of the island, and by their united forces Dermot was driven out of his dominions. He repaired to king Henry, who promised to aid him; but not being at leisure at the time, he gave him permission to treat with any of his subjects who might be willing to engage in the adventure at their own expense. Dermot applied to Strongbow, earl of Pembroke, a man of great strength and courage and of broken fortunes, who, on the promise of the hand of Eva, Dermot's only daughter, and the succession to his kingdom of Leinster, engaged to assist him. Two other ruined knights, named Fitz-Stephen and Fitz-Gerald, joined in the enterprize. They landed with a small body of men on the coast of the county of Wexford; and such was the superiority which their armour and their military skill gave them over the barbarous natives, that they proved victorious in every conflict. Strongbow espoused the Irish princess, and on the death of Dermot became sovereign of Leinster; and when Roderic at the head of fifty thousand men besieged him in Dublin, he routed him with great slaughter of that undisciplined rabble. King Henry himself then came over, and held his Christmas in Dublin, where, in a huge palace framed for him by the natives of wicker-work, he entertained a great number of the Irish princes, who acknowledged themselves his vassals.

Henry and his Sons.

It might have been expected that king Henry would have spent the concluding years of his reign in peace and tranquillity. But though he was a most affectionate father, his four sons, Henry, Richard, Geoffrey, and John, by their undutiful conduct, in which they were encouraged by their mother, and abetted by the kings of France and Scotland, led him a life of misery. They required him to surrender portions of his dominions to them, and on his refusal took up arms against him. He, however, proved himself superior in force to them and their royal allies. Some time after, prince Henry falling ill of a fever was filled with remorse for his undutiful conduct, and sent to request his father to come to see him; but the king apprehending treachery would only send him his ring in token of forgiveness. The dying prince pressed it to his lips, and then, in conformity with a usual practice in those times, caused himself to be laid on a bed of ashes, and in that position received the sacraments and expired.

The other princes still harassed their father, and at length, worn out by their continued ingratitude and turbulence, he breathed his last at the castle of Chinon in France.

Fair Rosamond.

King Henry had the defect of not being a faithful husband. His favourite mistress was a lady named Rosamond Clifford, commonly called Fair Rosamond. According to the tale, to save her from the jealousy of queen Eleanor he constructed a labyrinthine bower for her at Woodstock, which could only be entered by means of a clue of thread. But the queen contrived to get possession of the clue, and with its aid she threaded the mazes of the bower, and finding Fair Rosamond forced her to swallow a bowl of poison.

CHAPTER II.

RICHARD I. (CŒUR DE LION).

King Richard's Crusade.

HENRY II. was succeeded by his son Richard, named Cœur de Lion or Lion-heart, from his great intrepidity. As soon as this monarch ascended the throne he began to make preparations for a Crusade, which he was to lead into the East in conjunction with Philip, king of France; for the great Sultan Sáladin had lately given the Christians a total defeat, and had taken Jerusalem and all the other towns of the Holy Land, except a few places on the sea coast, and the only chance that remained for the recovery of the Christian dominion in the East was the presence of a powerful armament from Europe.

The two monarchs reviewed their troops, which counted one hundred thousand fighting men, on the plain of Vezelay in France; and as it had been determined that they should proceed by sea to Syria, they led them to the southern ports to embark in the vessels which had been prepared. The place of rendezvous was Messína in Sicily, and while they stayed in that town Richard espoused the daughter of the king of Navarre, to whom he had been for some time engaged. On his arrival in Syria he found a numerous Christian army, in which were the troops of the king of France besieging the city of Acre, while Saladin, at the head of a large force, was at hand seeking to relieve it. The valour of king Richard and his English troops soon gave such an impulse to the efforts of the besiegers, that the garrison was forced to surrender in the very sight of the sultan. It was agreed that two thousand five hundred of them should remain as hostages till Saladin should have released an equal number of Christian captives and paid a large sum of money. But when some delay had occurred with respect to the payment of the money, the king of England had the prisoners all led out and barbarously massacred in view of the sultan's camp. He then led his troops along the coast toward Jaffa; on the way he gave Saladin a great defeat, and he came at length within view of the Holy City; but such dissension prevailed in the Christian camp that no operations of any importance could be carried on, and Richard, who was extremely anxious to return to England, where his brother John, instigated by the king of France, was endeavouring to get possession of the throne, concluded a truce for three years with the sultan, and embarked with a few companions at Acre. He had spent only sixteen months in the East, where the impression made by his valour was such that the Saracens long used his name as a word of terror.

Imprisonment of Richard.

Richard had made so many enemies by his brutality and insolence, that he ran considerable risk of ill-treatment if he should fall into their hands. Among others he had mortally offended the duke of Austria by causing his banner to be pulled down and flung into the dirt, and his evil destiny caused him to become the captive of this very duke; for having been shipwrecked in the Adriatic, as he was proceeding homewards in disguise, through Germany, he was discovered and arrested at a village-inn near Vienna. When the emperor of Germany heard of the capture he made the duke surrender his royal prisoner to him, and Richard was transferred from one imperial castle to another, the object of the emperor being to extort a large ransom for him from the people of England.

There is a romantic tale respecting the captivity of king Richard. According to it the people of England could not for a long time learn any tidings of their king, and could only conjecture that he must be a captive somewhere. There was a minstrel named Blondel, who had been a great

favourite of the English monarch, who was himself a poet
and musician, and this Blondel resolved to travel all over
Europe till he should learn tidings of his beloved master.
He went from city to city and from castle to castle, but
nought could he hear. At length he learned that in a
certain castle in Germany there lay a prisoner of high rank,
but whose name was unknown: Blondel now hoping that
he had found what he was in search of, went before the
castle and played and sang the first stanza of a ballad, the
joint composition of the king and himself in happier days.
Richard, for *he* was the prisoner, took it up and sang the
remainder, and Blondel then hastened to England and informed the barons of the place of their king's captivity.

After more than a year's detention king Richard was set
at liberty on the payment of a large ransom. At his entrance into London, the citizens, it is said, made in their
joy such a display of their wealth, that one of the Germans
who were with him said, "If our emperor had known the
riches of England, thy ransom, O king, would have been
far greater." Richard immediately prepared for war against
the king of France, who had done all in his power to induce the emperor to detain him, and had attempted to rob
him of a part of his dominions; he also deprived his un-
grateful brother of all his possessions, but he was afterwards induced by his mother to pardon him. "I forgive
him," said he, "and hope I shall as easily forget his injuries
as he will my pardon."

Death of King Richard.

The death of king Richard occurred in the following
manner. The viscount of Limóges in France, who was his
vassal, having found a treasure of ancient coins, sent him
a part of them as a present, but Richard, as superior lord,
claimed the whole, and on the viscount's refusal to comply with his demand, he laid siege to the castle in which
the treasure was said to be deposited. During the siege,
as the king was one day taking a view of the castle, one of

the garrison, named Bertram de Gourdon, shot a bolt from his cross-bow which hit him in the shoulder, and owing to the want of skill of his surgeon the wound proved mortal. The castle had been taken, and all in it put to death except Gourdon, who was brought into the presence of the dying monarch. "Wretch!" said the king, "what have I ever done to thee that thou shouldst seek my life?" "You have killed," replied he, "with your own hands my father and two brothers, and you intended to hang me; I am now in your power, and you may torment me as you will; but I will endure with joy, happy in having rid the world of such a pest." Struck by this undaunted reply, Richard ordered him a sum of money and his liberty. But Márcadee, the commander of his troops, seized the unhappy man, flayed him alive, and then hanged him. Richard died next day, having at his own request been severely scourged by the clergy who attended him. He was only in the forty-second year of his age.

CHAPTER III.

JOHN (LACKLAND).

Fate of Prince Arthur.

THE next heir to the crown of England was Arthur, the young duke of Brittany, son of Richard's next brother, Geoffrey; but as he was only twelve years of age, the late king, urged probably by his mother, the old queen Eleanor, who hated Constance, the mother of Arthur, left the crown to his brother John. The king of France espoused the quarrel of prince Arthur, and a war ensued between him and John, but it was terminated by a marriage between Philip's son Louis and John's niece Blanche of Castille, and the cause of Arthur was abandoned by his royal protector.

Some years after, when a new quarrel had broken out between Philip and John, the former gave Arthur one of his daughters in marriage, and required that all the English dominions in France should be given up to him. A war ensued, and in the course of it, Arthur, learning that his grandmother, who was his most bitter enemy, was at the castle of Mirabeau in Poitou, set out with a party of horse in the hope of making her a prisoner. He had nearly taken the castle, when John, who had heard of his mother's danger, came to her aid, and Arthur was defeated and made a captive. He was confined at first in the castle of Falaise, in Normandy, where an attempt was made to murder him, but was prevented by the humanity of Hubert de Bourg, the governor. He was then conveyed to a castle on the banks of the Seine at Rouen. There one night he was awakened from his sleep at the midnight hour, and ordered to come out of the tower in which he lay. He obeyed, and found at the foot of the tower a small boat in which the king and one attendant were seated. He was ordered to enter the boat. He read his fate in the gloomy looks of his uncle, and throwing himself on his knees implored with tears for mercy. But he was instantly seized by the hair and a dagger plunged into his bosom. A stone was then fastened to his body, which was flung into the river.

This barbarous murder caused John to lose Normandy and the greater part of his French dominions. As both he and Arthur were vassals of the crown of France, Philip summoned him to appear and answer for the murder before his peers. As he refused to obey the summons he was condemned to death by the court, and all the territories which he held of the crown of France declared to be forfeited. Such was the general horror felt at John's murder of his nephew, that when Philip entered Normandy and the other provinces, no resistance was offered, and nothing but Guienne remained to John.

John's contest with the Pope.

John next engaged in a contest with the pope respecting the right of appointment to the see of Canterbury. His kingdom was in consequence laid under interdict; that is, the celebration of the rites of religion in it were prohibited by the pope. In return he deprived the clergy of their property. The pope then excommunicated him, and pronouncing him deposed from his crown, gave the kingdom of England to the king of France; for such was the power and authority claimed by the popes in those days. Philip had prepared an army to go and take possession of his new kingdom, when Pandolf, the papal legate or ambassador, frightened John so much by exaggerating the power of Philip and the disaffection of his own subjects, that he declared himself willing to submit to any terms. Pandolf required that he should acknowledge himself a vassal of the Holy See, and pay the pope seven hundred marks a year for England and three hundred for Ireland. To these humiliating terms John assented, and Pandolf then passed over to France and ordered king Philip to disband his army and not to molest a vassal of the Holy See; and though Philip refused compliance, he was at length forced to give up all hopes of the conquest of England.

Magna Charta.

John's next contest was with his own barons, who combined in order to restrain the enormous power of the crown, which when wielded by an unprincipled tyrant like John, was a source of most dreadful misery to all orders of the people. The prime mover of this patriotic resistance was Stephen Langton, the man whom the pope had forced John to admit to the see of Canterbury. This excellent prelate showed the barons a charter of Henry I., where they might see what English liberty had been even after the Conquest; and they swore on the high altar of the church in which they were assembled, to make war on the king till he should have confirmed their liberties by a charter. When they made their demands on the king he attempted to elude them, and the pope took his side warmly, and sent Pandolf to support him. But the archbishop preferred the interests of his countrymen, and of justice and humanity, to those of the Holy See. The barons brought all their retainers into the field; they made themselves masters of the city of London; and the king, finding himself abandoned by every one, was forced to consent to grant the charter that was demanded.

A meeting took place between John and his barons, in order to arrange the terms of a charter. The place of meeting was a mead on the banks of the Thames, named Runnymede, a spot ever dear to the lovers of true and rational liberty. On the one side appeared the flower of the English nobility, headed by Robert Fitz-Walter, the commander of their army; on the other the humbled tyrant, attended by the legate Pandolf and a few prelates, barons and knights. When the king had affixed his seal to the charter, the barons renewed their homage, and concord was to all appearance restored.

The charter thus granted is named the Magna Charta, or Great Charter. It is the foundation of all the abundant liberty which we now enjoy, and no other nation can produce such a monument of genuine patriotism and extended and enlightened humanity as it presents; and that too, it should be observed, in an age which we are apt to regard and despise as rude and barbarous. For those enlightened prelates and high-minded nobles who wrested the Great Charter from a reluctant despot, were not actuated by a selfish regard to their own peculiar interests. They provided for the security of even the lowest of the people. It was enacted by the Charter that *no man* should be imprisoned or otherwise punished but "by the legal judgement of his peers, or by the law of the land;" and it was also provided that fines should not be so enormous as to deprive any man of his means of living, for it is added, "a freeman shall be amerced according to his offence, saving his freehold; a merchant, saving his merchandise; and a villain (*i. e.* peasant), saving his waggonage."

War with the Barons.

But king John had no intention of keeping this good law. As soon as the barons went out from his presence he gnashed his teeth, gnawed sticks and straws, rolled his eyes, and acted like a maniac. He sent immediately to implore the pope to absolve him from his oath, and he commissioned some of his friends to hire mercenary soldiers for him on the continent. Ere long large bodies of these military ruffians landed in England, and the pope's absolution arrived, followed by a sentence of excommunication against the barons. But strong in the consciousness of innocence, they resolved not to heed it; and as the king, at the head of his foreign troops, was ravaging the country in a fearful manner, massacring the people and pillaging and burning castles, towns and villages, they deemed themselves justified in renouncing their allegiance, and they made an offer of the crown to Louis, son of the king of France. Louis soon landed with an army; large numbers of John's mercenaries went over to him; but on the other hand, several of the barons, suspicious of his designs, and gained by the lavish promises of John, were about to join their own king, when, as he was on his march to the town of Lynn, in Norfolk, he lost the waggons which carried his treasure by the overflow of the sea, and he was seized with a fever at the abbey of Swinstead, and breathed his last at Newark, to which he was removed. John was by far the worst king that ever reigned in England, for he did not possess a single estimable quality.

CHAPTER IV.

HENRY III. (OF WINCHESTER).

Character of Henry.—Confirmation of the Great Charter.

HENRY, the eldest son of king John, named of Winchester from the place of his birth, was only ten years old at the time of the death of his father. The prelates and barons of the royal party caused him to be crowned immediately, and the care of himself and kingdom was committed to the earl of Pembroke, an able and upright man. The nobles all gradually returned to their allegiance, Louis was obliged to depart, and the Great Charter was renewed.

The early years of the reign of Henry III. present few events of general interest. As he grew up his character proved to be one of great good nature, but of extreme weakness. He was lavish of the public money, and of places of honour and preferment to his own half-brothers and to the relations of his queen, who was daughter to the count of Provence in France; and he was the abject slave of the pope, whom he suffered to pillage the kingdom at his pleasure. These grievances and abuses at length produced a spirit of resistance among all classes of the people.

The clergy and barons first proceeded gently with their erring sovereign. Upon the occasion of his demanding a supply of money, the clergy deputed the primate and three other bishops to remonstrate with him. He was very free of his promises of amendment, and consented to confirm the Great Charter. The ceremony employed on this occasion was more solemn than usual; the charter was read aloud, the bishops and abbots all standing and holding lighted tapers in their hands. When it was read they pronounced the sentence of excommunication against whoever should violate it, and casting their tapers on the ground, exclaimed, " May the soul of him who incurs this sentence thus stink and corrupt in hell!" The king, laying his hand on his heart, replied, "So help me God as I shall observe and keep all these things, as I am a Christian man, as I am a knight, as I am a king crowned and anointed." Yet when the ceremony was over, he thought no more of this solemn promise.

Barons' War.

It was now apparent that it would be necessary to employ stronger measures to save the kingdom from being pillaged by the king and pope. A confederacy of the nobles was formed for the purpose of limiting the royal authority. At the head of it was Simon de Montfort, earl of Leicester, the king's brother-in-law, but a Frenchman by birth. Henry was obliged to consent to the formation of a committee of prelates and barons for correcting abuses and making good laws. But Leicester and the other members of the committee showed themselves to be too fond of power; they moreover did not continue at unity among themselves, and the nation in general was disappointed, so that the king was able to resume his power. The pope as usual absolved him from his oath, and the barons at last found it necessary to have recourse to arms. After sundry actions and negotiations a battle took place between the royal army and that of Leicester, at Lewes in Sussex, which terminated in the total defeat of the royalists and the captivity of the king, his son prince Edward, his brother, and his nephew.

Origin of House of Commons.—Prince Edward's Escape.

Leicester was now in effect the sovereign of all England; he carried the king about with him, and made what orders and regulations he pleased in his name. Among the other acts of this powerful nobleman at this time was the giving origin to the house of commons, a branch of the legislature which hitherto had no existence. In the year 1265, when summoning a parliament, Leicester directed the sheriffs "to elect and return two knights for each county, two citizens for each city, and two burgesses for each borough in the county."

At length prince Edward contrived to escape from the custody in which he was held by Leicester. His escape was effected in the following manner. Being at Hereford, he obtained permission to take an airing on horseback one day after dinner, and when at some distance from the town he proposed to his keepers to run races with their horses. Several matches were accordingly made, in which the prince and his friends took care not to engage. When the keepers' horses were pretty well tired, and a man mounted on a grey horse appeared and waved his bonnet (the signal agreed on) on the summit of an adjacent hill, the prince and his attendants set spurs to their horses and galloped off; the keepers pursued, but when they saw a body of armed men issue from a wood and receive the prince, they gave over the chase, and prince Edward hastened to meet the powerful earl of Gloucester and concert with him measures for opposing Leicester.

Defeat and Death of Leicester.

The armies of the prince and of Leicester encountered at Evesham, in Worcestershire. That of the former was by so much the more numerous, that when Leicester ascended a hill, to take a view of it, he cried, "The Lord have mercy on our souls, for our bodies are prince Edward's." In the battle he placed the old king in armour in the front, and one of the royalists, not knowing him, unhorsed, and might have slain him, but that he cried out, "Hold, fellow! I am Harry of Winchester!" The prince, who was at hand, then ran up, and had him conveyed to a place of safety. Leicester's horse was killed under him, and as he fought on foot, he demanded if they gave quarter: "Not to traitors!" was the reply; and he was slain. Of all the barons and knights in his army only ten remained alive.

Prince Edward's Crusade.

After the defeat and death of Leicester all opposition to the royal authority was at an end. Prince Edward took advantage of the calm to head a crusade to the East. He remained for eighteen months in the Holy Land, where he renewed the fame of the lion-hearted Richard. While there he nearly lost his life by treachery; for the prince of Jaffa, pretending a desire to embrace Christianity, sent an envoy to him, who, being admitted into the room in which he was lying on a couch during the heat of the day, drew a dagger and attempted to plunge it into his heart; but Edward received the blow on his arm, and then killed the ruffian with his own weapon. The dagger, it is said, was poisoned; and Edward's devoted wife Eleanor of Castille applied her lips to the wound, and thus extracted the poison at the risk of her own life. Edward was in Sicily, on his return to England, when he heard of the death of his father, who had breathed his last at Westminster, after a long reign of fifty-five years.

CHAPTER V.
EDWARD I. (LONGSHANKS).

Conquest of Wales.

EDWARD I., surnamed Longshanks from the extreme length of his limbs, proved to be one of the greatest monarchs that ever reigned in England. He was at the same time a gallant warrior, an able statesman and legislator, and in domestic life a faithful and affectionate husband to his excellent queen, and a good father to his children.

As Llewellyn, prince of Wales, had been on the side of Leicester in the late wars, and refused to come to perform his homage when summoned, king Edward led an army into Wales, and reduced him to submission. But ere long the Welsh resumed their arms; excited in part, as is said, by a prediction, ascribed to their ancient national prophet Merlin, who had, it seems, foretold that when English money became round a prince of Wales would be crowned at London; and as Edward had lately issued a circular coinage and forbidden the penny to be *cut*, as heretofore, into halfpence and farthings, they deemed that the prophecy was on the eve of its completion.

Their expectations were, however, wofully deceived. The whole country was speedily overrun and reduced; Llewellyn was slain as he was coming out of a barn, where he had slept, by a knight, who knew not his quality; and his head was brought to Edward, who in derision of Merlin's prophecy, placed it, crowned with ivy, or as some said, silver, on the Tower of London. Llewellyn's brother David, who had commenced the insurrection by surprising the castle of Háwarden, and murdering the garrison, was sentenced to be drawn on a hurdle to the gallows, to be there hanged, his bowels to be taken out and burnt before his face, and his body to be quartered and sent through the country. This was the first instance of what became the usual punishment of traitors.

The prophecy of Merlin was, however, to receive a certain degree of completion. While Edward was in Wales, his queen, who usually accompanied him, gave birth to a prince in the castle of Carnarvon, whom the king declared to be prince of Wales; and as this prince became afterwards king of England, it may be said that Merlin's prophecy was fulfilled. Ever since that time the eldest son of the reigning sovereign is called the prince of Wales.

Edward is charged with the commission of a very barbarous act while in Wales. Perceiving, it is said, the great influence of the strains of the Welsh bards over the minds of their countrymen, and fearing that they might again awaken the desire of independence, he assembled them all, and put them to death. It is gratifying, however, to observe that this event, which forms the subject of one of the finest lyric poems in the English language, is totally destitute of historic proof, and appears to be nothing more than the coinage of Welsh national feeling.

Conquest of Scotland.

Scotland next attracted the attention of king Edward. The feudal superiority of the crown of England over that kingdom had long been acknowledged; and on the occasion of a disputed succession to the throne, in consequence of the death of king Alexander III. without children, the decision was naturally referred to the king of England. The principal claimants were the descendants of the three daughters of David, brother of king William the Lion. Of these John Báliol was the grandson of the eldest daughter, Robert Bruce the son of the second, and John Hastings the grandson of the third.

Edward appeared with a large army on the frontiers of Scotland, and having made all the competitors acknowledge his feudal superiority, he appointed a council, composed of Scots and English, to examine their claims. He then retired, and at the end of a year he returned; and the council having decided in favour of Baliol, he pronounced judgement according to their award, and put that nobleman in possession of the kingdom.

Sometime after, however, Baliol having neglected to comply with some demands, which king Edward as his superior lord had made on him, the English monarch appeared again on the borders at the head o a numerous army. He took the town of Berwick-on-Tweed by storm, and sent a division of his army, under earl Warrenne, against the castle of Dunbar, whose garrison agreed to surrender if not relieved within three days. On the third day a Scottish army appeared on the adjacent hills; Warrenne caused his men to retire from the castle to prepare for battle. A cry of "They run! they run!" rose in the Scottish ranks, and their whole army poured down into the plain: but the English had now formed, and the Scots were defeated with tremendous slaughter. No further resistance was offered to king Edward: Baliol was deposed, and sent a prisoner to London; and earl Warrenne was set over the kingdom. Edward carried away the crown and the other regalia, and the stone on which the Scottish kings used to be crowned was deposited in Westminster Abbey.

William Wallace.

Scotland did not long remain tranquil: earl Warrenne being obliged to leave it, on account of ill health, committed the direction of affairs to Ormesby, the chief justice, and Cressingham, the treasurer. These men were tyrannic and oppressive, and their inferior officers followed their example. One of these last having offered an affront to a gentleman named William Wallace, the latter, who was a man of gigantic stature and great courage, struck him dead on the spot. Knowing that he had no mercy to expect, Wallace then fled to the woods, and led the life of an outlaw. He was joined by many others who hated the English or had felt their oppression, and in many parts of the country the people rose and massacred the English who were among them. But earl Warrenne soon returned at the head of an army, and most of the nobles and gentry who had joined Wallace, hastened to make their submission. Wallace and those who disdained to submit retired northwards; Warrenne followed them till he reached the Forth, at Stirling, near which, at a place called Cambuskenneth, on the opposite side of the river, the army of Wallace was posted. The earl prepared to pass over the only bridge that was near. It was of wood, and so narrow that only two persons could go abreast on it. Wallace waited quietly till about five thousand men were over, and he then poured down on them with an overwhelming force and slaughtered them all in the sight of earl Warrenne, who was unable to give them any relief. Cressingham was among the slain, and the Scots, it is said, flayed his body and made thongs for their horses of the skin.

After this victory Wallace was made governor of the kingdom; but his dignity was of short duration. King Edward once more entered Scotland with a powerful army and advanced to the Forth: want of provisions, however, obliged him to fall back toward the borders. Hearing on his way that Wallace lay with his army in the forest of Falkirk, he advanced in that direction. He found the Scottish troops posted behind a morass; but the English did not suffer this impediment to retard them: while one division moved directly through the morass, another, led by the bishop of Durham, a martial prelate, went round it, and the Scots, after a most valiant resistance, were all cut to pieces. According to some accounts the number of the slain was fifty thousand.

Want of supplies prevented king Edward from completing the conquest of Scotland at this time; but in about five years after he returned with an army which the Scots were totally unable to resist, and penetrated to the northern extremity of the kingdom. All submitted but Wallace and a few others; and some time after Wallace was betrayed by his servant to Sir John Monteith, who was in pursuit of him, and he was transmitted to London, where he was tried, found guilty, and executed as a traitor. His head was placed on the Tower, and his quarters were sent to Scotland, to be set up in various places.

Robert Bruce.

Scotland, however, though deprived of Wallace, was soon again in arms. Robert Bruce, the grandson of the claimant of the crown, and John Comyn, the nephew and nearest kinsman of Baliol, who was now dead, happening to meet in the town of Dumfries, Bruce requested Comyn to grant him a private conference in the church of the Minorite friars. They entered the church alone; high words arose between them, and Bruce drew his dagger and plunged it into Comyn's bosom. Bruce rushed out of the church pale and agitated: "I think I have killed Comyn," said he to his friends, whom he met outside. "You only think so!" cried one of them, "I will secure him!" and they all rushed into the church, where they despatched Comyn, who was still alive.

The Scottish historians relate this event with many romantic but probably fabulous circumstances. They say that Bruce and Comyn had agreed to rise against the English power; but that while Bruce was in London, having been summoned to the English court, Comyn wrote to king Edward, giving him a full account of the plot. The king charged Bruce with it, but he denied it, and Edward appeared satisfied. That very night, however, his friend the earl of Gloucester, sent to Bruce, while he was at his supper, twelve golden crown pieces and a pair of spurs. Bruce knew at once that he thus counselled him to make his escape, and he instantly set out, attended by a single groom. As the ground was covered with snow he caused the horses to be shod with the shoes reversed, in order to elude pursuit. On the borders of Scotland he met a man of suspicious appearance, whom he slew, and found on him letters from Comyn to Edward. He then punished that nobleman for his treachery in the manner above related.

After the murder of Comyn, Bruce assumed the title of king; but the English and their adherents drove him out of Scotland, and he was forced to conceal himself for an entire winter in a small island off the north coast of Ireland. King Edward again set out for Scotland, to take vengeance for the murder of Comyn. He reached Carlisle; but a disease with which he was afflicted caused his death, at a place a short distance from that town. It was reported that he made his son, the prince of Wales, swear that he would cause his body to be boiled in a caldron till the flesh was separated from the bones, and that he would always have them carried before him when marching against the Scots.

CHAPTER VI.

EDWARD II. (OF CARNARVON).

Piers Gáveston.

EDWARD II. was in all respects the opposite of his illustrious father. He was weak and devoted to pleasure, and immoderately attached to a worthless young man of his own age named Piers Gáveston. Instead, therefore, of prosecuting the war in Scotland he hastened to disband his army and return with his favourite to London. He heaped offices and lands upon him, and even committed the kingdom to his care when he himself went over to France, to espouse the princess Isabel, the daughter of the French king.

Gaveston, like most upstarts, behaved with great insolence, and the principal men in the realm became his personal enemies. A confederacy of the nobles was formed, headed by the potent earl of Lancaster; and after many fruitless attempts to induce the king to part with his insolent favourite, they besieged the latter in the castle of Scarborough, and forced him to surrender. They conveyed him to Warwick castle, and there debated how to dispose of him. Some were for sparing his life at least, but one observing, "You have caught the fox; if you let him go you will have to hunt him again," they resolved to put him to death. He was then led to an adjacent heath, and there beheaded. The king was filled with grief and rage when he heard of the fate of Gaveston. He, however, dissembled his resentment, and was soon to all appearance on cordial terms with his nobles.

Battle of Bannockburn.

The affairs of Scotland now claimed all the attention of the English monarch. Bruce had returned and gained nearly the whole kingdom, and the governor of Stirling castle sent to say that if not relieved he must surrender. Edward, therefore, hastily levied an army and marched to his relief. When he came to Stirling he found Bruce's army drawn up in three divisions, between the castle and the *burn* or brook of Bannock. The following morning, when the Scots were formed in line of battle, an abbot prayed aloud for their success, and at his prayer the whole army fell down on their knees. " They kneel!" cried some of the English, " they beg for mercy !" " Be not deceived," replied a knight, " they beg for mercy ; but it is only from God." In the battle which ensued both sides fought with the utmost valour ; but the skill of Bruce, who had sunk pits, filled with sharp stakes, and covered with sods, in front of a part of his line, and who brought up a strong reserve in due time turned the day in favour of the Scots, and the English were totally defeated. King Edward never halted till he reached the sea-coast; his baggage, his treasure, and all his military stores fell into the hands of the conqueror.

This victory of Bannockburn, the only victory ever gained by the Scots over the English, secured the independence of Scotland. No place remained to the English in that country, and they were obliged some time after to acknowledge the title of Robert Bruce.

Hugh Spenser.

Edward did not remain long without a favourite. His new minion was named Hugh Spenser. Like his predecessor, he speedily incurred the enmity of the barons; and they forced the king to banish him. But Edward soon found himself strong enough to recall him, and to set the barons at defiance. In the war which ensued the great earl of Lancaster was made a prisoner. He was conducted to his own castle of Pontefract*, where the king sat in judgement upon him, and without being heard in his defence he was condemned to be beheaded. He was forth-

* Pronounced Pomfret.

with placed on a grey pony without a bridle, and led out of the town, the common people cursing him and pelting him with mud as he passed along. "King of Heaven," cried the unhappy nobleman, "grant me mercy, for the king of earth has forsaken me." When he reached an eminence without the town, he was made to kneel down, and his head was struck off.

The queen like the nobles hated Spenser, and when she went over with her son prince Edward to France, on some affairs of the state, she refused to return. She also seems to have formed an improper attachment to Roger Mortimer, one of the confederate barons, who had made his escape from the Tower. She soon after landed in England with a body of troops, and she was joined by a great number of the nobility. Edward retired with his favourite to Bristol, and thence sailed with him for Lundy island, in the mouth of the Bristol Channel. The queen's troops soon appeared before that city, the command of which was held by Spenser's father, a venerable old gentleman of more than ninety years of age. But the citizens forced him to surrender, and after undergoing, like Lancaster, a mock trial, he was hanged as a traitor, and his body was cut into pieces and flung to the dogs.

Deposition and Death of Edward.

Edward, owing to the state of the weather, had not been able to reach Lundy. He attempted to conceal himself in South Wales, but was forced to surrender. Spenser had already been betrayed to his enemies, who hanged him on a gallows fifty feet high, with a wreath of nettles on his head. The unhappy king being without any friends was deposed by a parliament summoned by the queen, and his son prince Edward was proclaimed king in his place.

The deposed monarch was kept a prisoner under the charge of various persons, and conveyed from castle to castle. His final abode was Berkeley castle, near Bristol, where every kind of insult and indignity was offered him.

Thus, when one day he wished to be shaved, his keepers fetched dirty cold water from the castle ditch for the purpose. On their refusal to change it, the weak unhappy man burst into tears, crying that in spite of their insolence he would be shaved with clean and warm water. Worse, however, than this awaited him. One night dreadful shrieks were heard to ring through the castle, and in the morning the neighbouring gentry and the citizens of Bristol were invited to come and behold the dead body of the king. No marks of violence appeared, but the features were distorted, and the general belief was that Gournay and Maltravers, to whose charge Lord Berkeley had committed him, had produced his death by introducing a red-hot iron through a tube into his intestines. There was little doubt that the real author of his death was Mortimer, and probably with the queen's knowledge and consent.

CHAPTER VII.

EDWARD III. (OF WINDSOR).

Fall of Mortimer.

As Edward was not yet of age, the queen and Mortimer held the government in their own hands. Mortimer's insolence far exceeded that of Gaveston and Spenser, and he soon drew on himself the hatred of the nobility. The young king, as he grew up, was galled at the restraint under which he was held; and when he attained his eighteenth year, he readily listened to a project of lord Montacute for seizing the person of Mortimer, and assuming the government.

A parliament having been summoned to Nottingham, Mortimer and the queen repaired thither, and took up their abode in the castle. The keys of the gates were placed every night under the queen's pillow for security; but the governor being informed by Montacute of the king's pleasure, showed him a subterraneous passage into the castle; and Montacute, having ridden out into the country one day with a party of friends, returned at night and entered by the secret passage. They were joined by the king on the stairs of the tower which they had entered, and went on till they came to a room where Mortimer was in consultation with the bishop of Lincoln. They burst open the door, slaying two knights who defended it. The queen, in alarm, cried out from her bed in the adjoining apartment, "Sweet son, fair son, spare my gentle [*i. e.* noble] Mortimer!" but they made him a prisoner; and when parliament met, he was hanged at Tyburn for the murder of the late king, and other offences. The queen was confined to one of her manors, with an income of 4000*l.* a year.

Edward's Claim of the Crown of France.

Edward was soon after engaged in a war with Scotland, and he gave the Scots a great defeat at a place named Hálidon Hill, near Berwick-on-Tweed, when they came to the relief of that town, which he was besieging; and the southern part of the kingdom was ceded to him. But his attention was soon after drawn away from Scotland by the prospect of a more brilliant acquisition, that of the crown of France, which he claimed in right of his mother.

It is a remarkable fact, that from the very foundation of the French monarchy, the next heir to the crown had always proved to be a male; and an opinion seems thus to have grown up, that, by a law of the Salian Franks, who founded the monarchy (thence named the Salic law), the crown could not descend to a female. This supposed law had lately been acted on in three successive instances; for the three brothers of Edward's mother, who followed each other on the throne, had only had daughters. On the death of the last, his daughter had been excluded, and the crown given to his cousin, Philip of Valois; but Edward then, pretending that, though females could not inherit themselves, they could transmit a right to their male descendants, laid claim to the throne. This absurd claim was, however, at once rejected by the peers of France; and Edward, instead of persisting in it, did homage to Philip for Guienne. Matters stood thus for some years; at length Edward was induced by the enemies of Philip to assert his claim by force of arms; and his people gladly agreed to support him with their persons and purses in his unjust attempt on the crown of France.

Battle of Cressy.

We pass over the early events of the war; but in the month of July in the year 1346, king Edward, at the head of an army of thirty thousand men, landed at La Hogue in Normandy. He was accompanied by his son, the prince of Wales, though only fifteen years of age, and by his principal nobility. Having taken several towns, he moved along the left bank* of the Seine, which river he wished to cross, in order to join an army of Flemings in Picardy. But he found the bridges all broken, and king Philip, at the head of a numerous army, followed his motions on the opposite bank of the river. At length Edward contrived to repair one of the broken bridges, and to pass over unknown to Philip; and he then marched rapidly till he reached the river Somme; but he there again found all the bridges secured, and learned that Philip was at Amiens with one hundred thousand men. Being informed that there was a ford near the town of Ábbeville, which might be passed when the tide was low, Edward set out for it at midnight; but when the English reached it, the waters were not sufficiently low; and while they were waiting, a large body of French cavalry came down to oppose their passage. The

---

* It may be useful to mention that by the right and left banks of a river, is meant their position relative to a person going *down* the river from its source toward its mouth.

English horsemen, however, gallantly plunged into the stream, drove off the enemy, and gained the opposite bank. The whole army was over when king Philip arrived, and the rising of the tide obliged him to go round by the bridge of Abbeville.

Though the French army was nearly four times as numerous as his own, king Edward resolved to give it battle. He drew up his troops in three divisions on an eminence behind the village of Creci or Cressy. The prince of Wales, aided by the earls of Oxford and Warwick, led the first, the king himself commanded the last. At dawn, Edward, having heard mass and received the sacrament, rode along the lines, cheering his men, and at ten o'clock they sat down and took their breakfast in their ranks. The French, meantime, advanced from Abbeville in confusion and disorder. A storm of thunder and rain came on, and lasted through a great part of the day; but at five o'clock in the afternoon, the sky becoming clear, Philip ordered a body of Génoese cross-bowmen in his service to begin the battle. The Genoese gave a shout, and discharged their bolts; the English archers, who were posted in front, showered in return their arrows of a yard in length; and the Genoese, unable to re-charge their ponderous crossbows, fell into disorder. The count of Alençon then charged the first division of the English with a numerous body of cavalry. The second line advanced to its aid, and a knight was sent off to king Edward, who was viewing the battle from the top of a windmill, to pray him to send more help. "Is my son slain or wounded?" said the king. "No, sire." "Then," replied he, "tell Warwick, he shall have no aid. Let the boy win his spurs*." When this message was brought to the English, it redoubled their courage; and the French were at length totally routed, with immense loss. "Fair son," cried Edward to

* That is, show himself worthy of receiving the honour of knighthood, the putting on of the new knight's spurs being an important part of the ceremony.

the prince, as he clasped him to his bosom after the battle, "Fair son, continue your career. You have acted nobly, and shown yourself worthy of me and the crown."

The person of highest rank who fell in this great battle was John, king of Bohemia. This prince, who was blind from age, ordered four of his knights to lead him into the thick of the battle. They interlaced his and their own bridles, and rushed forward, and all were slain. The crest of the king of Bohemia, three ostrich feathers, and his motto, *Ich dien,* i. e. *I serve,* were adopted by the prince of Wales, and still are those of the heir-apparent of the crown of England.

Siege of Calais.

Edward now advanced, and laid siege to the town of Calais. He placed a numerous fleet before the port, and he constructed a large number of huts to shelter his men during the winter, for he resolved, instead of wasting the blood of his troops, to trust to the effect of famine. The governor of the town, John de Vienne, held out perseveringly for upwards of ten months. Philip came one time with an army of one hundred and fifty thousand men to attempt its relief; but he refused battle when offered by Edward; and the famine in Calais at length became so severe that De Vienne was obliged to surrender.

Edward, irritated by the obstinate defence of the citizens, demanded the lives of six of their principal men. While they were in perplexity as to how to act, Eustace de St. Pierre, one of the most eminent citizens, offered himself as one of the victims. His example was followed by others, and the number was thus completed. The gates were then opened; De Vienne came forth, mounted on a palfrey, on account of his wounds; he was followed by fifteen knights bareheaded; and then came the six voluntary victims, bareheaded, barefooted, in their shirts, and with halters about their necks. The governor fell on his knees, and presented the keys of the town to king Edward. He pleaded, but in vain, for the lives of the six citizens; the English barons interceded to as little purpose; the executioner had made his appearance, and their fate seemed inevitable, when the queen Philippa came forth from her tent, and falling on her knees, pleaded for their lives. "Dame," said Edward, "I wish you had been in some other place; but I cannot deny you." She took them to her tent, clothed and entertained them, and at their departure gave them each a sum of money.

Battle of Poitiers.

A dreadful plague, which ravaged all Europe, caused a cessation of war for some years. At length hostilities, of which the south of France was the scene, were resumed.

In the autumn of the year 1356, the Black Prince (as the prince of Wales was called from the colour of his armour), to whom his father had committed the government of Guienne, set out from Bordeaux at the head of about twelve thousand men, of whom only a third were English. He marched up the river Garonne to Agen, where he crossed; and he ravaged the adjacent provinces, slaughtering the peasantry, destroying the corn, wine, and provisions, and burning the farm-houses, villages, and towns. As he was returning through Poitou, he fell in, at a place named Maupertuis, near Poitiers, with the rear of a large army, led by John, the king of France, in person. "God help us," cried the prince, "it only remains for us to fight bravely." He then drew up his army on an eminence, the sides of which were covered with vineyards, a single lane, in which only four persons could ride abreast, leading to its summit. At the head of this lane he posted his cavalry, with a part of his archers in front of them; and he made the remainder of his archers line the hedges on each side of the lane.

The French army, which was seven times as numerous as that of the prince, was drawn up in three divisions on a moor at the foot of the hill. But ere the engagement commenced, the cardinal Tálleyrand Périgord, who dwelt hard by, came, and with uplifted hands besought the king of France to spare the effusion of Christian blood. With John's consent, he then rode to the prince to propose a negotiation. "Save my honour and the honour of my army," said Edward, "and I will hearken to any reasonable terms." He offered to surrender his conquests, booty, and prisoners, on condition of a safe retreat; but John would accept of nothing short of the surrender of himself and a hundred of his knights. These terms the prince indignantly rejected, and at dawn next morning both sides prepared for action. The good cardinal, having made another fruitless effort at conciliation, rode away, not to be a witness of the slaughter he had sought to avert. The first division of the French then charged up the lane, the archers showered their arrows on them from both sides; men and horses fell in heaps, and those who forced their way through, suffered equally from the shafts of the archers on the summit. This division being thus nearly destroyed, the archers quitted their covert, and boldly advanced into the plain and attacked the second division of the French in front, while a body of six hundred men, whom the prince had placed on an adjacent hill, came and assailed its left flank. After a little time it turned and fled. "Now, sir," cried sir John Chandos to the prince, "the field is won; let us mount and charge the French king. I know him to be a dauntless knight, who will never flee from an enemy; the attempt may be a bloody one, but please God and St. George he will be ours." They mount, they pour down the lane, and emerge on the moor; they cut to pieces the knights and soldiers who advance to oppose them; the king leads up his division on foot; he receives two wounds, and is beaten to the ground; a young knight advances, and, falling on his knees, implores him to surrender. "Where is my cousin, the prince of Wales?" cries the king; and finding that he is not at hand, he delivers his sword to the knight, and becomes his prisoner.

When the captive king was led to the tent which the prince of Wales had caused to be pitched for himself, the latter advanced to meet him with every mark of courtesy and respect. At table he waited on him, declaring himself, as his subject, not entitled to the honour of sitting with him. He then took him to Bordeaux, and shortly after they embarked for England. They landed at Sandwich, and thence proceeded to London. The citizens poured forth to meet their gallant prince; arches were thrown across the streets, tapestries and costly stuffs were hung from the windows. The king of France rode on a stately cream-coloured charger, the prince on a small pony by his side. When they reached Westminster-hall, where king Edward sat expecting them, amidst his prelates and nobles, the monarch rose, embraced the royal captive, and conducted him to a splendid banquet. The Savoy-palace in the Strand was then assigned as a residence to king John and one of his sons, who had been taken with him at the battle of Poitiers.

Last Days of the Black Prince and of the King.

Some years later a peace was concluded, and the ransom which the French king was to pay was agreed on. He was then set at liberty, but some difficulties arising about the payment of the ransom, he resolved to return to England. When his council remonstrated, he nobly replied, that if honour were banished from the rest of the earth, she should find an abode in the breast of princes. He was received with great respect by king Edward; but he fell sick shortly after, and died at the Savoy.

. Hitherto the reign of king Edward had been brilliant and glorious; but gloom now began to gather over it. The Black Prince had been induced to enter Spain in the cause of an odious tyrant, Peter the Cruel, king of Castille, against whom his subjects had risen on account of his oppression. He engaged and defeated his enemies; but the faithless Peter broke all his engagements with him, and he returned to Guienne with his health impaired, and deeply in debt. His necessities obliging him to lay heavy taxes on the people, they complained to the king of France as the superior lord, who summoned him to appear at his court. The prince replied that he would, but that it would be at the head of sixty thousand men. This, however, was only an empty boast; for when king Charles declared war against the English, the people of all the provinces favoured him; and the crown of England had less possessions in France at the end than it had at the beginning of king Edward's reign. So fruitless were the splendid victories of Cressy and Poitiers!

The Black Prince died soon after his return to England, leaving an only son; and he soon was followed to the tomb by his illustrious father. On the day of his death, this great monarch, we are told, was left in his expiring moments without a single friend or attendant. A priest at length came to his bedside, warned him of his situation, and bade him prepare to meet his Creator. He had just strength enough to thank him, and take a crucifix in his hand, which he kissed with tears, and then breathed his last.

The stately castle of Windsor was built by king Edward: for this purpose, every county in England was required to send him a rated number of carpenters, masons, and tilers. He also instituted the noble order of the Garter. At a ball, it is said, the countess of Pembroke, having dropt her garter when dancing, the king picked it up, and, seeing the courtiers smile, he said, "*Honi soit qui mal y pense*" (*i. e.* "Shamed be he who thinketh ill thereof"), which words are the motto of the order.

CHAPTER VIII.

RICHARD II. (OF BORDEAUX).

Rising of the Peasantry.

RICHARD, named, in the usual manner, from Bordeaux, the place of his birth, was the only son of the Black Prince, and his is the first instance in our history of a grandson succeeding his grandfather. As he was only ten years of age, a regency was appointed.

When Richard was about sixteen years old, a terrible insurrection of the common people broke out, in consequence of the imposition of what is called a poll-tax, that is, a tax imposed on every grown person. One of the collectors of this tax having demanded payment for the daughter of a tiler at Dartford in Kent, her mother objected to paying it, asserting that the girl was under fifteen years of age; the tax-gatherer affirmed that she was more, and behaved in so rude and indecent a manner, that her father, who just then came in from his work, struck him dead with the implement which he happened to have in his hand. His neighbours approved the act, and vowed to stand by him. The whole of Kent speedily rose, and Wat the Tyler became the leader of the insurgents. They were joined by the people of Essex under Jack Straw, and at Maidstone they liberated a priest named John Ball, who was in prison for preaching against the wealth and corruption of the clergy. At Blackheath, near London, Ball preached to them, taking for his text a rhyme very popular at the time:—

> "When Adam dalf [delved], and Eve span,
> Who was then the gentleman?"

and dwelling on the natural equality of man, declared that bishops, earls, barons, judges, and lawyers, should be all done away with, that all might be equally free and noble. His auditors highly relished his discourse, and they forthwith fell to pillaging the houses of the gentry, and cut off the head of every justice, lawyer and juror that fell in their way.

When the insurgents entered the city, they were joined by the populace. They broke open Newgate, they plundered and burnt the Temple, they pillaged the magnificent mansion of the duke of Lancaster, the king's uncle, in the Strand. Orders were given that no one should keep any part of the plunder, and one man, who had secreted a silver cup, was thrown, with the cup in his bosom, into the Thames. They repaired next morning to the Tower, where the king was residing, and at his desire they then followed him to Mile-end, where he agreed to give them a free pardon, and assented to their other demands, and they dispersed and retired to their homes.

During the king's absence, Wat Tyler and a party had broken into the Tower and murdered the archbishop of Canterbury and some other persons; and next day, when the king rode into the city with a small train, he was met by Tyler at the head of twenty thousand men. Tyler, leaving his men, rode up to him boldly. During the conference, he was observed to play with his dagger; and at length, though perhaps without any ill design, he laid hold on the king's bridle. William Walworth, the lord-mayor, instantly drew his sword, and stabbed him in the throat, and one of the king's esquires then despatched him. The insurgents bent their bows to avenge him, when the young king, with great presence of mind, galloped up to them, crying, "What are ye about, my lieges? Tyler was a traitor. Come with me; I will be your leader." They followed him to Islington, and he there directed them to disperse, and return to their homes in peace, promising the same terms that he had granted to their associates the day before. They obeyed his injunctions; but when the nobility and gentry had brought forty thousand men to the king's support, his promises and pardons were thought of no more; and Jack Straw, John Ball, and about fifteen hundred more, were publicly executed as rebels and traitors.

Limitation of the King's Authority.

From the energy and decision shown by the young king on this occasion, good hopes were entertained of his reign. But they proved illusive, for he was vain, haughty, arrogant, and luxurious. He also greatly offended the proud nobility by the favour which he showed to one Michael de la Pole, the son of a merchant, whom he made chancellor, and created earl of Suffolk. Hence arose a confederacy like those against Henry III. and Edward II., and parliament petitioned for a dismissal of the ministers. Richard insolently replied, that he would not remove at their desire the meanest scullion in his kitchen; but he was soon forced to give way, and Suffolk was impeached, and fined and imprisoned. A commission was then formed for the reformation of the state. Its head was the king's uncle, the duke of Gloucester, a man of a very violent arbitrary temper. The measures of the committee were harsh and tyrannical, and their influence gradually melted away; and in the twenty-second year of his age the king found himself strong enough to take the reins of government out of their hands. He then reigned for some years in undisturbed tranquillity, during which time he took an opportunity of going over to Ireland, and introducing some regularity into that barbarous country.

Murder of Gloucester.

Richard was all this time on terms of great cordiality with his uncles, and all those who had sought to limit his power. But he still secretly cherished thoughts of revenge, especially on Gloucester, who, when he was in power, had put several of his friends to death, and insulted himself. After a lapse of eight years, feeling himself strong enough to attack that prince, he went in person to his castle, and when the duke and his family came out to receive him, he ordered the earl-marshal to arrest him and convey him to the Tower. When they reached the Thames, on their way thither, the duke was hurried on board a vessel which lay ready, and conveyed to Calais; and when, some time after, orders were sent to bring him over to answer the charges made against him, word was returned that he was dead. There seemed to be little doubt that he had not died a natural death; and the most current report was that, by the king's orders, he had been smothered between two beds.

Quarrel between Norfolk and Hereford.

"The king," to use the words of the chronicler, "now began to rule more fiercely than before." Parliament had been induced (a thing without precedent) to grant him a revenue for life; he maintained a force of ten thousand men, and no one dared to gainsay his will. He was, to all intents, a despotic monarch; but he had lost his subjects' affection, and his downfall was approaching.

As the dukes of Hereford and Norfolk (the former the son of Lancaster, and the king's cousin) were one day riding from Brentford to London, they fell into discourse on the character of Richard, and his unforgiving temper, Norfolk observing, among other things, that he could not trust the king's oath. This discourse appears to have been secretly conveyed by Hereford to the king, who sent for him, and made him repeat it before the council. He then gave him a full pardon; and in the next parliament Hereford accused Norfolk as a traitor. Norfolk retorted the charge, and a court of chivalry decided, as there were no witnesses on either side, that the matter should be left to the judgement of God by wager of battle, at Coventry, in presence of the king. On the 16th of September, the day appointed, the combatants appeared in the lists. Their lances were in rest, and the signal was about to be given, when Richard flung down his warder or truncheon, and forbade the combat to proceed. He passed sentence of banishment on both, for life on Norfolk, for ten years on Hereford. The latter went to France, the former on a pilgrimage to the Holy Land, on his return from which he died of a broken heart at Venice.

Lancaster in Arms against the King.

The two banished noblemen had been allowed to appoint attorneys to receive any inheritance that might fall to them. Accordingly, on the death of his father, Hereford assumed the title of duke of Lancaster, and claimed the estates belonging to it; but Richard, asserting that an exile could not inherit, seized them to his own use. As discontent was now almost universal in England, Lancaster resolved to assert his rights, and probably obtain the crown by force; and taking the opportunity of the king's absence, who was gone a second time to Ireland, he embarked with his attendants in three small vessels at Vannes in Brittany, and landed at Ravenspur, in Yorkshire. He was joined immediately by the earls of Northumberland and Westmoreland. As he declared that he was only come to claim his rights, numbers flocked to his standard, and he reached London at the head of sixty thousand men. His uncle, the duke of York, who had been left regent, had assembled an army of forty thousand men to oppose him; but finding their leaders little inclined to act against the duke of Lancaster, he retired to Bristol, whither he was followed by his nephew. They had a private interview in the chapel of Berkeley castle, the result of which was the junction of their forces. The castle of Bristol surrendered at their appearance, and some of the king's friends who were in it were executed without even a trial. Lancaster then proceeded to Chester.

Capture of the King.

Owing to the state of the weather, it was some time before Richard was informed of what had taken place in

England. He then sent the earl of Salisbury over from Dublin with a body of troops, in order to raise the Welshmen, while he himself proceeded with the main body of his forces to Waterford. He made, however, so much delay, that by the time that he landed at Milford, the Welsh, after remaining a fortnight under arms, had dispersed, and returned to their homes; and on looking out of his window on the second morning, he saw that the greater part of his own troops had deserted. Some then proposed that he should fly to Bordeaux, others that he should try to make his way to Conway, where Salisbury was supposed to be now at the head of an army of Welshmen. This last plan was adopted, and the king assumed the disguise of a priest for the purpose. But on reaching Conway, he there found Salisbury with only a hundred men; and nothing now remained but to try to make terms with the duke of Lancaster. The king's half-brothers, the dukes of Exeter and Surrey, were then sent to that prince, by whom they were detained; and the earl of Northumberland set out with a sufficient force to try to obtain possession of the royal person.

As Northumberland feared that if the king should see his men he would put to sea, he concealed them behind a rock between Flint and Conway, and then proceeded to the latter place with only five attendants. He delivered to Richard the demands of the duke of Lancaster, which were, that he himself should be restored to his rights, that Exeter, Surrey, Salisbury, and the bishop of Carlisle, should stand their trial for having advised the murder of the duke of Gloucester, and that the king should engage to govern by law. These terms Richard accepted, without any intention of observing them, for he privately assured his friends that he would stand by them, and take ample vengeance on their enemies. Mass was then performed, and Northumberland swore on the sacrament to observe these conditions faithfully. He then departed, and after dinner the king set out for Flint. At a steep declivity near the sea he alighted from his horse, and began to walk it down; all of a sudden he stopped, crying, "I am betrayed. God of paradise, aid me! See ye not banners and pennons below in the valley?" Northumberland, who was now with him, affected ignorance. "If I thought you could betray me," cried the king, "it is not too late to return." "You cannot," said the earl, catching his bridle; "I have promised to convey you to the duke of Lancaster." A strong party of the soldiers was now come up, and the king, seeing that escape was impossible, submitted, saying to Northumberland, "May the God on whom you laid your hands reward you and your accomplices at the last day!" He was then conducted to Flint castle.

In the morning the king arose and ascended the tower, and beholding Lancaster's army of eighty thousand men advancing, he shuddered and wept. After dinner he was summoned down to the court-yard to meet the duke, who advancing, armed all save his head, bent his knee. "Fair cousin of Lancaster," said the king, "you are welcome." "My lord," replied the duke, "I am come before my time; but I will give you the reason. Your people complain that you have ruled them rigorously; but if it please God, I will help you to govern better." "Fair cousin, since it pleaseth you, it pleaseth me well," replied Richard. The king's horses were then called for, and he and Salisbury were mounted on two sorry jades, and thus conducted to Chester. At Lichfield Richard attempted to escape by letting himself down from a window, but he was taken in the garden; and when he reached London, he was consigned to the Tower. He was then forced to sign his abdication; and this instrument being read in parliament, his deposition was unanimously voted. Lancaster, who was present, then claimed the crown, and his claim was at once admitted, though there was a nearer heir, the earl of March, a boy, however, only seven years old.

Death of King Richard.

The unhappy Richard was confined in the castle of Pontefract; and shortly after, some of his friends having risen in his favour and perished, his death was announced to parliament. He had refused food, and starved himself to death, it was said, when he heard of the fate of his brothers, who were among the insurgents. Few, however, credited this account: the prevailing opinion was, that he had no doubt been starved to death, but that food had been withheld from him by order of the new king. There went another story, that one sir Piers Exton was sent, with seven assistants, from London to murder him; and that Richard, when they entered his apartment, guessing their design, sprang forward, and snatched a battle-axe from one, with which he killed some of them, but that Exton brought him to the ground with a blow on the back of the head, and then despatched him.

CHAPTER IX.
HENRY IV. (OF BOLINGBROKE).

Rebellion of Northumberland.

HENRY IV. had not long been on the throne when his great supporter, Northumberland, rose in arms against him. The occasion was as follows.

There was a Welsh gentleman named Owen Glendour, a part of whose lands had been seized by Lord Grey de Ruthyn, a relation of the king's; his application to parliament for justice being unheeded, Glendour resolved to right himself by the strong hand, and even to assume the sovereignty of Wales. His countrymen supported him, and the belief that he was versed in magic arts added greatly to his influence. Henry thrice in person led an army into Wales, and thrice he was obliged to retire, baffled by the weather, the country, and the skill of Glendour. Among the captives made by the Welsh was sir Edmund Mortimer, to whose sister Harry Percy, commonly called Hotspur, the eldest son of Northumberland, was married; and probably, because he was of the blood-royal, Henry refused permission to his relatives to ransom him. Hotspur, irritated at this conduct, and being supported by his father and his uncle, the earl of Worcester, and acting under the advice of the archbishop of York, resolved to proclaim the true heir and to levy war against Henry. He formed an alliance with Glendour, and with the Scottish earl Douglas, whom he had lately made his prisoner at the battle of Homildon; and their united forces advanced toward Wales to form a junction with Glendour. At Shrewsbury, however, they were met by the royal forces, led by Henry in person. The armies were about equal in number; the proposals of peace sent by the king were rejected through the influence of Worcester, and the battle was joined. Hotspur and Douglas, each with thirty followers, plunged into the centre of the royal army, seeking the king. They slew four different persons who wore the royal arms to deceive them, and the young prince of Wales was wounded in the face; but a chance arrow pierced the brain of Hotspur, and Douglas was made a prisoner. The rout of the rebels was complete. Worcester and two other persons were executed as traitors. Northumberland, who had not been present, was pardoned, but soon after he and the archbishop of York, and Mowbray, son of the late duke of Norfolk, were in arms against the royal authority. The king's son, prince John, and the earl of Westmoreland, were sent against them; and in a conference, having induced the prelate and

Mowbray to disband their forces, they made them both prisoners, and sent them to Pontefract, where they were shortly after beheaded. Northumberland escaped to Scotland, but he was afterwards slain in an engagement with the sheriff of Yorkshire, a just punishment for his treachery to king Richard.

Stories of the Prince of Wales.

The remainder of king Henry's reign was tranquil. The wild pranks of the prince of Wales caused his father, it is said, much annoyance; for the prince, carried away by his buoyant spirits, was too apt to indulge in riot and excess. Our wonderful dramatist, Shakspeare, has immortalised the memory of these youthful days of him who afterwards became one of England's greatest kings.

One of the riotous companions of the prince being taken for some misdeed, and brought before the chief-justice Gascoigne, the prince went, as we are told, and demanded his instant release; and being refused, had the audacity to draw his sword on the judge. Gascoigne instantly ordered him to prison for the offence; and the prince meekly submitted. "Happy the monarch," said the king, when he heard of it, "who has a judge so resolute in the discharge of his duty, and a son so willing to submit to the laws!" A suspicion, however, was instilled into the king's mind that his son aspired to the throne. When the prince heard of this, he demanded an audience of his father, and throwing himself on his knees, handed him a dagger, beseeching him to deprive him of life since he had deprived him of his favour.

Death of the King.

The king was only in the forty-sixth year of his age when symptoms of the approach of death began to appear. He became subject to fits of epilepsy; and one day, when he was lying in one of them, apparently dead, the prince came into the room, and taking up the crown, which, according to custom, lay by him on a cushion, carried it into an adjoining apartment. The king, on recovering, sternly asked what had become of his crown; the prince instantly brought it back. "Alas! fair son," said the king, at the close of their conversation, "what right have you to the crown when you know that your father had none?" "My liege," said the prince, "with the sword you won it, and with the sword I will keep it." "Well," replied the king; "do as you think best. I leave the issue to God, and hope he will have mercy on my soul." Shortly after, as Henry was praying in St. Edward's chapel in Westminster-abbey, he had another fit, and he expired in the abbot's chamber.

CHAPTER X.
HENRY V. (OF MONMOUTH).

Renewal of the Claim to the Crown of France.

THERE was great joy on the accession of Henry V., but the recollections of his youthful follies caused some apprehensions. These, however, were at once dispelled when he dismissed his former companions, with presents and promises of his future favour on their reformation, and continued his father's honest servants and ministers, especially chief-justice Gascoïgne, in their offices. He also set the earl of March (though the nearest heir of Richard II.) at liberty; and he removed the remains of that unhappy monarch to Westminster-abbey, himself attending as chief mourner. Every thing seemed to presage a happy reign, and prosperity to both the king and country.

But unfortunately the brilliant vision of the crown of France captivated the imagination of the king. The king of that country was a lunatic, and there was a furious and sanguinary contest going on for the administration of affairs between the dukes of Orleans and Burgundy, two princes of the blood-royal. Henry, resolving to take advantage of this confusion, claimed the crown. When his claim was rejected, he offered to be content with Normandy and some other provinces, and the princess Catherine, with a large dower, in marriage. The French were content to yield to a part of his demands, and on the subject of the princess, they only scrupled at the largeness of the dower. Henry, however, would not abate his terms; he resolved to assert his claim by an appeal to arms; and parliament, always liberal on such occasions, granted him a large supply of money, which he augmented by pawning his jewels and by raising loans.

Battle of Agincourt.

When all his preparations were completed, king Henry embarked at Southampton with a gallant army of thirty thousand men, and landing at the mouth of the river Seine, invested the town of Harfleur. After a brave resistance of five months' duration, the town surrendered; the inhabitants were expelled, like those of Calais, and an English garrison occupied it. To his mortification, Henry, at the end of 'the siege, found his army no longer in a condition for active operations; for it had suffered so severely from dysentery, that when the sick and wounded had been sent home, it did not count more than one half of its original number. In spite, however, of the remonstrances of his council, Henry resolved to march with his diminished forces to Calais. He reached unopposed the ford by which Edward III. had crossed the Somme, but found it secured by lines of palisades, behind which troops were posted. All the other fords were secured in like manner, and the bridges were broken. At length, finding a ford unguarded, the English passed over. The constable of France, who commanded the French army, fell back toward Calais, and having received orders from his court to fight without delay, he sent heralds to king Henry to ask which way he intended to march. Henry replied, by that which led straight to Calais, and dismissed the heralds with a present of a hundred crowns.

As the English were advancing, the duke of York, having ascended an eminence, descried the masses of the enemy. The troops were instantly formed in line of battle, but the French would not advance to attack them, the experience of Cressy and Poitiers having inspired them with a dread of the cloth-yard arrows of the English. But as their army presented an array of fifty thousand horsemen, they had no doubt whatever of the victory; and though the night was dark and rainy, they assembled round their banners, revelling and discussing the events of the coming day; and such was their confidence that they even fixed the ransoms of king Henry and his barons. The English, on the contrary, made their wills, and passed the night in devotion. Sickness, famine, and the smallness of their numbers, depressed their spirits; but their courage rose when they thought on Cressy and other victories, and on the gallant spirit of their king. Henry himself visited all their quarters, and he ordered bands of music to play all through the night to cheer their drooping spirits.

Before sunrise on the 25th of October, 1415, being St. Crispin's day, the English army, having heard mass, stood in order of battle. The king, wearing a helmet of polished steel, wreathed with a crown of sparkling stones, rode on a grey pony from rank to rank, inspecting and encouraging them. Hearing an officer say to another that he wished a miracle would transfer thither some of the good knights who were sitting idle at home, he declared aloud that "he would not have a single man more, as, if God them gave the victory, it would be plainly due to his goodness; if he did not, the fewer that fell, the less the loss to their country." Three French knights now came, summoning them to surrender. The king ordered them off, and cried out, "Banners, advance." The archers fell on their knees on the ground, then rose and ran on with a shout. They halted, and poured their hail of arrows on the first division of the French; and when they had thrown it into some confusion, they slung their bows behind their backs, and grasping their swords and battle-axes, killed the constable and his principal officers, and routed the whole division. They then advanced to attack the second division, led by the duke of Alençon. Here the resistance was obstinate. Alençon forced his way to the royal standard, killed the duke of York, and cleft the crown in the helmet of the king; but he was slain, and the division turned and fled. Henry was advancing to attack the third division, when word came that a large force was falling on the rear. The king gave hasty orders to put the prisoners to death, and numbers had perished before it was discovered that it was a false alarm, caused by an attempt of some peasantry to plunder the baggage. The slaughter was then stopped, but this cruel act tarnished the victory which was already won, for the third division offered but a slight resistance.

When Montjoy, the French king-at-arms, appeared, "To whom," said Henry, "doth the victory belong?" "To you, sir." "And what castle is that I see at a distance?" "It is called the castle of Agincourt." "Then," said the king, "be this battle known to posterity by the name of the battle of Agincourt." The prime nobility of France were taken or slain, and eight thousand knights and gentlemen lay dead on the field. The loss of the English had been only the duke of York, the earl of Suffolk, and about six hundred men.

Final Success of Henry.

After this great victory, the English king pursued his route to Calais; and as the season was too far advanced for any further operations, he returned, after a short stay, to England. The following summer he again landed in France, and he reduced Rouen, the capital of Normandy, and a great part of that province. Meantime, the French, instead of opposing the invader, were engaged in deadly animosities among themselves; the one party being headed by the queen, a profligate woman, and the duke of Burgundy; the other, by those who acted in the name of the young dauphin*. Both parties made proposals to Henry, who, like an able statesman, played them against each other. At length, in an interview between the dauphin and the duke of Burgundy, the latter was most basely assassinated. The queen and the son of the murdered duke instantly concluded a treaty with Henry on his own terms, which were, the hand of the princess Catherine, the regency during the king's lifetime, and the crown at his death. The royal marriage was then celebrated with the requisite ceremony, and Henry soon after conducted his bride to England. He returned to France in the following year, and reduced nearly the whole of that kingdom north of the Loire; but in the midst of his glory he was attacked by a fatal disease, which carried him off in the thirty-fourth year of his age.

CHAPTER XI.

HENRY VI. (OF WINDSOR).

Siege of Orleans.

Henry V. had left an only son, a child nine months old. A regency, therefore, was appointed, at the head of which was the duke of Bedford, the young king's uncle. The war was continued in France; and after some time it was

---

* The dauphin, so named from the province of Dauphiné, was the title of the eldest son of the king of France, like that of prince of Wales in England.

resolved to carry it beyond the Loire, and endeavour to drive the dauphin, who had now, his father being dead, assumed the royal title as Charles VII., out of the provinces which had acknowledged him. With this view, an English army laid siege to the strong city of Orleans, which is situated on the Loire.

The siege had lasted some time, and the city had actually offered to surrender to the duke of Burgundy, and Charles was thinking of quitting his kingdom and seeking an asylum in Spain or Scotland, when one of the most extraordinary personages in history appeared and restored the fallen fortunes of France.

The Maid of Orleans.

There lived in a village of the province of Champagne a peasant named Jacques d'Arc, who had several children, one of whom, a daughter named Joan, was remarkable for her piety and her serious turn of mind. This maiden brooded over the misfortunes of her king and country, till at length she began to fancy that some of the saints used to appear to her and urge her to undertake the deliverance of France from the English. She addressed herself to the lord of an adjacent town, praying him to send her to the dauphin as she was destined to crown him. He laughed at her pretensions, but he complied with her request. She appeared before the king in man's attire, and assured him that she was sent by Heaven to raise the siege of Orleans and conduct him to Rheims to be crowned. It is said, that though she had never before seen the king she recognised him at once among his courtiers, that she told him secrets known only to himself, and described and claimed a sword which had long lain forgotten in the church of St. Catherine. She was examined by a council of lawyers and divines, who pronounced her to be inspired. She was then exhibited to the people mounted on a stately grey charger, which she managed with great dexterity, and preceded by a banner, on which the Almighty was represented as a venerable old man with a globe in his hand.

The Maid, as she was styled, soon after headed a division of the French troops destined to convoy a supply of provisions to Orleans, and she succeeded in entering the town with her charge. The English soon after raised the siege, and the Maid then called on the king to proceed to Rheims for his coronation. Though the whole of the intermediate country was in the hands of the English and Burgundians it was resolved to comply with her desire, and Charles set forth with an escort of ten thousand horse. He reached Rheims in safety, and was there anointed with the holy oil which an angel, it was said, had brought from heaven at the coronation of Clovis, the founder of the monarchy. The Maid, who stood, holding her banner, at his side, then fell on her knees, and declaring her mission ended begged with tears to be dismissed. Unhappily for her, her presence was still deemed to be of importance, and the permission was refused.

Her good fortune had indeed deserted her, and the next year she fell into the hands of the English, being taken prisoner in an attempt to relieve a town which the duke of Burgundy was besieging. She was conducted to Rouen and tried on a charge of sorcery and imposture before a commission of prelates, of whom only one was English. She was condemned as a heretic and sentenced to be burnt; but on her owning that her visions were illusions of the devil, and swearing never again to wear man's attire, her sentence was commuted to imprisonment for life. Her enemies, however, it is said, having left men's clothes in her cell, she was tempted to put them on, and being caught in the fact she was adjudged to have relapsed, and she was burnt to death in the market-place at Rouen.

This barbarous execution of the noble Maid of Orleans was of little avail to the English. Fortune everywhere turned against them; their ally the duke of Burgundy became reconciled with king Charles, and finally, of all their possessions in France, Calais alone remained.

Deaths of Gloucester and Suffolk.

The young king of England as he grew up displayed a character the very opposite to that of his illustrious father. He was mild and pious, but feeble in intellect and ductile in temper. At the age of three-and-twenty he was married to Margaret the daughter of Réné duke of Anjou, a woman of masculine energy of mind, and he soon became little more than a puppet in her hands and those of her favourite Pole, duke of Suffolk. The king's uncle, Humphrey, duke of Gloucester, was by their means arrested on a charge of high treason; but ere he was brought to trial he was found dead in his bed, and his death was very generally ascribed to Suffolk, who got a large part of his estates. Suffolk's own fate, however, was at hand. He was impeached by the house of commons, and the king, to save him, ordered him to quit the kingdom for five years. He sailed from Ipswich with two small vessels, and proceeded to Calais. At that port he sent in a boat to know if he might land; but the boat was detained, and a large vessel named the Nicholas of the Tower, came alongside of his bark and ordered him on board. "Welcome, traitor, as men say," cried the captain as he came on deck. He was kept a prisoner for two nights, and then brought to a mock trial before the sailors. He was sentenced to death, and on the second morning a small boat with a block, a rusty sword and an executioner, came alongside, and he was lowered into it and his head was struck off. His body was laid on the sands at Dover, and by the king's orders it was delivered to his widow, and no inquiry was ever made into this murder.

Jack Cade.

The feebleness and corruption of the government gave occasion to much popular discontent, and soon after the death of Suffolk an insurrection broke out in Kent, and twenty thousand men, headed by one Jack Cade, but who called himself Mortimer, appeared in arms on Blackheath. When the king had collected a force they retired; but at Sevenoaks they turned and defeated and slew sir Humphrey Stafford who was in pursuit of them. Cade arrayed himself in the fallen knight's armour, and led his men back to Blackheath. The king retired to Kenilworth in Warwickshire, and Cade entered the city of London. He there made the mayor and judges sit at Guildhall, and arraigned before them lord Say and his son-in-law the sheriff of Kent, and he beheaded them at the Standard in Cheapside.

Every evening Cade led his men back to the borough of Southwark. Though no plunder had yet been committed, the citizens became apprehensive, and they agreed to join with lord Scales, who commanded in the Tower, in defending the bridge against the insurgents. Cade made several fruitless attempts to force it, and at length he and his men accepted the pardons that were offered them, and dispersed. Cade, however, afterwards collected more men, but finding them refractory he left them and fled to Lewes in Sussex, where he was slain in a garden, after an obstinate defence, by Iden the sheriff of the county.

Duke of York's Claim of the Crown.

The duke of Lancaster, through whom Henry VI. derived his title to the crown, was the third son of Edward III.; but Lionel, the second son of that monarch, had had issue, and the duke of York, descended on the father's side from the fourth son of king Edward, was through his mother the representative of Lionel. In the rigid order of succession, therefore, his right to the throne was superior to that of the king. But on the other hand, Henry IV. had obtained the crown by the choice of the people; it had been now in the undisturbed possession of his family for sixty years, and three dukes of York in succession had given it their allegiance and their services. It is probable that if the government of Henry had been like that of his father and grandfather his right would never have been disputed, for he was personally beloved, and the duke of York was a man of an extremely mild and moderate character. But the loss of France and the insolence of the queen and her favourites had exasperated the people, and they readily laid hold on a plausible pretext for overthrowing their power. Moreover, the right to the crown was regarded in general in the same light as that to a private property, and as want of possession does not destroy this last, people thought that the same rule should apply to the crown. The consequence was that a very large portion of the nation, particularly of the middling and lower orders, were in favour of the duke of York.

This prince had waited patiently, expecting the crown in the order of succession, for the king had been eight years married without having issue. But the birth of a prince at length showed the futility of this expectation, and as the king soon after fell into such a state of both bodily and mental debility, that he became merely a royal pageant at the disposal of Margaret and her friends, York caused himself to be appointed protector of the kingdom. Of this office, however, he was deprived on the king's showing some glimpses of returning reason, and he then retired to his estates and prepared to assert his claim to the throne by force of arms. Thus commenced a civil war called the War of the Roses, for the red rose was the cognizance or badge of the house of Lancaster, and the white of that of York. Most of the nobility were on the side of the king; the chief supporters of York were Mowbray duke of Norfolk and Neville earl of Salisbury, and his son the earl of Warwick.

War of the Roses.

The first encounter of the hostile parties was at St. Albans; for as the duke was advancing toward London with three thousand men the king met him at that town with a force of two thousand men. The royalists were defeated with a loss of about six score men, but several noblemen fell, and the king himself was wounded in the neck. He took refuge in the house of a tanner, where York waited on him and conducted him with all respect to the abbey. They thence proceeded to London, where the duke was again made protector; but he had soon after to resign that dignity, and though the primate and other moderate men did all in their power to avert the evils of civil war, both sides ere long resumed their arms, and the duke of York now for the first time advanced his claim to the crown.

Success was at first on the side of the royalists, and York and his friends were forced to fly to Ireland and France. But some time after, while a parliament was sitting at Westminster, York suddenly arrived with five hundred men, and entering the house of lords stood with his hand on the throne. The primate asked him if he would not go visit the king. He replied, "I know no one in this realm who ought not rather to visit me." He then took possession of the royal apartments, and some days after the rival claims to the throne being examined, the lords effected a compromise, by which the king was to retain the crown for life, but at his death it was to pass to the duke of York or his heirs.

Battle of Wakefield.

By this arrangement the young prince of Wales was in effect disinherited. His high-spirited mother would not tamely submit to such an indignity, and with the aid of Northumberland, Clifford, and some other northern nobles, she collected an army in the north. The duke of York set out at the head of only five thousand men to oppose her; and notwithstanding the inferiority of his numbers, he accepted the challenge of the enemy to meet them on the green of Wakefield in Yorkshire. Nearly one half of his troops were speedily slain, and he himself was made a prisoner. His captors placed him on an ant-hill, and set a crown of twisted grass on his head, and then bowing the knee in derision, cried, "Hail king without a kingdom! Hail prince without a people!" They then cut off his head, which Clifford presented on a pole to the queen, saying, "Madam, your war is done; here is the ransom of your king." She burst out into laughter, and sent the head to be fixed on the walls of York. In the pursuit Clifford had overtaken York's second son, the earl of Rutland, a youth of about seventeen years of age, whom his tutor, a venerable priest, was conveying to a place of safety. Rutland fell on his knees imploring for mercy. "Save him," cried the tutor, "he is the son of a prince, and mayhap may do you good hereafter." "The son of York," shouted Clifford, "as thy father slew mine, so will I slay thee and all of thy kin," and plunged his sword into his bosom.

Duke of York made King.

York's eldest son Edward, earl of March, was at Gloucester with an army of twenty-three thousand men when he heard of the death of his father. At a place named Mortimer's Cross, near Hereford, he engaged and defeated a royalist force of Welsh and Irish, and then moved toward London. The queen had also marched for that city, and had defeated lord Warwick at St. Albans; but on the approach of Edward she retired to the north. The young duke of York therefore entered London in triumph, and some days after lord Falconbridge and the bishop of Exeter having harangued the citizens, asked them if they would have Henry for their king. A general cry of " No, no!" arose; they were then asked if they would have Edward. "Yea, yea!" cried they, and shouted and clapped their hands. Edward was therefore proclaimed king.

CHAPTER XII.

EDWARD IV.

Battle of Towton.

THE indefatigable Margaret still upheld the rights of her son, and she was now at York at the head of not less than sixty thousand men. Edward marched from London without delay to oppose her with an army which counted nearly fifty thousand fighting men. Lord Clifford, who attempted to defend the passage of the river Aire at Ferrybridge, was defeated and slain, and the two armies encountered on the 29th of March, 1461, in the plain between the villages of Towton and Saxton in Yorkshire, under a heavy shower of snow which blew full in the face of the Lancastrians. The battle was continued with obstinacy till the evening, when the queen's troops gave way and fled. Edward had issued orders to give no quarter, and nearly one half of the Lancastrians were slaughtered.

Adventures of Queen Margaret.

Margaret made her escape to France, where having procured some supplies of men and money she returned to England to renew the contest. She landed in the north, and succeeded in obtaining possession of Scarborough and some other castles; but when Warwick arrived with an army of twenty thousand men, her troops were obliged to disperse. She also had the misfortune to lose all her treasure in a storm as she was going by sea to Berwick-on-Tweed. It is related that at this time, as she was riding with her son and a few companions through a forest, they were seized and stript by a party of bandits. While the robbers were quarrelling about the division of the spoil, the queen contrived to slip away with the prince, and plunged into the depths of the wood. Here, however, she encountered a single robber; and seeing escape hopeless she boldly went up to him and said, "Friend, I commit to thy care the son of thy king." The robber was not without generous feeling; he accepted the charge and conducted them in safety to their friends, and they once more sought a refuge in France.

The Lancastrians were defeated in two actions at Hedgeley-moor and at Hexham. King Henry, who was present at this last narrowly escaped being captured. He fled into Lancashire, where he was concealed by his friends for more than a year. At length a monk betrayed him, and he was seized as he was sitting at dinner at Waddington-hall. He was sent up to London; at Islington he was met by Warwick; his legs were then tied under the belly of his horse, and he was thrice led round the pillory, and finally consigned to the Tower.

Marriage of King Edward.

While Warwick and the other supporters of his throne were engaged in crushing the hopes of the Lancastrians, king Edward was devoting his days to love and courtship. As he was one day hunting in Northamptonshire he called to visit the duchess of Bedford, who had married sir Richard Woodville of Grafton in that county. While he was there the duchess's daughter Elizabeth, the widow of sir John Gray of Groby who had fallen on the Lancastrian side at St. Albans, came and implored him to restore her innocent children to their rank and property. Edward was moved to pity, and pity soon led to love; he offered his heart and hand to the fair relict. A monarch young and handsome as Edward was could not well meet with a refusal. About the end of the month of April (just at the time of the battle of Hedgeley-moor) he repaired to Stony Stratford, and on the morning of May-day he stole over to Grafton, where he was united by a priest to the lady Gray. He stayed an hour or two and then returned to Stratford. Two days after he invited himself and train to Grafton, where he remained for four days. His marriage was for some time kept a secret; but on the following Michaelmas Elizabeth appeared as queen, and her coronation took place in the month of May succeeding. Riches and honours were heaped profusely on her family; her five sisters were married to young noblemen of the highest rank, and her brother John, a youth of twenty years of age, was united in wedlock with the wealthy duchess of Norfolk, a dowager in her eightieth year!

Quarrel between the King and Warwick.

Various causes now contributed to estrange the king from Warwick and the rest of the powerful Neville family; but his brother, the duke of Clarence, in spite of all his efforts to prevent him, had married Warwick's daughter and joined cordially with that nobleman. Insurrections took place in various parts, apparently at their instigation, and they both found it expedient to seek a refuge at the court of Louis XI. king of France. There they met queen Margaret, and though no two persons hated one another more or with better reason than she and Warwick, their mutual interests made them, at the desire of Louis, consent to bury the past in oblivion and unite against Edward. Her son prince Edward married the lady Anne, Warwick's second daughter, and it was stipulated that if the prince should die without issue the crown was to go to Clarence. This prince, however, who had hoped to wrest the sceptre from king Edward, was by no means pleased with this arrangement, and he secretly became reconciled to his brother.

Flight and Return of Edward.

Preparations were now made for invading England, and Warwick soon after landed at Plymouth. He advanced into the heart of the kingdom proclaiming king Henry as he went along, and the number of his forces daily increased. Edward, who was with only a small force at Doncaster, was roused from his bed one night with tidings that Warwick was at hand. He mounted his horse with all speed and rode with only eight hundred followers to the port of Lynn, where he seized some small vessels and passed over to Holland. Warwick and Clarence then proceeded to London, where they took king Henry out of the Tower, and he once more walked in procession with the crown on his head to St. Paul's.

But Edward was not the man tamely to yield up his crown. Being secretly aided by his brother-in-law the duke of Burgundy, he embarked for England, and like Henry IV. landed at Ravenspur. Like him too he pretended that he had only come to claim the estates of the house of York, and his men shouted "Long live king Henry!" as they passed through the towns and villages. At York he swore on the altar that he had no design on the crown; but at Nottingham, when his force had swelled to the number of fifty thousand men, he cast off the mask. Clarence now openly joined him, having made the men whom he had raised in king Henry's name fling away the red rose and place the white on their gorgets.

Battle of Barnet.

Warwick, who was at Coventry, declined a proffered combat. Edward then marched to London; Warwick followed him; and Edward taking the poor old king Henry with him advanced to Barnet to give him battle. Clarence attempted to mediate. "Go tell your master," said Warwick to his messenger, "that Warwick, true to his word, is a better man than the false and perjured Clarence." On Easter-day this decisive battle was fought, and it ended in the total defeat of the Lancastrian army, owing in a great measure, it is said, to mistake; for as Edward's men wore on back and breast his badge, a sun, and the earl of Oxford's, on the Lancastrian side, a star with rays, the other Lancastrians taking these for enemies fell on and drove them off the field. The great earl of Warwick, surnamed the King-maker, found here the end of his life and hopes, and of all the Lancastrian leaders the earl of Oxford alone escaped. Edward returned in triumph to London, and Henry was again consigned to the Tower.

Battle of Tewkesbury.

The very day of the battle of Barnet queen Margaret landed at Plymouth. At the news of the defeat of Warwick she sank to the ground in despair; but the arguments of her friends soon awaked her natural courage, and she advanced to Bath. It was there resolved to try to effect a junction with the earl of Pembroke, who had a large force in Wales; but the people of Gloucester had secured the only bridge over the Severn, and at Tewkesbury it was found that Edward was at hand with a more numerous army. The Lancastrian leaders then drew up their forces without the town; the Yorkists, led by the king's brother, the duke of Gloucester, fell on them furiously, and after a short but gallant resistance the Lancastrians were totally routed. The queen and prince were made prisoners; the latter being led into the royal tent Edward demanded of him what had brought him to England. "To recover my father's kingdom and heritage, from his father and grandfather to him, and from him to me lineally descended," replied the undaunted youth. Edward struck him in the face with his gauntlet, and Gloucester, Clarence, and some others despatched him with their swords. Edward then set out for London, and on the evening of his arrival king Henry died in the Tower, of grief as was given out, but there can be little doubt that he was murdered by order of Edward. The guilt of the deed, though without any proof, was afterwards laid on the duke of Gloucester.

Fate of Clarence.

Queen Margaret was ransomed some time after by the king of France. As Warwick's immense possessions descended to his two daughters, the duchess of Clarence and the lady Anne widow of prince Edward, Gloucester was anxious to marry the latter, but Clarence, who wished to retain the whole of the property, did all in his power to conceal her. At length she was discovered in the disguise of a cook-maid in London, and Gloucester married her. Clarence was then obliged to divide the estates with him, and the two brothers continued to hate each other heartily.

It happened that as the king was hunting one time at Harrow in Warwickshire, the seat of a gentleman named Burdet, who was in the service of the duke of Clarence, he killed a favourite stag of the owner's. Burdet in his anger wished that its horns were in the belly of him who killed it. It is not certain that he knew it was the king: at all events he was condemned and executed for treason. Clarence, having expressed his indignation loudly, was committed to the Tower on a charge of high treason. He was tried before parliament and sentenced to die, and in about ten days his death was announced; the manner of it was uncertain; but the common report was that he had been given his choice, and had selected that of drowning in a butt of Malmsey, his favourite wine.

King Edward survived his brother only about five years. He had ruined his constitution by indulging in pleasures of every kind to excess. He died in the forty-second year of his age, after a reign of twenty-three years.

CHAPTER XIII.

EDWARD V.—RICHARD III.

Seizure of the King's Relations.

EDWARD, the eldest son of the late king, was only in his thirteenth year when he succeeded to the throne. He was then at Ludlow castle in Wales, under the charge of lord Rivers, his mother's brother. On the intelligence of his father's death he set out for London accompanied by his uncle, his half-brother lord Gray, and an escort of two-thousand horse. He had reached Stony Stratford, when he was waited on by his uncle of Gloucester and the duke of Buckingham, who with the greatest demonstrations of respect assured him that it was the intention of his uncle Rivers and his brother the marquess of Dorset to rule the realm and to destroy his noble blood. "What my lord marquess may have done in London," replied the prince, "I cannot say, but I dare answer for my uncle Rivers and my brother here that they be innocent of any such matter." Gloucester, however, arrested them both, and Sir Thomas Vaughan and sir Richard Hawse, and sent them prisoners to the north. He then himself conducted the young king to London and placed him in the Tower, it being the custom for the king to reside in that fortress previous to his coronation. Gloucester was at the same time named Protector.

Death of Lord Hastings.

It was the secret design of Gloucester to deprive his nephew of his throne, and with this view he determined previously to deprive him of all his friends. The seizure of Rivers and Gray had levelled the power of the queen's family; but lord Hastings, lord Stanley, the bishop of Ely and other nobles and prelates were atttached to the king on his father's account. Gloucester himself, Buckingham and his other partizans, used to hold their secret councils at Crosby-house, in Bishopsgate-street, in which he resided, while Hastings and the other friends of the king always sat in council at the Tower. One morning Gloucester went thither, and taking his seat at the board began to talk in a gay and cheerful tone, and praising the strawberries which grew in the bishop of Ely's garden at Holborn*, requested to have a dish of them for dinner. The bishop sent a servant to fetch them; the protector withdrew, and in about an hour he returned with a lowering countenance and sat down in silence. At length he cried, "Of what are they worthy who have compassed the death of me the king's protector by nature as well as by law?" "To be punished," said Hastings, "as false traitors." "And that," replied he, "hath that sorceress my brother's wife with others her accomplices endeavoured to do." "See," continued he, "in what a miserable manner that sorceress and Shore's wife with others their associates have by their sorcery and witchcraft miserably destroyed my body." He unbuttoned his sleeve and showed his left arm shrunk and withered. All present very well knew that his arm had always been so; Hastings, however, replied, "Certainly, my lord, if they have done any such thing they deserve to be both severely punished." "Do you answer me with *ifs* and *ands*, as if I charged them falsely?" cried the protector in a rage. "I tell you they have done it, and thou hast joined with them in this villany." He struck the table with his fist; a man without shouted Treason! armed men rushed in; "I arrest thee, traitor," cried Gloucester to Hastings. "Shrive [i. e. confess] thyself apace," he added, "for by St. Paul I will not dine till I see thy head off." Hastings then having confessed himself to a priest who was at hand was led down to the green before the

---

* The place is now called Hatton Garden, having been given to sir Christopher Hatton by queen Elizabeth.

Tower-chapel, and his head was struck off on a beam of timber that was lying there. Gloucester then ate his dinner. By the time he had dined the principal citizens appeared at his summons, and he and Buckingham came forth to them clad in rusty armour, which they had taken for their defence, as it were, in the Tower. He told them that Hastings had intended murdering him and the Duke of Buckingham, and that it had been only at ten o'clock that morning they had discovered the plot, and he requested them to inform their fellow-citizens of the real truth of the case.

The young Duke of York.

Lord Stanley and the bishops of York and Ely had been arrested at the same time with Hastings, and the king's party being thus weakened, Gloucester's next object was to get that prince's younger brother, the duke of York, into his power. But the queen when she heard of the affair at Stony Stratford had taken sanctuary at Westminster-abbey with that prince and her daughters. Gloucester therefore proceeded thither from the Tower in his barge attended by nobles and prelates. He was determined to take the young duke by force if fair means should prove unavailing; but the queen seeing that resistance was useless, yielded him up to a deputation headed by the primate, and the innocent victim was conveyed to the Tower, where he and his brother, little suspecting the fate that awaited them, met and embraced with the utmost delight.

Jane Shore.

In his discourse with Hastings, Gloucester it will be recollected had mentioned a person whom he called Shore's wife. This woman, better known by the name of Jane Shore, was the wife of a wealthy young citizen, but her virtue had been unable to resist the solicitations of king Edward, and she had been his mistress. "Proper she was and fair," says the good sir Thomas More, "yet delighted not men so much in her beauty as in her pleasant behaviour, for a proper wit had she, and could both read well and write; ready and quick of answer, neither mute nor babbling. Many mistresses the king had, but her he loved; whose favour to say the truth (for sin it were to bely the devil) she never abused to any man's hurt, but often employed to many a man's relief." After the king's death she had lived with lord Hastings, and she was now arrested as a sharer in his conspiracy. The protector seized her goods to his own use and then caused her to be tried in the spiritual court for lewdness and adultery. She was sentenced to do public penance; and stript to her kirtle with her feet bare, carrying a lighted taper and preceded by the cross, she was made to walk to St. Paul's. Jane lived more than forty years afterwards in poverty and neglect. The popular tale of the protector's having forbidden any one to relieve her, and her dying of hunger in the place named Shoreditch after her, is therefore entitled to no credit.

Gloucester's Usurpation of the Crown.

The prosecution of Jane Shore was designed to revive the memory of king Edward's licentious habits; and soon after a friar named doctor Shaw, the lord-mayor's brother, was employed to preach at St. Paul's Cross[*], and to insinuate the illegitimacy of king Edward's children on the grounds of his having been the husband of another woman at the time of his marriage with lady Gray. Doubts were even expressed of himself being the son of the duke of York. "But," cried the preacher, "my lord protector, that very noble prince, is the perfect image of his father; his features are the same, and the very express likeness of that noble duke." It had been arranged that Gloucester should appear at these words, and it was hoped that the

---

[*] This was a large ornamented cross which stood in the front of St. Paul's cathedral, and from which bishops and other clergymen used to preach to the people.

people might be induced to cry "God save king Richard!" but the affair was badly managed and the design miscarried. A day or two after Buckingham harangued the citizens at Guildhall on the same subject, and a few hired voices at the bottom of the hall having cried "King Richard!" Buckingham thanked them, and next morning he went with the lord-mayor and the principal citizens to Baynard castle, where the protector was residing, and demanded an audience. Gloucester appeared at one of the windows, and Buckingham read an address calling on him to assume the crown, to which he was the lawful heir. He affected great reluctance, and spoke of his affection for his nephews. "Sir," said Buckingham, "the free people of England will never submit to the rule of a bastard, and if the lawful heir refuses the sceptre, they know where to find one who will accept it." Gloucester then pretending that it was his duty to obey the voice of the people accepted the crown, and the farce thus terminated.

On the very day of Hastings' execution, Ratcliff, one of Richard's confidants, came to Pontefract, where the persons arrested at Stratford were confined, and after a mock trial caused their heads to be struck off. Sir Thomas Vaughan having appealed to God when on the scaffold, Ratcliff said with a sneer, "You have made a goodly appeal; lay down your head." "I die in the right," replied he: "take care that you die not in the wrong."

Murder of the Princes.

The coronation of Richard and of the lady Anne his queen was celebrated with extraordinary magnificence. After that ceremony he set out on a progress through the kingdom. When he was at Warwick on his way to the north he sent orders to Brackenbury, the lieutenant of the Tower, to put the two princes to death, for he did not deem his crown to be secure as long as they were alive. Brackenbury, however, refused, and orders were then sent to him to deliver the keys up to sir James Tyrrell for one night. He obeyed, and Tyrrell, taking with him two ruffians named Dighton and Forest, proceeded in the night to the chamber where the princes were sleeping. He stood himself outside of the door while his agents went in and smothered them in the bedclothes. They then called him in to view the dead bodies, and by his orders buried them at the foot of the staircase.

Fate of Buckingham.

At this very time there was a conspiracy to restore the young king to his rights, and it would seem to be the knowledge of it that caused Richard to hasten his death. At the head of the conspirators (from what motive is unknown) was the duke of Buckingham. When they found that the king and his brother were dead they agreed to offer the crown to Henry Tudor, earl of Richmond, who was now the head of the Lancastrian party, on the condition of his marrying Elizabeth the eldest daughter of Edward IV., and thus uniting the claims of the rival houses. Richmond, who was in Brittany, gladly accepted the offer of a crown. A simultaneous rising in the west and south of England was prepared while Henry should sail from Brittany with what forces he could collect. But fortune stood the friend of the usurper. Henry's fleet was scattered in a storm; and when Buckingham, who had assembled a body of Welshmen at Brecknock, led his men to the Severn, he found the bridges broken and the fords impassable, by reason of the heavy rains which had swollen the river. His followers lost spirit and dispersed, and he himself made his way in disguise to the house of one Banister, his servant, near Shrewsbury. He was there either betrayed or discovered, and he was led to king Richard at Salisbury, by whose order his head was struck off in the market-place of that city.

Battle of Bosworth.

Some time elapsed before Richmond was able to attempt the invasion of England. At length he put to sea and landed safely at Milford Haven in South Wales. He advanced northwards; but so few ventured to join him that when he reached Shrewsbury he had not under his banner more than four thousand men. Urged, however, by the secret assurances of many who could not venture openly to declare themselves, he still advanced toward Leicester, where king Richard lay with an army of about twelve thousand men. Richmond's great reliance was on lord Stanley, who was married to his mother; but Richard, to secure that nobleman's fidelity, kept his son lord Strange at court by way of a hostage, and this young man being detected in an attempt at making his escape, his father was obliged to join the royal standard.

Richard advanced to meet his rival as far as the town of Bosworth. Henry, who had been joined by some of the Stanleys, and whose army now counted six thousand men, had reached the neighbouring town of Atherton. Next morning both armies were set in battle-array on the moor called Redmore. Richard was dismayed when he saw the Stanleys opposed to him; but he soon displayed his wonted courage. Observing part of his troops inactive and others wavering, he resolved to make one desperate effort and conquer or fall, and crying out "Treason, treason!" and giving his horse the spurs, he rushed to where he saw Richmond. He killed his standard-bearer and made a furious stroke at Henry himself, which was warded off by sir William Stanley, and Richard was thrown from his horse and slain. Lord Stanley taking up the crown which he wore placed it on the head of Richmond, and shouts of "Long live king Henry!" were instantly raised all over the field. The loss on Richard's side in this decisive battle was three hundred, that on Henry's only one hundred men. The body of Richard was stript, and being thrown across a horse was conveyed to Leicester and there interred. This prince was only in the thirty-second year of his age when he thus perished, the victim of his criminal ambition.

HOUSE OF TUDOR.

CHAPTER I.

HENRY VII.

Title of Henry.

THE title of the new monarch was as weak a one as well could be. He claimed the crown in right of his mother, who was still alive; and her right only consisted in her descent from John of Gaunt; but she was only descended from one of that prince's natural children, who had been legitimated by Richard II., with the express condition of their never having any claim to the crown. Henry's real title, therefore, consisted in his marriage with the princess Elizabeth, and in the anxiety for repose from civil war felt by the nation in general.

Lambert Simnel.

There was still remaining a son of the late duke of Clarence, named the earl of Warwick. This poor youth had been kept a prisoner by the late usurper; and Henry, in whose bosom there was little of generosity or magnanimity, shut him up close in the Tower. As a good deal of discontent was shown by the Yorkists at the preference given by the king on all occasions to the Lancastrians, and at his want of attention to his queen, the name of Warwick was employed in one of the most extraordinary cases of imposture recorded in history.

There was at Oxford a priest named Simons, a man of a subtle, enterprising temper. He had a pupil named

Lambert Simnel, the son, as was said, of a baker, about fifteen years of age, and a handsome, engaging lad. From speculative motives of his own, or, more probably, acting under the direction of higher persons, Simons taught this youth to personate the earl of Warwick, who was reported to have escaped from the Tower. As the Irish were much attached to the family of the duke of York, who had been their governor in the reign of Henry VI., it was resolved to open the drama in Ireland. Simons, therefore, proceeded with his pupil to Dublin, and the pretender was at once acknowledged by the earl of Kildare, the chief governor, and by the nobility and people in general. Application was made to the duchess-dowager of Burgundy, the sister of king Edward IV., a woman of great wealth, and who bore an intense hatred to Henry and all the Lancastrian party, and she readily engaged to furnish a body of two thousand veteran German soldiers, under the command of an able officer named Martin Swartz. When these troops landed in Dublin, it was resolved to crown the impostor, and the ceremony was performed by the bishop of Meath in the cathedral of Christchurch, the crown used on the occasion being taken from the statue of the Virgin. In ten days after, the troops of the pretender landed at Furness, in Lancashire, where they were joined by sir Thomas Broughton, with his tenantry. The chief command lay with the earl of Lincoln, whom the late usurper had declared heir to the throne, and who probably was only using Simnel as his tool. The invaders advanced rapidly into the heart of the kingdom. At a place named Stoke they met the royal forces, which were advancing from Nottingham; and though Lincoln's army did not exceed eight thousand men, he hesitated not to engage the superior numbers of the king. The battle lasted for three hours, and ended in the destruction of the rebels, of whom the one half were slain. Lincoln, Swartz, Kildare, sir Thomas Broughton, and others, fell; Simons and his pupil were made prisoners. The former, after having been obliged to confess the imposture, was thrown into prison, and was never heard of more; the latter was made a scullion in the royal kitchen, and he afterwards attained to the higher rank of falconer.

Among those present on the side of the impostor at the battle of Stoke, was lord Lovel, who had been one of the principal friends and supporters of king Richard. He escaped from the battle, but he was never seen or heard of more. About two centuries afterwards, at his seat at Minster-Lovel, in Oxfordshire, a chamber was discovered under ground, in which was the skeleton of a man seated in a chair, with his head reclined on a table. It is not improbable that this was lord Lovel, who had fled thither for concealment, and had been starved to death from accident or neglect.

Perkin Warbeck.

Some years afterwards, the king's persevering enemy, the duchess of Burgundy, raised up a new pretender to his throne. The person now selected was one Peterkin or Perkin Warbeck, the son of a converted Jew at Tournay, who, by frequenting the society of the English merchants, had acquired a competent knowledge of their language. He was directed to personate the duke of York, who was reported to have been saved when his brother was murdered, and to have effected his escape from the Tower. Ireland was selected as the fittest place for Perkin's first appearance also, and he landed at Cork in that island. The mayor and citizens declared for him, as also did the great earl of Desmond. But just at that time, having received an invitation to the court of France, which was at war with Henry, he repaired thither. He was there treated as the true heir to the English crown; but when, shortly afterwards, a peace was concluded with Henry, Perkin was ordered to quit the French dominions. He retired to Burgundy, where he was received with great affection by the duchess, who styled him the White Rose of England, and assigned him a guard of honour.

About three years afterwards, the adventurer landed at Deal, in Kent; but the people rose, and drove him off. He then tried Cork again, but to no purpose, and he finally proceeded to Scotland. The Scottish king received him with great respect, gave him in marriage the lady Catherine Gordon, a near relation of his own, and poured, in his cause, his savage hordes of borderers into the north of England. But a peace between the two crowns soon made an end of Perkin's hopes in this quarter, and he put to sea once more. He landed in Cornwall, and when he raised his banner as Richard IV., three thousand brave Cornishmen repaired to his standard; and by the time he reached Exeter, the number was doubled. He laid siege to that city; but on the approach of the royal army to its relief, he lost courage, and departing in secret, took sanctuary at the abbey of Bewdley in the New Forest. His followers then laid down their arms, and were pardoned. Henry treated the lady Catherine Gordon with great respect, and placed her about the person of the queen. She afterwards married sir Matthew Craddock, a Welsh knight, and she lies buried at the church of Swansea in Wales.

A guard was placed round the sanctuary to prevent the escape of Perkin; and on receiving a promise of pardon he consented to leave it. He rode in the royal train to London, and on the way multitudes crowded to gaze on him. When he reached London, he was led on horseback through the city to the Tower, and back to Westminster. He was then left at his liberty, but commanded not to go beyond the bounds of the palace. He soon after, however, ran away, and made for the coast, but being closely pursued, he took sanctuary at Shene, now called Richmond. His life was again granted him, but he was twice set in the stocks, and made to read a confession of his imposture, and was then committed to the Tower.

Fate of Warwick.—Prince Arthur.

The adventurer, when in the Tower, soon contrived to form an intimacy with the poor young earl of Warwick. This unhappy youth, who had been suffered to grow up in such absolute ignorance, that, in the homely language of the chronicler, " he could not discern a goose from a capon," easily became his dupe, and listened to his projects for their escape. But their plans were discovered, and they were both brought to trial for treason, and condemned. Perkin was hanged at Tyburn, Warwick was beheaded on Tower-hill.

Thus perished the last male of the house of Plantagenet, the victim, as was generally supposed, of Henry's regard for his own tranquillity. But there is reason to suppose that he was actuated by a far more unjustifiable motive, namely, the desire of procuring a high matrimonial alliance for his son prince Arthur. He had been for some time in treaty on this subject with Ferdinand, king of Spain, whose daughter, the princess Catherine, he hoped to obtain for that youth, with a large dower. Ferdinand, it is said, had written to say, that, as long as the earl of Warwick lived, he could not regard Arthur's succession as secure. The consequence of this was, that the earliest pretext was laid hold on for depriving Warwick of life. The princess was then sent over to England, and married to Arthur, though he was not more than fifteen years of age. He survived his marriage only about four months, and Henry, who was anxious to retain the Spanish connexion and the princess's dower, arranged with her father that his second son, prince Henry, who was then only twelve years old, should espouse her as soon as he should have attained the age of fifteen.

Henry's Avarice.

Henry was extremely avaricious, and he made himself very odious to the people by the various modes which he adopted of depriving them of their money. He had two notorious agents of his extortion, named Empson and Dudley, whom he made barons of the court of Exchequer, with a view to their filling his coffers by various legal expedients; and if *he* was disliked by the people, these men were detested. The following incident will show to what his love of money could urge the king himself.

No man had been more active and zealous in the cause of Henry than the earl of Oxford. He had led the van of his army at the battle of Bosworth, and had always been distinguished for his loyalty. One time this nobleman entertained the king at his castle; and at the royal departure the servants and retainers of the earl, dressed in his livery, stood drawn up in two rows to do the monarch honour. "My lord," said the king, "I have heard much of your hospitality, but it is greater than the speech. These handsome gentlemen and yeomen that I see on each side of me, are surely your menial servants." "That, may it please your grace," replied the earl, "were not for mine ease; they are most of them my retainers, come to do me service at a time like this, and chiefly to see your grace." Henry gave a start. "By my faith, my lord," said he, "I thank you for your good cheer; but I may not endure to have my laws broken in my sight. My attorney must speak with you." A statute had been passed against this practice of giving liveries, as it was called; and the earl had to pay a fine of 10,000*l.* for thus having honoured his king.

Henry died of gout in the fifty-third year of his age, and his remains were deposited in the splendid chapel which he built at Westminster-abbey, and which still bears his name.

CHAPTER II.

HENRY VIII.

Commencement of Henry's Reign.

HENRY VIII. was only eighteen years of age when he succeeded to the throne of England. As the claims of the white and the red roses were united in him, all chances of a disputed title were removed. He was handsome in person, popular in manners, and liberal in disposition. His father had left him an exchequer well supplied with money, and men looked forward to glorious doings under a young and gallant monarch. Nor were their expectations disappointed. One of Henry's first acts was to celebrate his marriage with the princess Catherine. Their joint coronation was one of the most splendid that had ever been celebrated in England. Pleasure alone seemed to occupy the court. Tilts and other martial exercises, in which the king excelled, continually took place in the presence of the queen, the nobility of both sexes, and the foreign ambassadors, and the prize of skill and valour was often awarded to the king himself. Empson and Dudley, we may here observe, the agents of the late king's avarice, became the victims of the new monarch's love of popularity. Though they had done nothing contrary to, at least, the letter of the law, they were surrendered to the popular vengeance, and they were executed on a false and absurd charge of high-treason.

Battle of Spurs.

The early years of Henry's reign passed away in joy and festivity. At length, a war having broken out between England and France, the young monarch, who panted for military fame, passed over to Calais with a gallant army of twenty-five thousand men, and laid siege to the town of

Terouenne. The French king, Louis XII., advanced to its relief; his cavalry encountered that of Henry, which was commanded by Maximilian, the emperor of Germany, at a placed named Guinegate. A sudden panic seized the French, and they fled, almost without striking a blow, leaving several noblemen and gentlemen of high renown in war prisoners in the hands of the enemy. This action was named the Battle of Spurs, as the French made more use of their spurs than their swords. Terouenne surrendered, Tournai followed its example, and Henry then returned to England for the winter.

Battle of Flodden-Field.

While Henry was thus engaged in France, an English army, led by the earl of Surrey, gained a decisive victory over the Scots, commanded by their king in person. Ever since the time of Edward III. a common feeling of hostility to England and a dread of her power had caused a close connexion to subsist between France and Scotland; and war with the one was always sure to be war with both. Though James IV., the present king of Scotland, was married to Henry's sister, the tie of affinity did not prevent his sharing in the war against him, for which purpose Louis supplied him with large sums of money, and as James was of a gallant, chivalrous spirit, Anne of Brittany, Louis' queen sent him a ring from her own finger, and styled him her knight. James, therefore, summoned his vassals to his standard, and crossing the Tweed at the head of a numerous army, he entered England and besieged and took Norham, Ford, and some other castles. He then encamped on the hill of Flodden, the last of the Cheviot-hills, and awaited the approach of the English army.

Lord Surrey, who was at Pontefract, summoned the gentry of the north to meet him at Newcastle. When they had joined him, he advanced to within five miles of the Scottish camp, and sending a herald to James, required him to quit his strong position and meet him on equal terms on the plain. On his refusal, Surrey resolved to march toward Scotland, and then to return and take the Scottish army in the rear. He had just executed this manœuvre, when the Scots, aware of his object, set fire to their huts and prepared to occupy an eminence further to the north. But when the smoke cleared away, they saw the English army at the foot of Flodden-hill, and they then began to descend in five solid masses.

The Scottish spearmen fell boldly on the English vanguard. They threw a part of it into confusion; but a body of outlaws who suddenly came up restored the battle, and after a severe and bloody conflict, in which the earls of Crawford and Errol were slain, the Scots broke and fled. The king himself, followed by a numerous body of gallant warriors cased in armour, assailed the rearguard, and bearing down all opposition, had nearly reached the royal standard, when sir Edward Stanley fell on his rear, and threw it into confusion, and James was slain by an unknown hand. The Scots were now routed on all sides; though the battle had lasted only an hour, and was terminated by night, their loss had been ten thousand men slain, among whom were three bishops, two abbots, twelve earls, and thirteen barons. The day of Flodden-field was as fatal to Scotland as that of Poitiers had been to France, and it was long before she again attempted to measure her strength with England in a field of battle.

Marriage of Henry's Sister.

Henry created the earl of Surrey duke of Norfolk, and his son, lord Thomas Howard, earl of Surrey. The lord Lisle was made duke of Suffolk, and others who had distinguished themselves were similarly rewarded. A peace with France was concluded, and Louis, who was now a widower, though fifty-three years of age, married Henry's younger sister, Mary, a princess of only sixteen years. The king, however, died soon after his marriage, and lord Suffolk was sent to conduct the young widow to England Mary, whose first love Suffolk had been, gave him a challenge to marry her on a certain day, or to lose her for ever. Though he knew the risk he ran from the arbitrary temper of Henry, he resolved to act on the maxim of "faint heart never won fair lady," and he boldly married her. Henry was at first very angry, but Mary wrote, taking the whole blame on herself. Francis, the new French king, interceded for the lovers; cardinal Wolsey, Henry's great favourite, gave them his powerful influence, and a cordial forgiveness was the result.

Cardinal Wolsey.

The celebrated favourite, Thomas Wolsey, was said to have been the son of a butcher at Ipswich. Having received a learned education, he entered the church, and he became tutor in the family of the marquess of Dorset, the half-brother of the queen of Henry VII., to which monarch he was recommended by his patron. Henry, finding him active and intelligent, employed him, and gave him preferment in the church. When Henry VIII. ascended the throne, Wolsey became to him what Becket had been to Henry II.; he was the companion of his pleasures, and the director of his councils. Preferments of all kinds rapidly flowed in on him. The king made him chancellor and archbishop of York, and bestowed on him several other lucrative preferments in the church; the pope was induced to send him a cardinal's hat, and to appoint him the papal legate in England; and this pontiff, the king of France, and the emperor Charles V., granted him large pensions to secure his influence with his vain capricious master.

Field of the Cloth of Gold.

Francis I. of France, a prince of a gay and gallant temper, was extremely anxious to have a personal interview with the English monarch. Henry at length yielded to his solicitations, and it was arranged that the meeting should take place within the English territory in France, and a stately tournament be held on the occasion. The whole of the arrangements were by mutual consent committed to the English cardinal, whose taste and skill in all matters of magnificence and display were beyond dispute.

At the appointed time Henry and his court passed over to Calais. Two temporary palaces of framework, the walls of which were hung with tapestry and the ceilings covered with silk, were erected, at some distance from each other, for the two monarchs. When all the serious business had been concluded, and the kings had had a private interview in a rich pavilion pitched for the purpose in the vale of Andern, and conferred on the treaty which had been arranged by their ministers, the martial sports commenced.

On the first six days the kings tilted with spears against all comers; the tourney with the broadsword on horseback occupied two more, and on the last day the monarchs fought on foot at barriers. The two queens and their ladies looked on from their galleries and awarded the prizes, and the heralds duly registered the names, arms, and exploits of the knights. The French and English nobles vied like their sovereigns with each other in the display of magnificence, "many of them," a French writer observes, "carrying on their shoulders their mills, their forests, and their meadows." In the romantic language of the age, the place which was the scene of all this gorgeous display was named the Field of the Cloth of Gold.

Henry and Francis parted with suitable acts of gallant courtesy and with expressions of mutual esteem. But all the hopes of the latter founded on the chivalry and courtesy displayed on the Field of the Cloth of Gold were frustrated by a visit which Henry, immediately after parting with him, made to the emperor, who was the nephew of his queen, and ere long an English army spread its ravages over the fertile plains of Picardy, Henry being the ally of the emperor in a war with France.

The Reformation.

Hitherto the reign of Henry had been prosperous abroad and at home, and pleasure had chiefly occupied the hours of the king and his nobles. The scene is now to change, and the joyous, festive monarch is to appear in the character of the barbarous, capricious tyrant.

It was at this time that the great Reformation in religion commenced. Men of sense had grown weary of the frauds and superstitions of the church of Rome, and her avarice had turned the minds of the people against her. A German friar, named Martin Luther, a man of learning, of eloquence, of piety, and of undaunted courage, had boldly stepped forth as the champion of reason and of true religion, and in their cause had set at defiance the power of Rome. Among the supporters of the church in the literary warfare that ensued was the king of England, whose studies had lain much among books of divinity. He composed a work entitled "A Defence of the Seven Sacraments," which he dedicated to the pope, who received it with raptures of joy, and honoured its author with the title of Defender of the Faith. Little did either pope or king foresee that, within a few short years, a deadly, enmity and a final separation were to take place between the papacy and its champion, and that, under Heaven, Henry was to be the great agent in introducing the reformed religion into England.

Origin of Henry's Divorce.

Henry had, as we have seen, married his brother's widow. Though the consent of the pope had been obtained, many doubted if such a union was lawful in the sight of Heaven. Henry himself appears for many years to have felt no scruples on the subject; but the circumstance of the death of all his children by Catherine but one, the princess Mary, is said to have caused him some mental uneasiness, which was greatly augmented when a French prelate, who had come over as ambassador to England on the subject of the marriage of that princess with the son of the king of France, expressed some doubts as to her legitimacy. He confided his thoughts on the subject to Wolsey, who hated the queen because she used to rebuke him for the ill life he led, and the cardinal encouraged him in the idea of getting a divorce, a matter expected to be of little difficulty at Rome. It was Wolsey's design to have the king married to a daughter of the late king of France, and he went himself over to that country to try to arrange the affair.

Anne Boleyn.

But Henry had, unknown to Wolsey, already selected the person who was to occupy the place of his innocent and virtuous queen. When his sister went over to France to be the bride of king Louis, there was in her train a little girl, only seven years of age, the daughter of sir Thomas Boleyn, and niece of the duke of Norfolk. On the return of Mary to England, Anne Boleyn remained for some years at the court of the queen of Francis I. She was afterwards, when about fourteen years of age, brought back to England, and her father obtained for her a situation in the court of queen Catherine. Her beauty, sense, wit, and elegant manners, soon made her the object of general admiration. A proffer of the hand of lord Percy the heir of Northumberland, was not rejected by the fair maid of honour; but the king, who had other views for her, directed the cardinal, in whose family the young lord lived, to prevent the match. Percy at first was unyielding, but his father, when summoned from the country, soon reduced him to obedience, and he shortly after married another lady. Ere long the king himself became a suitor to Anne Boleyn; but her virtue was not to be overcome, and he at length promised to marry her as soon as he should be divorced from queen Catherine, a matter in which he reckoned that he should meet with no difficulty whatever.

Proceedings in the Divorce.

Under other circumstances there would probably have been no difficulty, but unluckily for Henry, the pope was at this time entirely at the mercy of Catherine's nephew, the emperor, whose troops had lately taken and sacked the city of Rome. After a good deal of delay, the pontiff at length issued a commission to Wolsey and to an Italian cardinal named Campeggio to try the cause in England.

The court of the cardinals was opened in a hall of the convent of the Black-friars, the king and queen having taken up their abode in the adjacent palace of Bridewell*, to be at hand. When the parties appeared before the court, Henry, on their names being called, replied, in a loud voice, "Here;" but the queen, rising from her place, went over, and kneeling before him, said that she was a poor woman, and a stranger in his dominions; that she had been his wife for twenty years, and had borne him several children; that if she had done anything amiss, she was willing to be put away with shame; that their fathers, who had been wise princes, had agreed on the match; that finally, she would not submit to the court till she had heard from Spain. She then rose and left the court, and Henry, when she was gone, bore public testimony to her virtues, declaring, that nothing but the uneasiness of his mind could have made him thus wound her feelings. The court held several other sittings, and Henry was in full expectation of a sentence in his favour, when Campeggio suddenly adjourned the court to a distant day. The duke of Suffolk, who was present, was so enraged, that, striking the table with his fist, he cried out, "By the mass, I see that the old saw [saying] is true; never was there legate or cardinal that did any good in England." Wolsey rebuked

---

* So named from the holy well of St. Bride. This palace was afterwards converted into a house of correction, and it has given its name to all places of the kind.

him, reminding him that *he* had been under much obligation to a cardinal, alluding to his marriage.

Fall of Wolsey.

This affair, however, proved the ruin of Wolsey. Norfolk, Suffolk, and other nobles, had long been his enemies, and now Anne Boleyn, viewing him as the means of preventing her from being queen, became inveterately hostile to him. It was about the end of the month of July that Campeggio had adjourned the court, and three days after, Wolsey, in the beginning of the following Michaelmas Term, had opened the court of Chancery with his usual pomp, when the dukes of Norfolk and Suffolk waited on him, by the king's command, and required him to deliver up the seals and retire to his house at Esher in Surrey. He refused at first, but on their bringing him a letter from the king, he submitted. Having caused an inventory to be made of all his plate and other valuables at York-house (the present Whitehall), the whole of which the king claimed, he entered his barge and proceeded up the river to Putney. He there landed and mounted his mule to go on to Esher. He had proceeded but a little way when a messenger met him, bearing a ring and a kind message from the king. He threw himself from his mule, took off his cap and knelt in the mire to receive the communication, and then proceeded in better spirits to his place of exile.

At Esher the cardinal fell sick, and Henry directed his own physician to attend him; he also sent him another ring, with kind messages from himself and Anne Boleyn. Henry also granted him a full pardon for the offences with which he was charged, and permission to reside at Richmond. But as the palace in which Henry passed most of his time was at that place, Wolsey's enemies, fearing that he might recover his influence, obtained an order for him to go and reside in his diocese of York. He accordingly set out in Passion week, and travelling by slow journeys and making long halts on the way, he reached the seehouse of Cawood, near York, about the end of September. As the ceremony of his installation had not yet been performed, he was preparing to celebrate it, when the earl of Northumberland (his former servant, lord Henry Percy) arrived and arrested him on a charge of high treason. On his way up to London he stopped for a fortnight at the seat of the earl of Shrewsbury, where he was attacked by a bowel complaint. He, however, went on to Leicester, and halted at the convent of that place. When the abbot and his monks came forth to receive him, he said to him, "Father abbot, I am come to lay my bones among you." He was then conducted to a chamber, which he never left. When he felt himself dying, he addressed sir William Kingston, the lieutenant of the Tower, who had him in charge, praying him to commend him to the king; and he concluded with these memorable words: "Had I but served God as diligently as I have served the king, He would not have given me over in my grey hairs. But this is the just reward that I must receive for my indulgent pains and study, not regarding my service to God, but only to my prince." He shortly after breathed his last.

Henry's Divorce and Breach with Rome.

Acting under the advice of a clergyman named Thomas Cranmer, Henry adopted the expedient of taking the opinions of universities and eminent divines throughout Europe on the subject of his divorce; and finding a sufficient number of them in his favour, he resolved to proceed in the affair without the pope, who was entirely under the influence of the emperor. He privately married Anne Boleyn, and then caused Cranmer, whom he had raised to the see of Canterbury, to pronounce the divorce between him and Catherine. This virtuous and ill-used princess survived the insult thus offered her only four years. A little before her death she dictated a letter to the king, which, unfeeling as he was, brought tears into his eyes.

In the course of the quarrel with the pope, Henry, by the advice of Thomas Cromwell, his present favourite, assumed to himself the supremacy over the church of England. The clergy in general were forced to yield to this assumption. Two men of great eminence, however, refused to acknowledge Henry in this new character: the one was Fisher, bishop of Rochester; the other the celebrated sir Thomas More, the late chancellor. They were both committed to the Tower on their refusal to take an oath relative to the succession to the crown, in which the marriage with Catherine was declared null and void; and after lying there upwards of a twelvemonth they were brought to trial on a charge of denying the king's supremacy, and sentenced to die as traitors.

Execution of Bishop Fisher and Sir Thomas More.

Bishop Fisher was a man of great piety, sincere, upright and conscientious. His death was perhaps hastened by the imprudence of the pope in raising him to the dignity of cardinal, for Henry is reported to have declared that "the pope might send him a cardinal's hat but that he should have no head to wear it." As for Fisher himself, he made so light of the honour, that he said, "If the red hat were lying at my feet I would not stoop to pick it up." On the morning of his execution he had himself dressed with great care. "My lord," said his servant, "surely you forget that after the short space of some two hours you must strip off these things and wear them no more." "What of that?" replied he; "dost thou not mark that this is my wedding-day?" On account of his infirmities he was carried in a chair to the place of execution. He opened a New Testament, which he held in his hand, at these words: "And this is life eternal, that they might know thee the only true God, and Jesus Christ whom thou hast sent. I have glorified thee on earth; I have finished the work which thou gavest me to do." He closed the book, saying, "Here is learning enough for me to my life's end." He ascended the scaffold without assistance, and his head was severed from his body at one blow.

More, like Fisher, met death with calmness and constancy. As his mind was pure and strong in innocence, the pleasant jocose humour which had distinguished him throughout life displayed itself even in his last moments. Observing the scaffold to be weak and tottering, he said, "I pray you, master lieutenant, see me safe up, and for my coming down let me shift for myself." When the executioner, in the usual manner, asked his forgiveness, he said, "Pluck up thy spirits, man, and be not afraid to do thine office. My neck is very short; take heed, therefore, thou strike not awry for saving of thine honour." As he knelt at the block he bade the executioner to stay till he had put his beard aside; "for," said he, "it never committed treason." One stroke of the axe terminated his existence.

Fall of Anne Boleyn.

The murders, for such they were, of More and Fisher, prove Henry to have been a barbarous tyrant; but that of his queen, of that Anne Boleyn whom he had loved so long, and for whose sake he had braved the resentment of the pope and emperor, and alienated the affections of many of his own subjects, places him almost without the pale of humanity. His motive too enhances his guilt, for it was to marry another woman that he deprived her of life.

Queen Catherine died in the beginning of January, in the year 1536. It could not be expected that queen Anne would mourn for her, but prudence might have taught her to conceal her joy. This, however, she did not do, and she appeared in a suit of yellow by way of mourning. Toward the end of the month she was delivered of a stillborn male child, on which occasion Henry reproached her in a most brutal manner, as if it had been her fault and not her misfortune. He had, in fact, transferred his affections to Jane Seymour, one of her own maids of honour, and he was anxiously seeking a pretext for divorcing or destroying her. Anne, who was volatile and imprudent, and somewhat of a coquette by nature, was not so guarded in her conduct and language as the wife of a jealous capricious tyrant like Henry should have been, and materials for a charge against her were easily obtained when the king's wishes were known. In the month of April a commission was appointed to investigate them, and on the following May-day there was a tilting-match at Greenwich, in the presence of the king and queen, in which her brother lord Rochford, and Norris groom of the stole, were principal actors. In the midst of it something occurred to disturb the king, and he rose abruptly and rode to Westminster. The queen also retired to her apartments in a state of great anxiety. Next day she entered her barge to proceed to Westminster; on the river she met her uncle the duke of Norfolk and some other noblemen, who had orders to convey her to the Tower. At the gate of that fatal fortress she fell on her knees and said, "O Lord, help me, as I am guiltless of that whereof I am accused!" When the lords were gone, she said to the lieutenant, "Mr. Kingston, shall I go into a dungeon?" "No, madam," said he, "you shall go into your lodging that you lay in at your coronation." "It is too good for me," she replied: "Jesu, have mercy on me!" She knelt down and wept, and then burst into a fit of hysteric laughter.

The charges against this unhappy lady were of the most monstrous character. She was accused of incest with her own brother, and of adultery with Norris and with Weston and Brereton, gentlemen of the privy chamber, and even with a musician named Smeaton.

On the 12th of May these last four persons were brought to trial before a jury, and were all found guilty. The three gentlemen boldly asserted the queen's innocence and their own, but Smeaton was induced to plead guilty. Three days after the queen and her brother were tried in the hall of the Tower by their uncle of Norfolk, and nine-and-twenty other peers, among whom it is to be feared their own father was compelled to sit. The queen was first tried. Her countenance was serene and cheerful, and she so easily refuted the charges made against her, that the by-standers all anticipated an acquittal; a majority, however, of her judges, valuing perhaps the king's favour more than justice and honour, pronounced her guilty, and she was sentenced by her uncle to be burnt or beheaded at the king's pleasure. When she heard this sentence, she raised her hands, and cried, "O Father and Creator! O thou, who art the way, the truth and the life! thou knowest that I have not deserved this death." Rochfort made a noble defence, but he also was found guilty, and two days after he and the other three gentlemen and Smeaton were executed. They all died asserting their innocence except Smeaton, who was the last executed, and who may therefore have had hopes of mercy. He said that he well deserved death, but did not give a reason. When the queen heard of what he said, she indignantly exclaimed, "Has he not then cleared me from the public shame he has done me? Alas, I fear his soul will suffer from his false accusation."

Execution of Anne Boleyn.

The following day the order came to the Tower for the execution of the queen. It found her firm and undismayed. "I have seen," said Kingston, "many men, and also women executed, and that they have been in great sorrow; to my knowledge this lady hath more joy and pleasure in death." When conversing with him, she said, "Mr. Kingston, I hear say I shall not die afore noon, and I am sorry, therefore, for I thought to be dead and past my pain." He said "it would be no pain, it was so subtle." She replied, "I heard say the executioner was very good, and I have a *little neck*;" and she put her hands about it, laughing heartily.

Next day, a little before noon, she was led to the scaffold. She ascended it and addressed those present in the following words: "Good Christian people, I am come hither to die, for according to the law and by the law I am judged to die, and therefore I will speak nothing against it; I am come hither to accuse no man, nor to speak anything of that whereof I am accused and condemned to die; but I pray God to save the king and send him long to reign over you; for a gentler [nobler] nor more merciful prince was there never, and to me he was ever a good, gentle and sovereign lord; and if any person will meddle with my cause I require them to judge the best. And thus I take my leave of the world and of you all, and I heartily desire you to pray for me. O Lord, have mercy on me! To God I commend my soul." She calmly took off her hat and collar, knelt down and uttered a pious ejaculation, and one blow of the executioner's sword terminated her existence. Her remains were thrown into an elm chest and interred without any ceremony in the Tower chapel.

The very day after this murder of his innocent wife the tyrant married Jane Seymour. But Heaven had decreed that he should not long enjoy the fruit of his crime, for Jane died of fever on the birth of her first child, a son, who survived and was named Edward.

Suppression of Monasteries.

One of the most remarkable acts of Henry's reign was the suppression of all the monasteries throughout the kingdom, and the seizure of their revenues for the use of the crown. Visitors were sent to inquire into their condition, and in many of them gross irregularities of life and morals were discovered. The pious frauds by which the monks and friars used to beguile the credulity of the people were also detected and exposed. Thus it was found that eleven different religious houses boasted of the possession of the Virgin Mary's girdle, and that eight others had some of her milk to show. The teeth of St. Apollonia, which were said to cure the toothache, were so numerous that they filled a ton when collected. At Reading there was a wooden angel with only one wing, and yet it had flown to England as the bearer of the spear-head that pierced our Saviour's side. The monastery of Hales in Gloucestershire had in a vial a portion of our Saviour's blood, to see which pilgrims resorted from all parts; but when the vial was displayed to their view the sacred blood was often not to be seen. The reason, as they were told, was that they had not purchased enough of masses, and when they had paid more money the blood became visible. It was found that the vial, which contained the blood of a duck, had one opake side, which the priest used to turn to the pilgrims till they had given money enough. At Boxley in Kent was a crucifix, called the Rood of Grace, which by secret springs and wires was made to move its head, lips, etc., to the great amazement of the ignorant people. These were all brought to St. Paul's, and the impostures there exposed. Some of the lands of the monasteries were sold; but the greater part were given by the king to his rapacious courtiers; and hence at the present day the seats of so many noblemen and gentlemen are called Abbeys and Priories. Such, for example, are Woburn abbey and Newstead abbey. In many cases the magnificent churches and other buildings of the abbeys were stript of their roofs and let go to ruin. Many of these noble ruins, such as Fountains, Tintern and Netley, may still be seen, and they will in some bosoms awake a sigh at the barbarous rapacity which reduced them to such a condition.

Anne of Cleves.—Fall of Cromwell.

Henry did not remain very long a widower. He was rather perplexed in his choice of a wife, for as he was now grown very large and corpulent, he fancied it was only fitting that his wife should be of suitable dimensions. He had the indelicacy to propose to the king of France a conference at Calais, to which the latter should bring the finest ladies of his court; but Francis declared that he would not treat the French ladies as men did nags at a fair.

At length Cromwell proposed to his master Anne, daughter of the duke of Cleves. Her portrait having satisfied him, he proposed for her, and was accepted. When she landed in England he went to meet her, but his expectations were terribly disappointed; for though she was tall, large and fair, her features were coarse and her manners ungraceful. Henry swore that they had brought him a great Flanders mare; but seeing no remedy, "I *must*," said he, in a sorrowful tone, "put my neck into the yoke;" and the marriage ceremony was performed by Cranmer.

This marriage proved the ruin of Cromwell. Henry began to hate him as the means of his being united to so disagreeable a yoke-fellow, and his enemies soon obtained the advantage over him which they sought. At dinner one day at the bishop of Winchester's, Henry met with Catherine Howard, a niece of the duke of Norfolk's. His fancy for large portly women being now pretty well ended, he was greatly pleased with Catherine, who was little and agreeable, and he became her captive. His dislike of his queen and his hatred of Cromwell were thereby augmented. He forthwith resolved to divorce the former, and by his orders the latter was arrested as a traitor by the duke of Norfolk at the council-board. As Henry's will was always a law to his parliament, the affair of the divorce was easily managed, and Anne was obliged to resign her royal rank for the palace of Richmond, £3,000 a year, and the title of the king's sister. As for Cromwell, the parliament pronounced him guilty of the charges made against him, and though the despot whom he served shed tears at the letter which he wrote to him imploring for mercy, his ruthless heart was not to be moved. The fallen minister was therefore beheaded on Tower-hill, and he died with piety and constancy.

Catherine Howard.

The king now married Catherine Howard, and according to his own account led a most happy and virtuous life with her for upwards of a twelvemonth. At the end of that time, Cranmer, after mass one day, put into his hands a series of charges relating to her incontinence before marriage against his seemingly virtuous consort. Henry was thunderstruck at the information; he asserted that the charges were forged, but he nevertheless ordered inquiry to be made, and they proved to be but too well founded. Catherine herself, when examined, confessed her ill conduct before marriage; but she asserted, and probably with truth, that she had never been unfaithful to the king. This assertion, however, availed her nothing; when parliament met, she and lady Rochfort, her friend and confidant, were sentenced to death, and they were both beheaded within the Tower.

In the act of parliament passed on this occasion it was declared that any woman whom the king should be about to marry should be guilty of treason if she did not inform him of any slip she might have previously made. It was therefore jocularly said that the king must not now look for any but a widow. True words are often spoken in jest, for Henry's next choice *did* fall on a widow. This was Catherine Parr, the relict of lord Latimer, a woman of sense and virtue, and inclined to the new opinions in religion.

Attempt to ruin Cranmer.

These new opinions, or what now were called the *protestant* doctrines, had been making great progress through the nation. Henry sided now with one now with the other party, and most impartially hanged some for denying his supremacy, and burned others for denying the real presence of Christ in the elements of the Lord's supper. The reformers were headed by Cranmer and favoured by the queen; the catholics regarded Gardiner, bishop of Winchester, and the lord-chancellor, Wriottesley, as their chiefs.

Gardiner, who was a man of considerable talent, had, it is said, "bent his bow in order to shoot at some of the head-deer." The first at whom he let fly a shaft was the primate. Henry was told that his throne was in danger from that guileless man, and was advised to send him next day to the Tower. He gave a seeming consent; but at midnight he summoned the primate to his presence, and informed him of what was intended. Cranmer said that he cared not about it, as he could easily prove his innocence. " O Lord God!" cried the king, " what fond [foolish] simplicity have you so to permit yourself to be imprisoned, that every enemy of yours may take advantage against you! Do you not know that when they have you once in prison three or four false knaves will soon be procured to witness against you and condemn you?" He then gave him a ring, and bade him appeal to *him* if he should find the council hostile.

Next morning Cranmer was summoned before the council. After having been made to wait a long time in an outer room, among servants and low people, he was admitted and informed of the charges against him. His demand to be confronted with his accusers being refused, he produced the ring, at the sight of which they were struck dumb, and when they waited on the king he rated them well for their malice to the primate. He then made them shake hands with that placable prelate, by whom they were all entertained a few days after at his palace at Lambeth.

Attack on the Queen.

Gardiner had shot covertly at the primate; he aimed a shaft openly against the queen. Henry, who was grown peevish and irritable from disease, was annoyed by her urging him on points of religion. He mentioned this one day to Gardiner, just as she had left the room, and that artful prelate made such good use of his opportunity that he obtained permission to have articles of accusation drawn up against her. Henry approved of them when shown to him, but luckily for the queen, the paper containing them was dropt by accident or design, and was picked up by one of her friends. The alarm brought on a fit of illness; the king came to visit her, and behaved with kindness. Next day she returned the visit, and when Henry asked her opinion on a matter of religion, she modestly replied, that the man was the woman's natural superior, and her judgement should be directed by his. "Not so, by St. Mary; you are become a doctor, Kate," said he, "to instruct us, as we take it, and not to be instructed by us." She assured him that her only object in arguing with him had been to divert his mind, and to obtain instruction. "And is it even so, sweetheart?" cried he; "then perfect friends are we now again. It doth me more good to hear these words of thine own mouth than it would have done had I heard the news of a hundred thousand pounds fallen unto me." He embraced and dismissed her. The following day he sent for her to the garden, and while they were there the chancellor came to arrest her. She retired at a sign; the chancellor knelt, and Henry saluted him with "knave, fool, beast, avaunt from my sight!" and similar strong phrases. The queen came forward to intercede. "Ah, poor soul!" said Henry, "thou little knowest how evil he hath deserved this grace at thy hands. Of my word, sweetheart, he hath been toward thee an errant knave, and so let him go." Orders were then given that Gardiner should appear no more in the royal presence.

Last Days of Henry.

The days of Henry were now drawing to their close; but one more act of injustice was to be perpetrated. The duke of Norfolk and his son, the earl of Surrey, were committed to the Tower on some absurd charges of treason. Norfolk was a man who had often done good service to the crown; Surrey was the most accomplished nobleman of the age, and his poems may still be read with pleasure. Yet both were found guilty of the trifling charges made against them, and Surrey was executed, and Norfolk only escaped by the accident of the king dying the night before the morning on which he was to have appeared on the scaffold.

Henry had been growing every day worse and worse, but no one ventured to tell him of his danger. At length sir Antony Denny took courage; he received the intelligence with meekness, saying that he relied on the merits of his Saviour. Being asked what divine he would have to attend him, he said, "Let me take a little sleep first, and when I awake again I shall think more about the matter." On awaking, he directed that Cranmer should be sent for, but when that prelate arrived he found him speechless. He desired him to give a sign of his faith in the merits of Christ; the king pressed his hand and expired.

Henry left three children; a daughter, named Mary, by Catherine of Aragon; another daughter, named Elizabeth, by Anne Boleyn; and a son, named Edward, by Jane Seymour.

CHAPTER III.

EDWARD VI.

Fate of Lord Seymour.

As Edward VI. was only in the tenth year of his age, his father had by his will appointed a council of sixteen persons to administer the government. The leading person in this council was the young king's maternal uncle, Seymour, duke of Somerset, with the title of Protector; and as this nobleman held the reformed doctrines, the true religion made great progress in this reign.

Somerset was on the whole a good man; yet his evil destiny, as we may perhaps term it, forced him to spill the blood of his own brother on a scaffold. This brother, who had been ennobled under the title of lord Seymour of Sudeley, and raised to the post of lord high admiral, was a man of a haughty aspiring temper. He married the queen dowager, to whom he had been long attached, and on her death soon after in childbed, he turned his thoughts to the lady Elizabeth, who was now in her fifteenth year; and he sought to gain influence over the mind of her royal brother by supplying him secretly with money. His evident object was the overthrow of his brother's power, and it would appear that he had other designs of a dangerous nature. He was therefore committed to the Tower by the council, and articles of accusation against him were exhibited in parliament. A bill of attainder, as it was termed, was rapidly passed, and the admiral was beheaded on Tower-hill, his own brother and Cranmer being among those who signed the warrant for his execution.

Fall of Somerset.

Though Somerset's love of power thus urged him to shed the blood of his brother, he was not able to avert his own fall. He possessed an able, ambitious and unprincipled rival in Dudley, earl of Warwick, the son of the agent of Henry the Seventh's rapacity, whom the late king had taken into his service and raised to the peerage. The execution of his own brother had drawn on Somerset much odium; people were also displeased at beholding the great fortune which he had amassed at the expense of the crown and church, and at the magnificent mansion, named Somerset-house, which he was building for himself in the Strand. To procure a site for this edifice he had pulled down a church and three bishops' houses, and he had demolished some other sacred edifices for the sake of the materials. Warwick and his other enemies in the council soon therefore found themselves strong enough to attack him.

He was committed to the Tower on sundry charges, the truth of which, to save his life, he was obliged to acknowledge on his knees before the council, and he was deprived of all his offices, and of a part of his landed property. An apparent reconciliation, however, soon after took place between him and Warwick, cemented by a marriage between lord Lisle, the latter's eldest son, with the lady Anne Seymour. But nothing but the total destruction of Somerset would content the criminal ambition of Warwick. He bribed the duke's servants to convey him intelligence of all he said; and he provoked him by menaces and insults, in order that he might give utterance to expressions on which charges might be founded. At length, having obtained what he deemed sufficient, he caused him to be committed to the Tower on a charge of intending to dethrone the king and to seize the earl of Warwick. He was brought to trial before a court composed of twenty-seven peers, one of whom was Warwick himself. They acquitted him of the treason, but found him guilty of the felony, and Warwick, who was resolved to have his blood, never ceased till he had prevailed on the young king to sign the warrant for his execution. Somerset was accordingly beheaded on Tower-hill. Though strict orders had been given for people to stay at home, the place was crowded by day-break, though it was toward the end of the cold month of January; and when the axe had stricken off his head, numbers rushed forward and dipped their handkerchiefs in his blood, as in that of a martyr; for his zealous attachment to protestantism, and his sympathy for the sufferings of the poor, had made him the most popular nobleman of the age.

Last Days of King Edward.

Warwick, who had lately been created duke of Northumberland, now took a higher flight of ambition, and even aimed at bringing the crown into his own family. The young king, who had inherited the delicate constitution of his mother, had lately had both the measles and the smallpox, and his frame had become so delicate that it was plain he could not live many years. Northumberland had married his son, the lord Guilford Dudley, to the lady Jane Grey, daughter of the marchioness of Dorset, to whom the capricious will of Henry VIII. had given a kind of claim to the crown, in preference to the children of his sister the queen of Scots. As Edward was a bigoted protestant, and his sister the lady Mary was as bigoted a catholic, Northumberland, by working on his religious feelings, induced him to make a devise of the crown in favour of the lady Jane Grey. The claim of the lady Elizabeth, Northumberland expected to be able to set aside on the pretext of her not being legitimate. To make the matter more sure, he insisted on the members of the privy-council all putting their names to the instrument of devise. Cranmer long refused, and he only yielded at last to the earnest entreaties of the dying king.

Edward, who was in a consumption, did not long survive this act. His last words were, "O my Lord God, defend this realm from papistry, and maintain thy true religion, that I and my people may praise thy holy name, for Jesus Christ's sake." He was very generally regretted, for he was of a most amiable temper, and was sincerely religious. His abilities were considerable, and had he lived he would probably have proved an excellent king.

CHAPTER IV.

MARY.

Lady Jane Grey.

THE lady Jane Grey, to whom her late royal relative had bequeathed his crown, was only sixteen years of age. She was of an agreeable person, and a gentle and amiable temper. Her talents also were considerable. She read both Greek and Latin, and also understood some of the modern languages. When Northumberland and some other lords came to announce to her the death of her cousin, and her elevation to the throne, she burst into tears and fell senseless to the ground. When she recovered, she looked up to heaven, and said, "If the right be truly mine, O gracious God, give me strength, I pray most earnestly, so to rule as to promote thy honour and my country's good."

But the good and virtuous lady Jane was not destined to rule on earth. From a persuasion of the lady Mary's right to the throne, and from detestation of Northumberland, the people in general declared in favour of that princess. The efforts of Northumberland to oppose her proved fruitless; she entered London in triumph, and the unhappy lady Jane, after enjoying the pageantry of royalty for the brief space of ten days, found herself a captive in the hands of her rival.

Execution of Lady Jane Grey.

Northumberland was brought to trial on a charge of high-treason. He pleaded guilty, and made the most abject supplications for life. "Alas," cried he, "let me live a little longer, though it be but in a mouse-hole." But the queen was determined not to spare him, and indeed there was no good reason why she should; and he suffered the fate which he had brought on the far more estimable duke of Somerset. All the other prisoners were set at liberty except lady Jane and her husband.

But this innocent young couple were not to be spared. In the following year, when an insurrection, headed by sir Thomas Wyat, and caused by apprehension of Mary's catholic bigotry, had been suppressed, she signed the warrant for the execution of "Guilford Dudley and his wife," as it was expressed. Dudley was beheaded the first; lady Jane, who had refused to see him lest the meeting should overcome their fortitude, beheld him from her window as he went forth, and she gazed on his lifeless remains as they were brought back in a cart. When led to the scaffold herself, she mounted it with a firm step, and addressing the spectators, acknowledged that she had committed an unlawful act in taking the crown, but asserted that she had done it in innocency, and declared that she died a true Christian. As she was placing herself before the block, she said to the executioner, "I pray you, despatch me quickly;" adding, "Will you take it off before I lay me down?" "No, madam," replied he. Her eyes being bandaged, she groped about for the block, and not finding it became a little agitated, and said, "What shall I do? Where is it? where is it?" Her head was then guided to the right spot; she stretched forth her neck, saying, "Lord, into thy hands I commend my spirit!" and a single blow terminated her existence.

Danger of Elizabeth.

Thus perished this admirable lady, the victim of the crimes of others. A fate similar to hers was near befalling the lady Elizabeth. The queen, who hated her as the daughter of Anne Boleyn and as a professor of the reformed religion, under the pretext of her being engaged in the late conspiracy, caused her to be arrested at her residence in the country and brought up a prisoner to London, though the season was cold and she was in a delicate state of health. In about a fortnight after she was committed to the Tower. At the gate of that fortress she sat down on a stone to rest her, though it was raining. "Better sitting here than in a worse place," said she to the lieutenant, when he pressed her to come in out of the rain. She was then led to her apartment, and the doors were locked and bolted on her, and she remained in solitude to meditate on the fate of her mother and of lady Jane Grey, a fate which so soon might be her own. Some of the members of the council were for bringing her to the block, but Gardiner, bishop of Winchester, who was chancellor, and a man of great influence, strongly opposed this course; and after a confinement of some months, she was sent to Woodstock-castle, and placed under the charge of sir Henry Bedingfield, a bigoted Catholic. This knight proved so rigorous a jailer, that the princess, it is said, hearing one day the blithe song of a milkmaid, could not refrain from wishing that she were a milkmaid, that she might carol thus gay and free from care. She, however, soon found a powerful friend and protector in a quarter where it was least to be expected.

The Queen's Marriage.

Two subjects had engaged the thoughts of the queen ever since her accession: the one was the choice of a husband, the other the restoration of the catholic religion. The fortunate person in the former case proved to be her cousin Philip of Spain, the son of the emperor, a prince eleven years her junior in age, but who was easily induced to overlook the difference of years when a kingdom was in prospect. The extreme fondness of Mary, however, proved disagreeable to him, and his indifference increased when he found that there were no hopes of her having children; for she and her friends had made themselves very ridiculous on the occasion of her supposed pregnancy, when even the household of the future prince of Wales was arranged. What she fancied to be pregnancy proved to be the commencement of a dropsy. This circumstance was favourable for the lady Elizabeth, for Philip, seeing now no prospect of children, and knowing that if she were removed the next heir was the queen of Scots, who was married to the dauphin of France, became, from political motives, her protector. Hatfield was now assigned to her as a residence, under the care of sir Thomas Pope, a gentleman of honour and humanity, and she was frequently received at court.

Change of Religion.

The other great object of the queen's anxiety was, as has been said, the bringing back of England into the bosom of the catholic church. Immediately on her accession the pope had appointed her kinsman, cardinal Pole, to be his legate in England, in which country he arrived shortly after the queen's marriage. A parliament had been summoned, and on a sufficient assurance being given that the holders of the church-lands would not be called on to surrender them, it readily agreed to a national change of faith. The cardinal then solemnly absolved the whole realm, and restored it to a communion with the church of Rome. Religious toleration was at that time rarely practised by any party, and it has never been practised by the church of Rome. The leading protestant divines were in prison, mostly on account of their adhesion to the cause of lady Jane Grey, and they now were brought to trial as heretics. Of these Cranmer, Ridley, bishop of London, and Latimer, formerly bishop of Worcester, were lying in prison at Oxford, the primate being in the common jail, which was named Bocardo; Hooper, bishop of Gloucester, and Rogers, Taylor, Saunders and other eminent divines, were in the prisons of London.

Burning of Rogers and Hooper.

The chancellor Gardiner, aided by that most brutal man, Bonner, bishop of London, and other prelates, and the duke of Norfolk and two more lay-lords, held his court, under the legate's authority, for the trial of heretics. Hooper and Rogers were first tried; the charges made against them were the denial of the real presence of Christ's body in the sacrament, and their having married, though in holy orders. In reply to the former charge, Hooper said, "I have done so, and I now affirm that the very natural body of Christ is not really and substantially present in the sacrament of the altar. I assert, moreover, that the mass is idolatrous and the iniquity of the devil." Rogers denied the doctrine in equally decisive terms, and both were sentenced to be burnt at the stake. The following was the manner of this cruel death. A large stake or post was fixed in the ground with a ledge or step to it, on which the victim was set, stript to his shirt. He was fastened to the stake with chains, but his arms were left at liberty. Faggots and bundles of reeds were then piled round him, to which fire was set, and he was thus consumed.

The scene of Rogers' martyrdom was Smithfield. He proceeded thither singing a psalm and cheered like a triumphant conqueror by the assembled crowds as he passed along the streets. Among the spectators he beheld his wife with her ten children, one of them an infant at the breast. Yet, mindful of the crown of glory promised in Scripture to those who persevere to the end, he committed them to Heaven, and spurning a pardon which was offered him if he would recant, he gave his body to the flames, and died with faith and constancy.

Hooper was transmitted to his own diocese of Gloucester. He performed the journey on horseback, under the charge of six men of the royal guard. On the second day after his arrival he was led to the stake, which was set in front of his cathedral. A box containing his pardon was laid before him, in the hope that it might induce him to recant. "If you love my soul," cried he twice over, "away with it." He stripped himself, fire was set to the pile, but most of the wood being green, it would not kindle, and the wind also blew the flame away from him. Some bags of gunpowder, which one of his guards had humanely placed about him in order to shorten his sufferings, exploded to little purpose. His tortures endured for three quarters of an hour; one of his arms was seen to drop off, yet his lips were observed to move constantly in prayer. At length nature gave way, and he expired.

Burning of Ridley and Latimer.

A commission, headed by Brookes, bishop of Gloucester, was sent down to Oxford to try the three prelates who were confined there. Ridley and Latimer were required to subscribe five articles relating to the mass, the real presence, and other disputed points. They steadfastly refused to sign them; they were then excommunicated and degraded from their sacred office. The appearance of Latimer, a venerable old man of primitive simplicity of manners, was striking and interesting. He was clad in a threadbare frieze gown, fastened round his loins by a common leathern girdle; he had a nightcap on his head covered by a handkerchief, over which was a tradesman's cap, with flaps buttoned under his chin. His Testament was suspended from his girdle, and his spectacles from his neck, and he held his hat in his hand.

The two prelates suffered together in the old city-ditch opposite Baliol-college. When they met at the fatal spot, they embraced each other, and Ridley said, "Be of good heart, brother, for God will either assuage the fury of the fire, or else strengthen us to abide it." When they were stript, Latimer appeared arrayed in a new shroud; and though he had been enfeebled by age and infirmity, he now, we are told, "stood bolt upright, as comely a father as one might lightly behold." When they were fastened to the stake, and a lighted faggot had been flung at their feet, "Be of good comfort, Master Ridley," said Latimer, "and play the man. We shall this day, by God's grace, light in England such a candle as I trust shall never be put out." As the flames ascended, he washed his hands, as it were, in them, and then stroked his face, and crying, "Father of Heaven, receive my soul," speedily expired. The sufferings of Ridley were more protracted. The bottom of the pyre being composed of furze, the flame at first was strong, and burned his lower extremities; but as the faggots which were heaped on the furze did not kindle, the flame subsided. He cried out in agony, "Oh, for Christ's sake, let the fire come unto me!" His brother-in-law, hardly knowing what he was about, heaped on more faggots. The victim became enveloped in a dense smoke, whence he kept crying, "I cannot burn. Oh, let the fire come unto me!" Some of the faggots were then removed, a brisk flame sprang up, to which he eagerly turned, some gunpowder which had been placed about him exploded, and his sufferings at length terminated.

Death of Cranmer.

Cranmer still lay in the common jail. At length Bonner and Thirlby, bishop of Ely, came to Oxford as papal commissioners to condemn him. They took their seat in the choir of Christ-church. The prisoner was conducted before them. The various Romish vestments, made of canvass, by way of insult, were put on him, a mock mitre was placed on his head, a mock crosier in his hand. The brutal Bonner then began to scoff at him, but Thirlby, who was a man of gentle nature, and had in better days been very intimate with the unhappy primate, shed floods of tears. When the ceremony of degradation was completed, Bonner, who was a vulgar-minded as well as cruel man, could not refrain from insulting his venerable victim. "Now you are no longer 'my lord,'" said he, and he continued to speak of him as "this gentleman here."

Cranmer had not the firmness of Ridley or Latimer, and the artifices of his enemies working on his natural love of life, induced him to injure his character by signing more than one recantation of his opinions. But it was determined not to save him, and the writ for his execution was sent down to Oxford. It was, however, concealed from him till he was actually on his way to the stake, when, as the morning was wet, he was led into St. Mary's church to hear the sermon usually preached on these awful occasions. The sermon was preached by Dr. Cole, and was chiefly occupied with giving reasons why he should be burnt as a heretic, though he had recanted his opinions. When it was concluded, Cole called on him to make a confession of his faith, and show that he died a catholic indeed. "I will do it," said Cranmer, "and that with a good will." He took off his cap, and addressed the people; then drawing a written prayer from his sleeve, he repeated it aloud, and then on his knees said the Lord's prayer, in which all joined. He rose, and again addressed the people, declaring his belief in the creed and in all things taught in the Old and New Testaments. He concluded by expressing his sincere grief and regret for the recantations which he had made; "and forasmuch," said he, "as my hand offended in writing contrary to my heart, my hand, when I come to the fire, shall first be burnt. And as for the pope, I refuse him, as Christ's enemy and Anti-christ, with all his false doctrine." When he would say more, Cole cried out, "Stop the heretic's mouth, and take him away!" He was hurried to the stake, where he stripped himself with haste, and stood in his shirt. When he took off his cap, his head appeared quite bald: his beard was long and flowing. The pile was kindled, and he stretched forth his right hand and held it in the flame till it was consumed, crying with a loud voice, "This hand hath offended." As the fire burned intensely, his sufferings were short. His heart, it was observed, was found entire among the ashes, an emblem, as it was considered, of his constancy in death. "His death," said a catholic who was present, "much grieved every man; his friends for love, his enemies for pity, strangers for a kind of common humanity, whereby we are bound to one another."

Last Days of the Queen.

Though Cranmer and the other prelates were the principal, they were not the only victims to the blind bigotry and cruel fanaticism of the queen. The records of her reign enumerate nearly three hundred persons, who, in the space of three years, perished in the flames sooner than deny their faith; and had not a merciful Providence abridged its duration, the catalogue there can be no doubt would have been much more copious. Of these victims sixty were women and forty were children. Some of the women, we are assured, were so far advanced in pregnancy that the heat of the flames brought on their labour, and the babes were flung into the burning faggots by the ruthless catholics, and thus ended their life, as we may say, before it had well begun.

Cruelty and injustice often bring their punishment with them. There probably was not in her dominions a more unhappy person than queen Mary. She was neglected and deserted by her husband, on whom she doted. She was suffering from disease, and she saw that the crown would come to her sister, whom, though prudence made her disguise her religion, she knew to be a protestant in her heart; and all her labour for the extirpation of what she regarded as heresy would thus be rendered of no avail. She finally had aided her husband in a war with France, and the valour of the English troops had gained for him the battle of St. Quintin; but the French, in return, surprised Calais, and this town was thus lost for ever to the crown of England, after a possession of two hundred years. The loss of Calais deeply affected the queen, who, with all her defects, had an English heart. On her death-bed she said to her attendants, "When I am dead and opened, ye shall find Calais lying in my heart."

While queen Mary's mind was thus agitated, she was attacked by an epidemic fever, and she breathed her last during the celebration of mass in her chamber, in the forty-third year of her age. Cardinal Pole, who was ill of the same fever, died on the following day.

CHAPTER V.

ELIZABETH.

Accession of Elizabeth.

As in the natural world, when, after a night of gloom, of storm, wind and rain, the sun in the morning comes forth in his splendour, all nature revives beneath the influence of his cheering rays; so did England revive, when the sceptre passed from the hands of the gloomy fanatic, Mary, to those of the noble, majestic Elizabeth, whom Heaven had destined to be the glory of her sex and the brightest ornament of English history.

When a deputation of the council waited on this princess at Hatfield to announce to her her accession to the throne, she fell on her knees and said, " This is the Lord's doing, and it is marvellous in our eyes." On her reaching the Tower, in which, according to usage, she was to reside previous to her coronation, her religious feelings were again awakened by the thought of the alteration in her fortunes since she had last entered that fortress, and she fell on her knees and humbly returned thanks to Heaven.

On the day before that appointed for her coronation, the queen left the Tower and proceeded through the city in a splendid carriage, preceded by the trumpeters and heralds, and followed by a train of nobles, ladies and gentlemen on horseback, all richly arrayed in crimson velvet. As she passed along she was greeted with joyous shouts by the assembled multitudes. The companies of the city erected across the streets gorgeous *pageants*, as such exhibitions were named. One displayed the eight Beatitudes or blessings of our Lord's sermon on the mount, all suitably attired, and each appropriated to the queen. In another were seen the opposite images of a decayed and a flourishing commonwealth, emblematic of the late and the present reign. From a cavern issued Time, leading forth his daughter, Truth, who presented an English bible to the queen. Elizabeth took the book, and pressing it to her heart and lips, said she thanked the City more for it than for all the cost it had bestowed on her. At the end of Cheapside the recorder met her, and presented her, according to ancient usage, with a purse filled with gold, so weighty that she was obliged to take it in both her hands. Over Temple-bar stood the huge giants Gog and Magog, holding out Latin verses; and a child richly dressed as a poet pronounced a farewell in the name of the city of London.

The pompous ceremony of the coronation took place the next day; and it being the custom to release prisoners on such occasions, as the queen on the following morning was on her way to the chapel one of the courtiers put into her hand a petition, praying that four or five more prisoners of importance might be set at liberty: these were the four Evangelists and St. Paul, who had long been shut up in an unknown tongue, so that they could not converse with the common people. The queen replied with great gravity, that it were better first to inquire of themselves whether they would be released or not.

First Years of Elizabeth.

The protestant religion was now finally established in England. The popish prelates of queen Mary were deprived of their sees, but none of them were put to death, even Bonner being only kept in prison. The nation put on a new character; the queen, who was young and handsome, loved gaiety and magnificence. She made stately *progresses* through the kingdom, in which she was entertained by the nobility at their mansions. She was at peace with all foreign powers; many princes sought her hand, but she would lend an ear to none of their solicitations. Among her own subjects, lord Robert Dudley, son of the duke of Northumberland who had been beheaded in the late reign, was her especial favourite. She created him earl of Leicester, and showered honours on him, and it long was thought that she intended to give him her hand. But she had early formed a resolution of living and dying a maiden queen; and though she indulged her natural vanity and coquetry at the expense of many, it may be doubted if she ever seriously thought of espousing any man.

Thus passed the ten first years of the reign of Elizabeth, her halcyon days, as they were justly called. The arrival of the queen of Scots in England put an end to this tranquillity, and henceforth until the death of that queen conspiracies and warlike menaces disturbed her government.

The Queen of Scots.

Mary, Queen of Scots, was the only child of James V. of Scotland. As her mother was of the house of Guise, in France, the young princess was sent to that country for her education, and she was some time after married to the Dauphin, a boy of only fifteen years of age. Mary was brought up in the Romish religion, and as the church of Rome denied the legitimacy of queen Elizabeth's birth, and Mary, as the descendant of the elder daughter of Henry VII., was the next heir to the crown of England, the king of France, on the death of queen Mary Tudor, made his son and daughter-in-law assume the arms of England. When Elizabeth complained an evasive answer was returned; and seeing that she might have to contend for her crown, and knowing that her own catholic subjects were naturally inclined to Mary, she judged it expedient, in self-preservation, to form a party among Mary's subjects, and she became the supporter and protectress of the Scottish protestants. Thus, of the two British queens, the one was at the head of the protestants, the other of the catholics; and as Elizabeth was prudent and cautious, and Mary was rash and imprudent, there could be little doubt on which side the victory would lie.

Return of Mary to Scotland.

The Dauphin Francis succeeded his father on the throne, and Mary thus became queen of France as well as of Scotland. But her glory was of brief duration, for Francis, a puny delicate youth, soon sickened and died. The queen-mother, the famous Catherine of Medicis, who was all-powerful under her son Charles IX., hated Mary, and the latter, finding her residence in France no longer agreeable, and being urged to return to her own kingdom, where her mother, who had administered the government with great prudence, was now dead, at length resolved to abandon France and take up her abode in the bleak regions of the north. She embarked at Calais, and remained on deck till it was dark, gazing on the shores of France which she was quitting, as she believed, for ever. She caused her bed to be made on the poop, and directed the steersman to awake her at daybreak, if France should be still in sight. The man obeyed her command; she rose and gazed on the coast till it ceased to be visible. "Farewell, France," said she; "it is over; I shall never see thee again." She arrived in safety at the port of Leith, near Edinburgh; the people received her with every demonstration of loyalty and respect, but she could not avoid comparing their rudeness, barbarism and poverty, with the gaiety and splendour of the court in which she had all her life resided, and the contrast cost her many a sigh.

First Years of Mary's Reign.

Though Mary was a bigoted catholic, and a lover of gaiety and splendour, and her Scottish subjects in general had adopted the most morose and repulsive form of protestantism, which viewed the masks and revels in which she delighted with a pious horror, still harmony existed for some years between her and them, and might long have continued, had she not given the reins to her passions. This was owing to her having the prudence to bestow her confidence on her half-brother, the earl of Murray, the head of the protestant party, and to the friendly conduct of queen Elizabeth, although Mary still maintained her claim to the crown of England.

Love was the rock on which the happiness of Mary made shipwreck. As she was young, handsome, highly accomplished, and the mistress of a kingdom, she naturally had many suitors. It was a matter of much importance to Elizabeth whom the queen of Scots should select for a husband; for should she marry into any of the great catholic houses of the continent, retaining as she did a claim to the crown of England, she might cause that princess much uneasiness, and even put her throne in jeopardy. It was therefore Elizabeth's desire that Mary should marry an English subject, and the person on whom she wished her choice to fall was no other than lord Robert Dudley, whom she created earl of Leicester, in order to give him suitable rank. But Mary gave an evasive reply to the English ambassador; and as Dudley at this time was not without hopes of obtaining the hand of Elizabeth herself, he showed no great eagerness for the Scottish match.

Lord Darnley.

The choice of Mary (and a most unfortunate one it proved to be) was destined to fall on another English subject. This was lord Darnley, the son of the earl of Lennox, and grandson of Margaret Tudor, queen of Scotland, by her second husband, the earl of Angus. He was therefore Mary's cousin; and when Lennox, who was a Scottish peer, had, with Elizabeth's permission, gone to Scotland to seek the restoration of his titles and estates, he spoke so advantageously of his son, that Mary became desirous of seeing him, and Elizabeth, when applied to, made no objection to his visiting Scotland. Darnley was a tall thin stripling of nineteen years of age, straight as an arrow, and he danced well, and played on the lute, and had the usual accomplishments of the age. He pleased the eye of Mary, who was some years his senior; she made no trial of the qualities of his mind and heart, but fell in love at once; and Darnley, among whose good or ill qualities bashfulness was not to be reckoned, lost no time in making proposals to her. She affected to be angry, but was secretly determined to make him her husband.

Elizabeth and her council, on maturely considering the probable consequences of this match, were strongly opposed to it. Murray, to testify his dissatisfaction, withdrew from court; but nothing would check the impetuosity of the love-sick queen; and as soon as the necessary dispensation arrived from Rome, she gave Darnley her hand and the title of king. She then outlawed Murray and some other lords, and when they appeared in arms in the western counties, she took the field against them in person, riding at the head of her troops with loaded pistols in her girdle; for Mary was by no means the delicate, shrinking, sensitive female into which the romantic fancy of later times has converted her. She pursued the lords hotly, and forced them to cross the border and seek refuge in England.

Murder of Rizzio.

Mary's affection for Darnley soon began to cool; she found, to her cost, that all his merits lay in his person, that he was brutal in temper, and addicted to the grossest intemperance. She, therefore, gradually estranged herself from his society, and passed her hours among those whose pursuits were more congenial to her inclinations. There was at her court a man named David Rizzio, an Italian, who having come to Scotland in the suite of the ambassador of Savoy, had won the favour of Mary by his musical talents. She induced him to remain in her service, made him her French secretary, and it was soon observed that all her graces and favours passed through his hands. The proud semi-barbarous nobles of Scotland were galled at being obliged to become suitors to the Italian upstart; and as Rizzio, like upstarts in general, did not bear his faculties meekly, they hated while they flattered him. Darnley, when courting the queen, did not disdain to engage the influence of Rizzio in his favour; but soon seeing how much more agreeable to the queen was the society of the foreign secretary than his own, he conceived a strong suspicion that the cause was an improper attachment.

While Darnley was in this state of mind he happened one day to say to his uncle Douglas, "It is a sore case that I can get no help against that villain David." "It is your own fault," replied Douglas; "you cannot keep a secret." This led to an understanding, and a league was soon formed between Darnley on the one part, and the lords Morton, Ruthven and others on the other. *They* were to put Rizzio to death and procure for Darnley the crown matrimonial, which the queen withheld; *he* was to bear them harmless, to obtain a pardon for Murray and the other banished lords, and to secure the protestant religion.

The attack on Rizzio was fixed for a Saturday night. At the appointed time lord Ruthven rose from a bed of sickness and cased himself in armour; he and his associates were then conducted by Darnley up a private staircase which led to the apartment where Mary, who was now six months gone with child, was sitting at supper. Her only companions were Rizzio and her natural sister, lady Argyle. Darnley entered and stood by her chair with his arm round her waist. Ruthven then appeared, pale and haggard from disease, and supported by two of his men. He required that Rizzio should quit the room; the queen replied it was her will he should be there. Rizzio then ran behind her chair for protection, a tumult ensued, the table was overturned, and Rizzio was dragged out and despatched in the antechamber with fifty-six wounds. When the queen, who had been vainly interceding for him, found that he was no more, she said, "No more tears; I must think of revenge." She was never again heard to lament him; but she steadily, though secretly, adhered to her resolution of vengeance. She contrived to detach her weak and worthless husband from his associates, whom she chased into England; and she paid much court to Murray on his return. Her great favourite now was James Hepburn, lord Bothwell, between whom and Murray, though they were bitter enemies, she effected a reconciliation.

Bothwell.—Murder of Darnley.

In due time the queen was delivered of a son. A special ambassador was immediately despatched with the glad tidings to the court of queen Elizabeth, and with a request that she would stand godmother to the new-born prince. Elizabeth, who had just recovered from a severe fit of illness, was at her favourite palace of Greenwich when the ambassador arrived. She was dancing after supper (an exercise in which she delighted) when her minister Cecil whispered the news to her. Elizabeth, with all her great qualities, was still a woman, and the desire of offspring is most women's first impulse; she instantly stopped dancing, and sat down, resting her cheek on her hand. At length she gave vent to her feelings in the natural reflection of " The queen of Scots is mother of a fair son, while I am but a barren stock." Next morning, however, she received the Scottish ambassador with a cheerful countenance, and readily consented to be the prince's godmother.

The alienation of Mary from her husband became every day more apparent; her whole favour was engrossed by Bothwell, and suspicion was strong that her intimacy with him was not of the most innocent nature. On one occasion, when Bothwell, who held the office of warden of the marches, or governor of the borders between Scotland and England, happened to receive a wound in a scuffle with one of the border freebooters, and was conveyed to his castle of Hermitage, the queen, who was at Jedburgh, became so uneasy about him that she resolved to visit him, and ascertain his real condition. Though the distance was twenty miles, though the roads were in a most wretched state, and the weather was cold and wet, it being then the month of October, she set out with a few attendants, rode to Hermitage, and having ascertained that his life was in no danger, she rode back the same day to Jedburgh. This exploit (no trifle even to a robust man) was, however, near costing her dear; she was attacked next day by a fever, in which her life was for some days despaired of; but the vigour of her constitution triumphed over it, and she was reserved for more vicissitudes of fortune.

The baptism of the young prince was celebrated in the following month of December at Stirling-castle, and though Darnley was there at the time he did not appear at it. The task of regulating the ceremony and of receiving the French and English ambassadors was committed to Bothwell. On Christmas-eve Darnley left Stirling, and set out for his father's house at Glasgow, and immediately after his arrival there he was attacked by the small-pox. The queen sent her own physician to him, and toward the end of the month of January she went herself to Glasgow to visit him. She manifested the greatest fondness for him, and she finally induced him to return with her to Edinburgh. Pretending there that the situation and noise of the palace of Holyrood-house would be injurious to him, she placed him in a lone house without the city-walls, named the Kirk of Field, and she had a chamber fitted up for herself under his, in which she sometimes slept. One Saturday night she stayed with him till ten o'clock, and then recollecting that she had promised to give a mask on the occasion of the marriage of two of her servants, she took leave of him, and returned to the palace. At two in the morning a loud explosion was heard, and when daylight came the Kirk of Field was seen to be in ruins. The dead body of Darnley was found at some distance in the field, but without any marks of violence.

Marriage of Mary and Bothwell.

It appeared that the house had been blown up with gunpowder; people were unanimous in fixing the guilt on Bothwell, and the queen herself was accused as an accomplice. Lennox demanded justice, and so strong was the popular feeling, not only in Scotland, but on the continent, that Mary found it impossible to elude the demand for a trial. She, however, took good care that Bothwell should run no risk, for she left to himself the arrangement of the manner of the trial, and when it came on he made his appearance at the head of such a body of armed men that neither accuser nor witnesses ventured to appear. He was of course acquitted; and when the queen went to open the next parliament, Bothwell carried the sword of state before her.

A few days after Mary went to Stirling to visit her son. On her return she was met by Bothwell at the head of a party of armed men. He dispersed her train, took her horse by the bridle and led her to Dunbar. There can be little doubt that this whole proceeding had been previously arranged between the queen and him, for when, after detaining her some days at Dunbar, he conducted her to Edinburgh, she bestowed additional marks of honour on him, and in about a fortnight after openly married him, a divorce having previously been effected between him and his wife, the lady Jane Gordon.

Deposition of Mary.

One short month, however, put an end to the joys of the guilty pair. An extensive association of the nobles was formed for the defence of the prince. Bothwell was forced to fly to Dunbar, and his flight was accompanied by Mary in male attire. Having collected some troops she advanced to Carbury-hill, near Edinburgh, to meet the confederate lords; but finding that they would not fight in her cause, she was obliged to take a farewell (a final one as it proved) of Bothwell, and surrendered to her subjects. The lords received her with respect, and conducted her to Edinburgh; but as she passed along her ear was assailed with maledictions and the foulest epithets from the tongues of the populace, especially the women. When she rose in the morning the first object that met her view was a white flag, which was displayed before her window, and bore on it the image of the body of her husband lying beneath a tree, and her infant son on his knees, saying, " Judge and avenge my cause, O Lord!"

The lords soon discovered that the promise which the queen had made to give up Bothwell could not be relied on. They, therefore, sent her as a prisoner to the castle of Lochlevin, which stood on an island in a lake, and its owner, Douglas, was married to the mother of Murray. While there she was forced to sign an abdication of her crown in favour of her infant son, who was crowned with great solemnity at Stirling, and Murray was appointed regent during the minority.

Flight of Mary into England.

The ill-conduct of Mary had been so flagrant that hitherto hardly any one had ventured to appear in her favour. But soon jealousy of Murray caused the Gordons and others to take up arms, and communications were opened with the captive queen, who very artfully, when Murray visited her, proposed to him (to show how sincere she was in her intention of giving up all thoughts of Bothwell,) to marry his own half-brother, George Douglas, the son of the lady of Lochlevin, a youth of only eighteen years of age. She had, in fact, been making amorous advances to this stripling; but her object was to engage him to aid her in making her escape. This she very nearly effected in the following manner. Having changed clothes with a laundress who used to come to the island from a village near the lake, she got into the boat undiscovered. She had nearly reached the shore, when one of the boatmen, saying " Let us see what sort of a dame this is!" attempted to raise the muffler which covered her face. She put up her hand to prevent him; its whiteness excited suspicion; the boatmen then refused to land her, and carried her back to the island.

Her next attempt was more successful. As the lady of

the castle and her eldest son were sitting one night at supper, a youth, named the little Douglas, stole the keys and opened the gate. Mary then hastened into a boat which lay ready, and Douglas having locked the castle-gate on the outside flung the keys into the lake as they rowed along. On the shore Mary was met by George Douglas and some of her other friends; she mounted a horse and rode to Niddry, the house of lord Seaton, and having rested there for about three hours she mounted again and rode to Hamilton, where she was received by the nobles of her party at the head of three thousand of their followers. It was proposed that they should wait for the lords Huntley and Ogilvie, who were gone to the north to raise their tenants, and that meantime the queen should be placed, for security, in Dunbarton-castle. But as they were on their way to that fortress, they were met at a place called Langside Hill by Murray with a superior force. In the space of a quarter of an hour their troops were totally routed, and Mary, who was viewing the encounter from an adjoining eminence, seeing that all was lost, galloped off at full speed for Dunbarton. Failing in her hope of reaching that castle, she directed her course to Dundrennan abbey, on the Solway Firth, a distance of sixty Scottish miles, accompanied by the French ambassador, by lord Herries, and a few others.

Nothing now remained for the unfortunate queen but a flight into England, whose sovereign had of late acted a very friendly part toward her. She, therefore, wrote to the governor of Carlisle to know if she might come thither in safety; but fearful of again falling into the hands of her enraged subjects, she did not venture to wait for his reply, and next day she embarked in a fishing-boat and landed at Workington. She was conducted by the gentry of the county thence to Carlisle, and she wrote immediately to queen Elizabeth. She had little or no money with her, and not even a single change of clothes.

Having thus far related the history of this guilty queen,

we will now tell the wretched fate of the partner of her crimes. Bothwell had fled to the Orkney islands, where he hired some ships with the intention of passing over to Denmark; but all his vessels, with the exception of the one he himself was on board of, were captured by those sent in pursuit of him. He escaped to Norway, where, having no proper papers to produce, and his ship having once belonged to a noted pirate, he was cast into prison on suspicion, and he died some years after in a Danish fortress deprived of reason.

Detention of Queen Mary.

To return to the queen. Elizabeth and her council determined on detaining her till she should have cleared herself from the suspicion of being concerned in the murder of her husband. A conference for this purpose was opened at York, whither Murray and other Scottish nobles repaired, and produced the proofs of the queen's guilt which lord Herries, and her other advocates found it totally impossible to refute. Her criminality being thus proved, Elizabeth and her ministers resolved, though they knew the danger of that course, to detain her, come what might, and for a space of nearly twenty years she remained a captive in England, being moved about from castle to castle according as she was committed to the charge of different noblemen and gentlemen. During all that time she was incessantly engaged in forming schemes for recovering her liberty and dethroning her son and queen Elizabeth, and conspiracies and rebellions on her account disturbed the repose and endangered the life of this great princess.

Fate of the Duke of Norfolk.

The duke of Norfolk, a nobleman of the highest rank and consideration in England, the relative of Elizabeth on the mother's side, and the very person who had presided at the Conference in which Mary's guilt was proved, became the first victim of her intrigues. Leicester and other favourites and ministers of Elizabeth, jealous of the influence of Cecil, now lord Burleigh, proposed a marriage between Norfolk and the queen of Scots. The approbation of the kings of France and Spain were obtained, and it was expected that Elizabeth might be forced to give her consent. Mary, on her part, wrote the most affectionate letters to Norfolk, whom she had never seen, and that weak nobleman suffered himself to be beguiled. But Elizabeth, who knew what was going on, gave him timely warning. "Be careful," said she to him one day, "of the pillow on which you are about to lay your head." He knew what she meant, and replied, "I will never marry a person with whom I could not be sure of my pillow." Some time after Leicester confessed the whole affair to the queen, and she then taxed Norfolk with his designs, and advised him to abandon them. He spoke contemptuously of the queen of Scots and her kingdom, saying that his estates in England were nearly equal to it in value, and that when he was in his own tennis-court at Norwich he thought himself a petty prince. Shortly after, however, it was thought necessary to commit him to the Tower, but he was not long detained. He still kept up a correspondence with Mary, and it soon appeared that a plan had been arranged for the duke of Alba, the Spanish governor of the Netherlands, to land at Harwich with ten thousand men, where Norfolk was to join him, and they were to march to London and compel the queen to consent to his marriage with the queen of Scots. Norfolk was in consequence brought to trial on a charge of high treason; his peers unanimously pronounced him guilty; the queen, after much hesitation and many a struggle with herself, signed the warrant for his execution, and he was beheaded on Tower-hill.

Massacre of St. Bartholomew.

On the eve of St. Bartholomew's day, the 22nd of August, 1572, was perpetrated in France a most atrocious massacre of the professors of the reformed religion. Their leading men were all invited to Paris, to be present at the marriage of the young king of Navarre, the head of their party, with the sister of the king, Charles IX. The marriage was celebrated with the usual magnificence, and nothing occurred to awake the suspicions of the protestants, when on the appointed night the *tocsin* or alarm-bell sounded; the catholics, who were in readiness, immediately fell on the protestants and massacred them in their beds, or slaughtered them in the streets, as they were flying for their lives. Similar massacres took place in Orleans, Rouen, Lyons, and the other cities of France. The whole number of protestants thus cruelly and treacherously slaughtered amounted to about thirty thousand persons.

At Rome the tidings of this atrocious deed were received with rapture, and the pope and his cardinals went in solemn procession to the church of St. Louis, to return thanks to Heaven. But in England it was viewed with dismay and horror. When the French ambassador went to Woodstock, where the court was then residing, to make an excuse for it, he was conducted through rooms in which reigned a silence like that of the tombs. The lords and ladies, who were habited in deep mourning, took no notice of him as he passed. Elizabeth received him with cool courtesy, and calmly listened to the excuse which he was instructed to offer, namely, that a conspiracy of the protestants had been detected, and thus anticipated. She merely said that she trusted that the king would institute an inquiry and punish the authors of the charge if it should prove to be a calumny.

Revolt of the Dutch.

The massacre of the protestants in France is supposed to have been only a part of a plan formed by the pope and the courts of France and Spain for the extirpation of Protestantism all over Europe. Philip of Spain, the husband of the late queen of England, was one of the most bigoted catholics in existence, and the cruelties which he caused to be exercised on his protestant subjects in the Netherlands were such, that in their despair they at length resolved to fling off the yoke of Spain, and win civil and religious liberty or perish in the attempt. Their leader in this glorious cause was the great prince of Orange, and Elizabeth secretly assisted them. They made an offer to her of their crown, but she declined the tempting gift; when, however, the prince of Orange had been assassinated by an agent of Philip and the church of Rome, and the affairs of the Dutch, as the revolters were named, seemed nearly desperate, she hesitated no longer. She was now the head of the protestant cause throughout the world, and she resolved openly to aid the brave struggles of the Dutch with the power of her kingdom, and as the king of Sweden expressed it, take the diadem from her head and hazard it on the chance of war.

An army of six thousand men was sent to the aid of the Dutch; but in the choice of a commander Elizabeth did not act with her usual judgement. Her partiality for Leicester made her confide the charge to him, who though brave, had never had any military experience, and send him where he was to be opposed to the prince of Parma, the greatest general of the age. His career of war was therefore not very brilliant, and his haughtiness and insolence alienated the minds of the Dutch senators and statesmen. The queen, therefore, after some time, found it necessary to recall him, and the Dutch placed Maurice, son of the late prince of Orange, at the head of their armies, the English troops being commanded by Lord Willoughby.

Sir Philip Sidney.

The most remarkable event which took place in Leicester's first campaign was the death of his nephew, sir Philip Sidney, the most accomplished knight of his time, who united in his person the scholar, the writer, the courtier, and the soldier. At the siege of Zutphen, sir Philip, in an encounter with some troops sent by the prince of

Parma to the relief of that place, was wounded by a musket-ball in the thigh; loss of blood making him thirsty, he called for drink; a bottle of water was given him; he put it to his lips, but seeing a wounded soldier looking wistfully at it, he said, "Thy necessity is yet greater than mine," and handed it to him. After lingering for about three weeks, he breathed his last with the greatest piety and resignation. His death was the subject of sincere regret to the queen and to the people of England.

Babington's Conspiracy.

Conspiracies against the life of Elizabeth had of late become more frequent and formidable. The new society of the Jesuits, who were the most active and devoted supporters of the church of Rome, and who scrupled at no crime in her cause, were the soul of all these projects, of which the grand object was the placing of Mary on the throne of England. Various conspiracies had been detected, and those concerned in them punished. At length one of greater magnitude, and which involved Mary in the ruin, was discovered by Elizabeth's faithful and sagacious minister Walsingham.

Some of the English priests, at their seminary of Rheims in France, conceiving the murder of Elizabeth to be a meritorious act in the sight of God, had sent a soldier named Savage over to England to perform the pious deed. At the same time a priest named Ballard came over from Paris in the disguise of an officer, calling himself Captain Fortescue, in order to induce the catholics to rise and liberate Mary while the queen's troops were away in Holland. Ballard, on arriving in London, made the plan known to Antony Babington, a young man of good property in Derbyshire, who approved of it, but said that there was no chance while Elizabeth lived. Ballard then told him of Savage, but he said, that one man was not enough for a matter of such importance, and he proposed to join five of his friends who could be depended on with

Savage. Babington, who had been already in correspondence with Mary, now wrote her an account of the whole plan, which met with her entire approbation. She was now at a place named Chartley, in Staffordshire, under the charge of sir Amias Paulet.

Most of the conspirators were thoughtless imprudent young men, and their projects did not long escape the knowledge of Walsingham. Some of their associates were actually in his pay, and when one Dr. Gifford came over from Rheims to urge on Savage, he secretly made a tender of his services to Walsingham. As Gifford was to be the agent of communication with the queen of Scots, Walsingham wished Paulet to connive at his bribing one of his servants, but Paulet, who was a very religious man, would only consent to a brewer's boy, who supplied the house with beer, being the agent. The letters to and from Mary were therefore conveyed through a hole in the wall, which was stopped with a loose stone, and the whole correspondence thus passed through the hands of Walsingham, who communicated his knowledge to no one but the queen.

Walsingham was desirous to give the conspirators more time, in order to come at a more perfect knowledge of the plot, but the queen said that further delay would be only a tempting of Providence, and accordingly Ballard was arrested. Babington and his friends, when they found that their plot was discovered, stole out of London, and concealed themselves in St. John's Wood and other places near the city; but in a few days they were taken and cast into prison. Of their own accord they confessed their guilt, and revealed all the particulars of the plot. They were tried, sentenced, and executed as traitors. As it was the barbarous custom in such cases to cut down the criminal before he was dead, and take out his bowels and burn them before his face, Ballard, Babington and some others were thus treated; but when the queen heard of it, she gave strict orders that all others should be suffered to hang till they were dead.

Trial of the Queen of Scots.

As soon as the conspirators were arrested sir Thomas Gorges was sent from court with the tidings to the queen of Scots. She was on horseback going out hunting when he arrived; she wished to return to her chamber, but she was not permitted, and during her absence her cabinets were broken open and all her correspondence was seized, and her two secretaries were carried prisoners to London. She was conveyed from one gentleman's seat to another, and at length to Fotheringay-castle in Northamptonshire. Her keeper was still sir Amias Paulet, with whom was now associated sir Drue Drury.

Abundant evidence having now been procured to prove the participation of the queen of Scots in the late conspiracy, it was resolved to bring her to trial on a late act of parliament; and a commission, consisting of Burleigh, Walsingham, and several other noblemen and privy councillors of both religions, proceeded to Fotheringay for this purpose.

The hall of the castle was fitted up for the trial. At one end was placed, under a canopy, a chair of state for the queen of England; at some distance opposite was a chair for the queen of Scots; the commissioners sat on benches at each side, the law officers at a table in the centre. The trial lasted two days; the confessions of Babington and his accomplices, and of her own secretaries were read, as also were her own letters. She defended herself with dignity, spirit, and acuteness, but the evidence against her was too strong to be repelled, and the commissioners on their return to London, after having once more examined her secretaries, pronounced her guilty of all the charges made against her. Parliament approved of the sentence, and petitioned the queen to have it executed. When the sentence was published the citizens illuminated their houses, and the bells of all the churches rang out joyful peals.

Execution of the Queen of Scots.

The king of France, and her son the young king of Scotland, sent ambassadors to intercede for Mary, but Elizabeth confuted their arguments, and despised their menaces. Still she was in great doubt how to act. She had a natural aversion to bloodshed, she viewed in Mary a queen and a kinswoman, and she feared the judgement of posterity. On the other hand, her ministers and all her protestant subjects were urgent for the execution of the royal criminal, and rumours of plots and invasions were every day carried to her ears. In this state of uncertainty, one day while she was at the palace of Richmond, she directed her secretary Davison to bring her the warrant which had been drawn out some time before by Burleigh. She signed it, and directed him to take it to the chancellor and have it sealed, and to send it down to the commissioners, and not to trouble her any more on the subject. Davison went straight to Burleigh and Leicester, and showed them the warrant, and then proceeded to London and got it sealed by the chancellor. Next day a messenger came to him from the queen to tell him if he had not been with the chancellor not to go till he should have seen her. He therefore hastened to Richmond and informed her that the warrant was sealed. She blamed his haste, but did not intimate any change of purpose, and Davison then went and delivered it to Burleigh. In the morning the council met, and it was resolved to send off the warrant, and letters were written to the earls of Kent and Shrewsbury relative to the execution of it, and despatched by the clerk of the council. During the succeeding days the queen, who did not know that the warrant had been sent off, evinced no change of purpose. Her secret wish was that the queen of Scots might be despatched by poison, a course which Leicester had suggested; but Paulet and Drury, when sounded, positively refused to be the agents.

When the two earls, with the sheriff of the county, came

to Fotheringay on their melancholy errand, they waited on the unhappy prisoner, and bade her prepare for death in the morning. She heard them with composure, and requested that a minister of her own religion might be permitted to visit her and prepare her for death; but this request, according to the intolerant practice of the age, was refused, and she declined the aid of a protestant minister. When the earls were gone she sat down to supper, she drank to her servants' health and happiness, and when they craved pardon for any offences they might have committed, she asked their pardon in return. She looked over her will and wrote some letters; she then went to bed and slept for some hours. When she awoke she rose and spent the remainder of the night in prayer.

At eight o'clock next morning, the 7th of February, the sheriff came to summon her. She had arrayed herself in her richest clothes for the occasion, and rising from her devotions and taking her crucifix in one hand and her prayer-book in the other, she gave her blessing to her servants and followed him. At the foot of the staircase Melville her steward met her, and bursting into tears, lamented that he should be the bearer of such sorrowful tidings to Scotland. She bade him rather to rejoice than lament, as the end of her troubles was arrived, and she kissed him and bade him pray for her. She then entered the hall, Melville bearing her train. A reluctant consent had been obtained from the earl of Kent for two of her maids and four of her men to attend her in this last scene of her earthly existence.

The hall was thronged with spectators. In its centre stood the scaffold, two feet high, and covered with black. She ascended it with the aid of Paulet, and sat down on a stool while the warrant was read out. She then asserted the injustice of her sentence, and denied all thoughts of injuring the queen. The dean of Peterborough commenced a cruel and ill-timed address; she bade him not to trouble her as she would die in the faith in which she was reared. When, holding her crucifix, she prayed in Latin with her servants, the fanatic earl of Kent said, "Madam, settle Jesus Christ in your heart, and leave those trumperies." She took no heed, but continued her prayers. Her women then began to undress her, the executioner advanced to assist, but she said that she was not used to employ such grooms, or to strip before so numerous a company. She checked the lamentations of her servants, and bade them farewell; a cloth was then put on her face, and she was led to the block. She laid down her head, saying in Latin, "Into thy hands, O Lord, I commend my spirit." Her head was struck off at the second blow. The executioner held it up, streaming with blood. "So perish all the queen's enemies," cried the dean. "Such end of all the queen's and the Gospel's enemies," said the earl of Kent, standing over the body. All the rest were silent from pity or from horror.

The real or pretended grief of Elizabeth when she was informed of the execution of Mary was extreme. She shed copious tears, her voice was broken by sighs, she drove her ministers from her presence, and she put herself and her whole court into deep mourning. The whole weight of her vengeance fell on the unfortunate Davison, who was committed to the Tower, and fined in so large a sum as proved his utter ruin, and she could never be prevailed on to restore him to favour.

The young king of Scots readily listened to the excuses of Elizabeth, whose throne he hoped to inherit. The king of France was in secret not displeased at what had occurred. Philip of Spain alone resolved to make the death of Mary a pretext for the invasion of England.

Sir Francis Drake.

It was in the reign of Elizabeth that England's naval glory commenced its brilliant career. A trade with Russia carried on by sailing round the north of Europe to the port of Archangel, and attempts made to discover a north-west passage to India, gave origin to a race of hardy, skilful, and enterprising mariners. Such were John Hawkins and Martin Fróbisher, and the most distinguished of all, the renowned sir Francis Drake.

Drake was the son of the vicar of Upnore, on the Medway, in Kent. He was bound apprentice to the master of a trading ship. After some years he joined Hawkins in an expedition to America, but their vessels were destroyed by the Spaniards, and it was some time before Drake could again attempt anything of importance. At length he found himself strong enough to attack and capture a Spanish town on the isthmus of Pánama, and as he advanced into the interior to intercept a caravan of mules laden with silver, he caught from the summit of a mountain a view of the Pacific ocean. He instantly fell on his knees and made a vow to visit that sea, in which an English sail had hitherto never been spread.

Five years after he sailed from Plymouth with five small vessels. In his voyage to the Pacific, he lost, or found it necessary to destroy four of them, and he appeared in that sea with only a single ship. He made plundering descents on the coasts of Chili and Peru, till finding that the alarm was given, he saw he could remain no longer with safety in those parts; but instead of attempting to return by the way he came, he resolved to stretch boldly across the Pacific, and thus to sail round the globe. He reached the Molucca islands, thence proceeded to Java and the Cape of Good Hope, and on the 3rd of November, 1580, he landed at Plymouth, after an absence of nearly three years. He then went round to the Thames, and his ship was laid up at Deptford, where the queen condescended to partake of a banquet on board, and conferred the dignity of knighthood on the adventurous mariner.

The Spanish Armáda.

The talents of Drake and all the other able English seamen were now to be displayed on a more extensive field. Philip of Spain, after some years of preparation in all the ports of his extensive dominions, had assembled in the river Tagus a fleet of one hundred and thirty large vessels, carrying nearly thirty thousand men, and the prince of Parma had collected in the ports of the Netherlands ships and boats for the embarkation of an equal number of his veteran troops. To resist these formidable preparations, Elizabeth had only a navy of thirty-four ships, but the nobility and the sea-ports fitted out such a number of vessels at their own expense, that there soon was at sea a fleet of one hundred and eighty vessels of all kinds, large and small. The chief command was committed to Howard of Effingham, lord high-admiral of England, and Drake, Hawkins, and Frobisher held commands under him. The fleet was stationed at Plymouth. A land army of thirty thousand men was posted at Tilbury, in Essex, under the command of lord Leicester, for the protection of the city of London, while another of equal strength was destined for the guard of the queen's person.

On the 29th of May, 1588, the Invincible Armáda (i. e. *Fleet*), as it was proudly styled, sailed from the Tagus, but owing to a storm which it encountered, it did not appear off the coast of England till the 19th of July. On that day it was descried near the Lizard point, in Cornwall, by a Scottish pirate, who made all the sail he could to convey the intelligence to Plymouth, and the admiral got his fleet out to sea with as little delay as possible.

As the Spanish admiral had orders not to engage in hostilities till he should have seen the prince of Parma's army landed in England, he took no notice of the English fleet, but steadily directed his course up the channel. The Armada sailed in the form of a crescent, of which the horns were seven miles asunder. Its motion was slow though every sail was spread, "the winds," says the historian, "being as it were tired with carrying the ships, and the ocean groaning beneath their weight." The English ships, which were smaller and more active than those of the

Armada, followed to harass it and cut off stragglers, and during the six days which it took to reach Calais, it suffered considerably from their persevering attacks. At Calais the admiral learned that the prince could not embark his troops for want of stores and sailors, and while he waited the Armada narrowly escaped destruction from fire-ships sent into it by the English. A violent tempest succeeded, which drove it among the shoals on the coast of Zealand; and a council of war determined that, as it was now in too shattered a condition to attempt anything against the enemy, it were best to return to Spain without delay; but as the passage down channel was so full of hazard, it was resolved to sail round Scotland and Ireland. The Armada, therefore, set sail; the English pursued it as far as Flamborough-head, where want of ammunition forced them to give over the chase. Storms, however, assailed the Armada, and several of the vessels were cast away on the coast of Ireland, where the crews were butchered by the barbarous natives. The total loss was thirty large ships and ten thousand men. Philip received the intelligence with great tranquillity, and ordered public thanks to God and the Saints for the calamity not having been greater.

In this great danger of herself and kingdom, Elizabeth had shown the spirit of a heroine. She visited the camp at Tilbury, rode along the lines mounted on a white palfrey, and cheered the soldiers by her animated language. When the danger was over she went in state to St. Paul's, and publicly returned thanks to Heaven. She granted pensions to the disabled seamen, she created the admiral earl of Nottingham, and bestowed honours and rewards on his officers. The sudden death of Leicester shortly after he had disbanded his army, intercepted the favours she might have designed for him.

Taking of Cadiz.

Thus was England saved by Providence from that greatest of calamities, a foreign invasion, aided, perhaps, by an insurrection of the catholic part of the population. Elizabeth, to take vengeance on Philip, immediately began to send out expeditions against his dominions. Of these the most celebrated was that to Cadiz in the year 1594.

This expedition was composed of one hundred and fifty ships, English and Dutch, carrying fourteen thousand soldiers. On board of the fleet was also a gallant band of fifteen hundred gentlemen volunteers. The chief command was held by the lord high-admiral Howard, with whom were the illustrious sir Walter Raleigh, the brave Vere, Carew and Clifford, and the queen's present favourite, the gallant and generous, but rash and impetuous earl of Essex. On reaching the bay of Cadiz they saw in it fifteen large men-of-war; and as the English ships were small the admiral hesitated to attack them. He at length, however, yielded to those who were eager for action, at which Essex was so delighted, that, regardless of his dignity, he flung his hat up into the air. After an engagement of six hours three of the men-of-war were taken and three burnt. Essex then landed with six hundred men, and advanced against the town. He drove off the troops that opposed him, and entered the town pell-mell with them. The admiral had meantime landed and forced his way in at another side. The inhabitants made no resistance; they agreed to give up all the property in the place, and pay a ransom for their lives. As the queen had given strict orders to spare the women, the aged and the children, and put none to the sword but those who resisted, the capture of Cadiz was not sullied by the excesses usual in towns taken by storm. The nuns and other women, to the number of three thousand, were sent under an escort to a place of safety, and they were even permitted to take with them their clothes and jewels, and this noble and generous conduct of the English gained them general admiration and respect. When all the booty was removed, the whole town was burnt with the exception of the churches, and the expedition returned to England after an absence of only ten weeks, having in that time caused an enormous loss to the king of Spain.

The Earl of Essex.

The young earl of Essex, of whom we have just had occasion to speak, was the step-son of the late earl of Leicester, by whom he had been introduced to the notice of the queen. The generous chivalrous spirit which he showed on all occasions quickly won him the favour of that great princess, and he soon occupied the place of Leicester in her affections. She even used to put up with and pardon acts of insolence in him which she would not have tolerated in another. When, some time after the expedition to Cadiz, in a council held in presence of the queen, the appointment of a chief-governor of Ireland was under consideration, Elizabeth wished to appoint one person, while Essex, with all the warmth of his character, was strenuous in favour of another. In the heat of the argument he so far forgot his duty as to turn his back on her with a kind of contempt. She gave him a box on the ear, and bade him go to the d—l; the earl clapped his hand on his sword, swore he would not put up with such an affront even from Henry VIII. himself, and left the court in a passion. The coolness between the queen and her favourite lasted for about five months. He then re-appeared at court, but he seems not to have recovered his place in her affections.

Essex in Ireland.

The chief government of Ireland, where a native chief named O'Nial, whom the queen had created earl of Tirone, was in arms against the crown, now tempted the ambition of Essex. In the council, when he was giving a description of the kind of person who should be sent to that country, he drew so accurate a likeness of himself that no one could doubt of his wishes. His enemies, who wished to remove him from court, gladly forwarded his views; the new title of Lord Lieutenant was conferred on him, and he set out for Ireland amid the acclamations of the people, with whom he was a great favourite, and followed by a gallant train of nobles and gentlemen.

The troops placed at the disposal of Essex amounted to eighteen thousand men. With such a force, judiciously directed, Tirone might have been reduced in a very short space of time; but Essex acted so imprudently that his army melted away by disease and desertion; and though he received reinforcements from England, he was not able to lead more than four thousand men against the northern rebels. As this force was too small for effective operations, he listened to Tirone's proposal for a conference. They met on the opposite banks of a stream, and a truce was concluded till the month of May in the following year. Essex then, though he had received strict orders not to quit Ireland, conscious that he had given his enemies an opportunity of injuring him, resolved to anticipate them, and on the morning of Michaelmas-eve the queen was surprised by seeing him enter her chamber before she had finished dressing, and throw himself on his knees before her. Taken thus by surprise she gave him her hand to kiss, and he retired thanking God that though he had met with many storms abroad, he had found a sweet calm at home. His exultation, however, was short; the queen, who would have her authority respected, ordered him into custody; yet, when his mental uneasiness had brought on an attack of illness, she sent him some broth from her own table, and with tears in her eyes desired her physician to tell him that were it not for her honour she would visit him herself.

Fall of Essex.

Some time after the queen directed that he should be examined on the charges made against him before the privy-council. He made no defence, throwing himself entirely on the queen's mercy. He was ordered to confine himself to his own house, and, but for his own imprudence, which hurried him on to his ruin, he would probably have regained his station in the queen's favour.

He conceived that his enemies were bent on his destruction, and he was gradually led by those about him to resolve on a recourse to violent means for his security. As he had great influence among the citizens of London, he hoped, with their aid, to be able to seize the palace and force the queen to dismiss her present ministers. But these men had intelligence of all his plans, and on a Sunday morning they sent the lord-keeper of the great seal and some others to Essex's house to bring him before the council. But Essex locked them up in one of the rooms, and then sallying forth at the head of a party of his friends, went toward St. Paul's, shouting out, "For the queen, my mistress! there is a plot laid for my life." No one, however, joined him, and he soon after heard himself proclaimed a traitor. He then attempted to return home, but he was repulsed by the guard at Ludgate, and he found it necessary to proceed thither in a boat by water; he found his prisoners gone; soldiers soon began to surround the house, and cannon were brought from the Tower; he therefore surrendered himself on the promise of a fair trial.

Essex and his friend, lord Southampton, were tried and found guilty of high treason. For himself Essex said he would neither solicit nor refuse mercy, but he hoped that the life of his friend would be spared, as he had only acted from affection to *him.* Southampton threw himself entirely on the mercy of the queen. It cost Elizabeth many a struggle before she could be induced to sign the warrant for the execution of her noble-minded but imprudent favourite. At length his enemies wrung it from her, and Essex died on the scaffold within the Tower, acknowledging the justice of his sentence. The life of Southampton was spared.

There went a story, that in the days of his favour the queen had taken a ring from her finger and given it to

Essex, telling him to send it to her whenever he should be in danger, and that he gave this ring, after his condemnation, to the countess of Nottingham, wife of the lord-admiral, to convey to the queen, but that the countess, acting under the advice of Essex's great enemy, sir Robert Cecil, did not deliver it, and that Elizabeth, indignant at his not applying to her, signed the warrant. It is added, that the countess, when on her death-bed, sent for the queen and confessed to her what she had done, imploring forgiveness, and that Elizabeth shook the dying woman violently, saying, "God may forgive you, but I never will." For the credit of human nature we are happy to say that there is very little foundation for this tale.

Death of Elizabeth.

Elizabeth did not long survive her unhappy favourite. She was taken ill at her palace of Richmond, and she daily grew worse. Her ministers, seeing that her death was at hand, were urgent with her to name a successor, a thing she could hitherto never be induced to do. She named the king of Scotland, and then became speechless. By signs she replied to the primate, when examined by him of her faith, and she shortly after gently breathed her last in the seventieth year of her age.

HOUSE OF STUART.—PART I.

CHAPTER I.

JAMES I.

The Gunpowder Plot.

JAMES the Sixth of Scotland, and the First of England, was descended from Margaret, the eldest daughter of Henry VII. He was, therefore, the direct lineal heir of the English crown, and the nation gladly acquiesced in his accession. He was a prince of considerable talent and learning, but he was mean and cowardly in disposition, and he possessed none of the lofty qualities of the late illustrious queen. He was also, like Scotsmen in general, too partial to his own countrymen. Altogether, in a very short time, he ceased to be popular with his English subjects.

James had not been more than a year on the throne when a horrible plot was formed by some desperate and fanatic Roman catholics, to blow up the parliament-house with gunpowder, when the king, the royal family, and all the peers of England should be assembled. Of this atrocious plot, named the Gunpowder Plot, the following are some of the leading circumstances.

The idea was first conceived by Robert Catesby, a gentleman of good birth and property, which last, however, he had squandered in riot and dissipation. He communicated it to two of his friends, John Wright and Thomas Winter, which last went over to the Netherlands, and there engaged in the plot one Guy Fawkes, a gentleman of good family in Yorkshire, who having run through his small patrimony, had entered the Spanish service. When Winter and Fawkes came to London the plan was communicated to Thomas Percy, a kinsman of the earl of Northumberland, to whom he acted as steward, and a house adjoining the parliament-house was taken in his name, and Fawkes, as his servant, was put in charge of it. Another house was taken at Lambeth, in which the powder, timber and other things requisite for their purpose, might be kept.

These preparations were made in the spring of the year, and as parliament was not to meet till the February of the following year, the conspirators did not commence operations till the beginning of December. Catesby and his associates then entered the house in Westminster, well supplied with tools and with hard eggs and baked meats for their support, and began to run a mine thence under the parliament-house, Fawkes standing sentinel while they wrought. They never stirred out, or even went up stairs, lest they should be seen, and every night they spread over the garden the matter which they had extracted during the day. They thus wrought till Christmas-eve, when learning that the meeting of parliament was put off till the following October, they separated for the holydays.

Their number was increased when they renewed their labours in the month of February. The new associates were Wright's brother Christopher, Winter's brother Robert, and John Grant of Norwood, near Warwick. And we may here observe, that, with the exception of Catesby's two servants, Keyes and Bates, all engaged in this diabolical conspiracy were gentlemen, and all but Percy and Catesby men of unexceptionable moral character and of independent fortune. We may hence learn how baneful are the effects of false religion on the mind and heart when it could engage such men in such an undertaking.

We need hardly observe that the conspirators were superstitious men. Accordingly, we are told, that as they were urging on their mine they one day distinctly heard the tolling of a bell under the parliament-house. Fawkes, when called down, heard it also; but when they had sprinkled the place with holy water the sound ceased, and the same remedy always proved efficacious whenever it was renewed. Some time after they were startled by a rushing noise over their heads; they thought at first that they were discovered, but on inquiry they found that it was caused by a man named Bright, who was selling off his coals from a cellar under the house of lords. They now saw that by taking that cellar they might terminate their labours, and it was accordingly taken in Percy's name, and twenty barrels of gunpowder were conveyed to it from the house in Lambeth, and covered over with billets and faggots of wood, and lumber and empty bottles were scattered over the ground to deceive those who might happen to enter the cellar.

During the summer the plot was communicated to three gentlemen of good birth and large fortune, namely, sir Everard Digby, Ambrose Rookwood, and Francis Tresham. As parliament was certainly to meet on the 5th of November, the conspirators made their final arrangements. Fawkes was to fire the mine by means of a slow match, and as soon as he had lighted it he was to hasten on board a small vessel which would be lying ready in the river, and carry the news over to their friends in Flanders. Digby was on the same day to assemble a number of the catholic gentry under pretence of a hunting party at Dunchurch, in Warwickshire, and seize the king's only daughter, the princess Elizabeth, who was in that neighbourhood, and proclaim her queen.

On the 26th of October, as lord Monteagle, a catholic peer, was sitting at supper at his house at Hoxton, near London, an anonymous letter was handed to him by a page, who said he had received it from a strange man in the street. It desired him to make some excuse for not attending parliament, "for God and man," it said, "had concurred to punish the wickedness of this time," with other mysterious hints. Lord Monteagle went that very evening to Whitehall, and showed the letter to lord Salisbury and other lords of the council, and next day, when the king, who had been out hunting, returned to town, a council was held on the subject of the letter. James himself was the person to discover its meaning, but it was determined not to search the cellar till the last moment. Accordingly, on the eve of the meeting of parliament the lord chamberlain and some others entered the cellar. They saw Fawkes there, but made no remark; in the night a magistrate was sent, who arrested him as he was coming out, and six and thirty barrels of powder were found in the cellar when it was searched. Fawkes, when taken before the council, avowed and gloried in his design, but refused to name his accomplices.

Such of the conspirators as were in London fled as soon as they heard of the apprehension of Fawkes. When they came to Dunchurch their dejected looks told their story, and all who were there dispersed to provide for their security. As they went along the catholic gentry drove them from their doors with reproaches. At length they reached Holbeach, the house of Stephen Littleton, one of their friends. There, as they were drying some of their powder which had been wetted, a burning coal fell into it, and Catesby and some others were much injured by the explosion. Next day the sheriff of the county appeared and summoned them to surrender. On their refusal he ordered an assault on the house. Rookwood, Thomas Winter and the two Wrights were wounded. Catesby and Percy, who had placed themselves back to back, were shot through the bodies by two balls from one musket, and both of them died of their wounds. The whole party were then made prisoners. Digby and others who were not there were captured in different places, and all were conveyed to London. They all, like Fawkes, confessed their crime, and all were executed as traitors. They died glorying in the deed for which they suffered.

From the confessions of some of the conspirators it appeared that Father Garnet, the superior of the Jesuits in England, was acquainted with the plot. A warrant was issued for his apprehension, and as it was suspected that he was concealed at Hendlip Hall, the seat of Mr. Abington, near Worcester, the sheriff of the county surrounded and searched the house. So well, however, were the places of concealment contrived, that it was not till the eighth day that Garnet was discovered. He was brought up to London, and being tried and found guilty, he was hanged on a gallows in St. Paul's churchyard.

Though there can hardly be a doubt of Garnet's guilt, the church of Rome has made him one of her saints, and therefore an object of worship to pious catholics. As miracles are required to prove sainthood, we are told that a new kind of grass sprang up on the spot where he last stood in Hendlip lawn of the form of an imperial crown, and that the cattle never touched it. A spring of oil, too, burst out of the earth at the place where he suffered martyrdom. But the miracle that made most noise at the time was that of Father Garnet's Straw. This was an ear of the straw used at his execution, which a young catholic picked up, and on which appeared the face of the martyr. The privy council found it necessary to institute an inquiry into the matter, and it of course proved to have been a pious fraud.

The Favourites.—Somerset.

King James, like Edward II. and most weak princes, was greatly under the influence of favourites. As Edward had his Gaveston and Spenser, so James had his Somerset and Buckingham. The first of these was a young Scotsman named Robert Carr, who was selected by one of the Scottish nobles to bear his shield and device to the king in a tilting-match. As Carr approached the royal seat, his horse became unruly and threw him. His leg was broken, and James, affected by his youth and beauty, had him removed to a room in the palace, where he visited him after the tilt. Pleased with the manners of the youth, James gradually became attached to him, and he resolved to raise him to wealth and honour. He created him viscount Rochester and lavished riches on him; and as the favourite had the good sense to let himself be guided by sir Thomas O'verbury, a prudent and able man, he might have led a happy and respectable life (for he was not by any means a bad man), had he not become connected with an abandoned woman.

It was the custom at that time among the great families to marry mere children to each other. A match of this kind had been effected between the earl of Essex (the son of Elizabeth's favourite), and lady Frances Howard, the daughter of the earl of Suffolk. Immediately after the ceremony the young bridegroom was sent to the continent to travel for his improvement, and lady Suffolk, instead of keeping the bride at home in privacy, carried her to court, where her beauty and accomplishments soon procured her many admirers. Among these the viscount Rochester was the only one who made an impression on her heart, and she agreed to marry him if she could obtain a divorce from the earl of Essex. Accordingly, when that young nobleman returned from his travels, she treated him with such coldness that he at length consented to a divorce, and she was married to Rochester, whom the king, that she might not lose in rank, created earl of Somerset.

When the favourite communicated to his friend Overbury his intention of marrying lady Essex, the latter did all in his power to dissuade him from such a proceeding. Somerset weakly told her all that Overbury had said to her disadvantage, and she, who was a most abandoned and revengeful woman, determined to have Overbury's life. She first offered 1000*l.* to a person who was his enemy to assassinate him, and on his refusal she managed to have Overbury committed to the Tower. While there he was poisoned by a person whom the countess had contrived to set about him, with the connivance of sir Gervase Elways, the lieutenant, and of her own uncle the lord Northampton. The principal agent of the countess in the dark procedure was one Mrs. Turner, the widow of a physician, a woman of infamous character. The crime, however, did not go unpunished. All concerned in it were brought to trial. Somerset, who perhaps was innocent, and his wife, who pleaded guilty, were condemned to death, but the king pardoned them, and allowed them to retire into the country with an allowance of 4000*l*. a year, and they lived there for many years, hating and shunning each other. Elways was beheaded, Mrs. Turner and some of the inferior agents were hanged. As this woman had been the introducer of a yellow starch for stiffening ruffs, the executioner, in mockery of her, wore yellow bands and cuffs, and the yellow starch went out of use for some years.

Buckingham.

The successor of Somerset in the royal favour was George Villiers, the son of a knight in Leicestershire, who by the elegance of his dress and manners, and his showy person, made an instant impression on the king's mind. The enemies of Somerset resolved to set up Villiers as his rival, and the queen herself was induced to favour his advancement. James was glad of a pretext for gratifying his own inclination. He heaped wealth and offices on Villiers, whom he raised at length to the rank of marquess of Buckingham; and Villiers, more fortunate, though perhaps less deserving than his predecessor, contrived to retain his influence to the last over his royal master, whom he even ventured to treat with insolence and rudeness.

Fate of Sir Walter Raleigh.

The great sir Walter Raleigh, one of the favourites of Elizabeth, and one of the most distinguished men whom England has produced, had been sentenced to death on a false charge of treason in the beginning of James's reign. He had lain for several years in the Tower, when the king, induced by the hopes which he held forth to him of the great wealth that might be obtained from the gold-mines of Guiána in South America, to which he had made a voyage in the late reign, consented to allow him to proceed thither with an expedition fitted out at the expense of himself and his friends. But he refused to grant him a pardon, and straitly charged him not to make any attempt on any of the Spanish settlements; for as James had set his heart on a marriage between the prince of Wales and one of the Infántas or daughters of the king of Spain, he was extremely anxious not to give any offence to the Spaniards.

Raleigh sailed from Plymouth with fourteen vessels, and after losing a great number of his men by disease, he at length reached the mouth of the great river Orinoco. He sent five of his vessels up the river in search of the mines, giving their commander, captain Kemys, strict orders not to molest the Spaniards, who, since Raleigh had been last there, had built a sort of town, named St. Thomas, some way up the Orinoco. As the English were passing by that place the Spaniards attacked them in the night, but they were repulsed, and the English pursued them to their town, and took and plundered it. In the action, Raleigh's eldest son and the Spanish governor, a kinsman of Góndomar's, the ambassador at the court of London, were both slain. Kemys having sought in vain for the mine, returned to Raleigh, who reproached him so bitterly for what had occurred, that he went into his cabin and blew out his brains. Raleigh was arrested and committed to the Tower the moment he landed in England. Gondomar ceased not to call for vengeance, and James offered to give him up to the king of Spain; but that monarch said he would rather that Raleigh should be executed in England. The judges of the court of King's Bench were therefore directed to proceed to execution against him on his former sentence. Raleigh in vain submitted to the court, that the commission, giving him, as commander, the power of life and death over others, amounted to a pardon; execution was granted, and the scholar, the writer, the warrior, and the statesman (for Raleigh was all these), was led to a scaffold in the sixty-sixth year of his age, in order to cement by his blood (like the innocent earl of Warwick on a former occasion), a marriage with a daughter of Spain. He mounted the scaffold with that courage which never deserted him. When he had taken off his gown and doublet, he asked the executioner to let him see the axe. He poised it, and running his thumb along the edge, said with a smile, "This is a sharp medicine, but it will cure all diseases." The executioner was going to blindfold him, but he refused to let him, saying, "Think you I fear the shadow of the axe, when I fear not the axe itself?" He gave the signal by stretching out his hands, and his head was struck off at two blows.

The Prince's Expedition to Spain.

Though James thus put to death one of the greatest men in his dominions to conciliate the court of Spain, the marriage-treaty went on very slowly. Buckingham, who had at first treated the prince of Wales with his usual insolence, soon began to reflect that, as the king was growing old, the time might not be far distant when the sceptre would pass into the hands of the prince, who would then have the power, and, if he did not conciliate him in time, might have the inclination, to make him feel his vengeance. He therefore used his utmost diligence to ingratiate himself with the prince; and so complete was his success, that his influence over him became greater than even over the king himself.

One day Buckingham took an opportunity of remarking to the prince how tardily the treaty for his marriage went on, and he ascribed all the delay to the slowness and indifference of those engaged in it. He then hinted, that if the prince were to go in person to Madrid, he might conclude that matter at once, and gain various other advantages for his family. Charles was of a romantic temper, and his imagination kindled at the prospect of thus distinguishing himself. Buckingham proposed that they two, with a few attendants, should proceed in disguise to Madrid. Charles then went to his father, and throwing himself on his knees, craved his permission to undertake the journey. Buckingham urged his suit, and the king at length gave a reluctant consent.

But when James had time to reflect, he saw all the danger and absurdity of the wild project, and when they came to him next day he recalled his consent. The prince shed tears and remonstrated with his father; but Buckingham, who was in the habit of treating the king in a different style, told him that no one would in future believe anything he said; that he had, contrary to a promise he had given the prince, revealed the matter to some rascal, who had furnished him with the pitiful reasons he had given, but that *he* would find out who that counsellor was, and the prince would make him suffer for it. The poor weak king, thus bullied, renewed his consent, and the prince and Buckingham went to a house belonging to the latter in Essex, to prepare for their romantic expedition.

Having furnished themselves with false beards and periwigs, they went down to Dover, and under the names of Jack and Tom Smith passed over to France. At Paris they saw the young king, Louis XIII., and his mother and his sister Henrietta Maria, at dinner and at a masked ball, but the prince did not reveal his rank, and they stopped only one day in that city. They travelled rapidly through France, and in little more than a fortnight from the time of their leaving England, they found themselves within a day's journey of Madrid. Leaving their attendants, they went on by themselves, and came to the house of lord Bristol, the English ambassador. The prince stayed in the street while Buckingham went in, bearing their portmanteau. Bristol received the prince with all suitable respect, and next day the arrival of the heir of the English crown being made known at court, the prime minister waited on him, and in the evening the king in person came to visit him. He was treated with the utmost respect, the prisons were thrown open on his account, the king gave him precedence on all occasions, and presented him with two golden keys, which gave him admittance whenever he wished to the royal apartments. When it was known in England that the prince of Wales was in Spain, numbers of the young nobility repaired thither to do him honour, and Madrid presented an unwonted appearance of gaiety and festivity. Meantime the marriage articles were in the course of settlement; and though Spanish etiquette did not permit of any intimacy between the prince and his future bride, he saw her frequently at court.

Various delays having occurred, chiefly on account of the death of the pope, the prince was summoned home by his father. He took a solemn leave of the queen and the infanta, who now assumed the title of Princess of England, and had a separate court formed for her. The king accompanied him on his way as far as the palace of the Escúrial, where they parted as brothers, and several of the Spanish nobility attended him to the place of embarkation. He went on board at St. Andéro, and landed at Portsmouth after an absence of more than seven months.

Breaking off the Match with Spain.

The marriage was to be performed by proxy when the pope's permission should arrive; but Buckingham, whose vanity had been mortified in Spain, was resolved that it should never take place, and he easily drew the prince and king into his views. The Spanish court was treated with insult, and when parliament met, Buckingham, by dint of lying and misrepresentation, persuaded the members that the court of Spain had been insincere throughout the whole business. Money was voted for a war, and the people, who hated the Spaniards, testified their joy by illuminations and bonfires. The prince, meantime, transferred his affections to the princess Henrietta, whom he had seen at Paris, and a marriage-treaty was speedily concluded with the court of France.

The king did not live to witness the marriage of his son. He died of gout in his stomach, after a fortnight's illness, in the fifty-ninth year of his age.

Anecdote of King James.

King James had very high notions of the extent of the royal power, and he thought his subjects' money was all his own, and that he might take it when he pleased. One day, when he was at dinner, with Dr. Andrews, bishop of Winchester, and Dr. Neal, bishop of Durham, standing behind his chair, he said, "My lords, cannot I take my subjects' money when I want it, without all this formality of parliament?" "God forbid, sir, but you should; you are the breath of our nostrils," replied the bishop of Durham. "Well, my lord, what say you?" said the king, turning to the other prelate. "Sir," replied the bishop, "I have no skill to judge of parliamentary matters." "No put-offs, my lord," said the king. "Then, sir," said he, "I think it is lawful to take my brother Neal's money, for he offers it."

CHAPTER II.

CHARLES I.

Charles' first Parliament.

CHARLES was in the twenty-fifth year of his age when he ascended the throne. He was grave and decorous in his manners, a lover and patron of the fine arts, and sincerely attached to the protestant religion. To his misfortune he had learned from his father to hold the most extravagant notions of the royal authority, and he was blindly devoted to the vain and insolent Buckingham.

One of the first acts of the new king was to celebrate his marriage with the princess Henrietta Maria. He then summoned a parliament in order to obtain money for the war with Spain, and other purposes; but the members had discovered that Buckingham had deceived them by false statements, and that the Spaniards had not behaved so ill as they had been led to suppose. They were therefore by no means desirous of war, and they were aware of many grievances and oppressions in the government, the removal of which would be of far more real benefit to the nation than any triumphs over the fleets and armies of Spain. Accordingly they declined giving the people's money, except on the condition of a redress of grievances, and they showed an inclination to impeach the duke of Buckingham, as the favourite was now styled. To save him, Charles dissolved the parliament.

War had not been declared against Spain, and there was no necessity for declaring it. Yet such was Buckingham's influence with the king, that a fleet carrying a force of ten thousand men was fitted out and sent to make an attack on the port of Cadiz. But it was not now as in the days of Elizabeth; the commanders wanted skill and the soldiers wanted discipline, and the attempt on an unoffending people proved a disgraceful failure.

Buckingham's Insolence.—War with France.

Not content with having engaged his sovereign in an unprofitable contest with Spain, Buckingham would also have him at war with France, purely to gratify his own passion for revenge; for when he was sent over to convey Henrietta to England, he had the audacity to make love to the young queen Anne of Austria, who did not reject his advances. He got a hint, however, that if he persisted in his attentions he would be assassinated, and he quitted France, vowing vengeance. He immediately made every effort in his power to turn Charles against his queen, and he himself treated her with the greatest insolence and rudeness. With his usual arrogance he insisted on his mother, who had been only a servant when his father married her, being treated with as much respect as if she were born a princess; and when something occurred one day to prevent the queen from calling on her at an appointed hour, he told her that she should repent it; she replied with some quickness, and he then added, that "there had been queens in England who had lost their heads," alluding to those whom Henry VIII. had put to death on charges of adultery.

When he found that he could not provoke the court of France to a declaration of war, he resolved to commence hostilities himself. He therefore entered into an alliance with the French protestants, and having assembled a fleet of one hundred ships, carrying about seven thousand men, he embarked at Portsmouth and sailed for Rochelle, a seaport then in the hands of the protestants. But the people of that town would not venture to admit him; they would only engage to supply provisions if the English remained in the neighbourhood. Off the coast of France, near Rochelle, there are two islands named Rhe and O'leron, of which the latter, the nearer to Rochelle, was well supplied with wine, oil, etc., and was slightly garrisoned, while the former was more distant, and was defended by a citadel and a strong garrison. Buckingham proposed to attack Oleron, but he changed his mind, and landed his troops in Rhe. He drove off the garrison, but instead of attacking the fort at once, spent five days doing nothing. This gave the French time to send fresh troops into the fort, and after committing a series of military blunders, he was obliged to retire from before it. He conducted his troops along a narrow causeway, on each side of which were deep salt-pits. The French, waiting till a part of the troops were on the causeway, made a furious attack; the English were thrown into confusion, and numbers were forced into the pits, and there drowned. Their total loss was two thousand men. Buckingham, who had shown much personal courage on the occasion, then embarked his troops, and returned to England.

Murder of Buckingham.

Some time after, Rochelle being hard pressed by the troops of the king of France, another fleet and army were assembled at Portsmouth to proceed to its relief. Buckingham was to take the command as before, and he went down to Portsmouth for the purpose. One morning, as he was passing from his chamber to his carriage, he stopped as he was crossing the hall to listen to something which one of the officers whispered to him. Suddenly, an unknown hand plunged a knife into his heart, and left it sticking there; the duke cried "Villain!" plucked it out, staggered against a table, and died. Some French gentlemen with whom he had been talking with loud words in his chamber, were suspected of the deed, and they narrowly escaped instant death. The real assassin, who had reached the kitchen, and might have escaped, on hearing a sudden alarm, drew his sword, crying, "I am the man." When seized, he said that his name was John Felton, a protestant, and a lieutenant in the army, but that he had retired from the service when he saw junior officers put over his head, and his arrears of pay withheld. He had been convinced that the duke was the cause of all the national calamities, and that by killing him he should serve God, his king and his country. He said that he had no accomplices, he had travelled seventy miles to do the deed, and so little personal enmity did he bear the duke, that as he struck the blow he prayed "May God have mercy on thy soul!" When brought to trial, he pleaded guilty, owned the enormity of his offence, and prayed that the hand that did the act might be struck off before he died. He was hanged as a murderer.

The king, who was staying at a private house near

Portsmouth, was at his prayers when the news reached him of the murder of the duke. He preserved his usual calm and unmoved air; but he felt deeply. He wished to have the murderer put to the rack, but the judges declared torture to be contrary to the laws of England. He caused the duke to be buried in Westminster-abbey, styling him "the martyr of his sovereign;" he paid his debts to the amount of 60,000*l.*, and took his family under his protection.

Despotism of Charles.

After the death of Buckingham, Charles had no favourite; but he was greatly influenced by his queen, a vain, selfish, self-willed woman. He was also his own minister, and his government became a perfect despotism. For a space of twelve years he summoned no parliament, he took his subjects' money from them as he pleased, and gave no account of it; for he considered himself accountable only to God for his conduct as a sovereign. In the church, too, a similar despotism was exercised, with the king's approbation, by Dr. Laud, archbishop of Canterbury; and all who ventured to oppose were most cruelly punished. As an instance we may mention the case of the father of that most excellent and pious man, archbishop Leighton. This divine, who belonged to the church of Scotland, and not to that of England, had printed a book in Holland against bishops, styling them men of blood, and calling on the parliament utterly to root out prelacy. He also, when speaking of the queen, termed her, in the controversial language of the time, a daughter of Heth, that is, an idolater or papist. For this offence he was brought before the court called the Star Chamber, and sentenced to be committed to the Fleet-prison for life, to be fined 10,000*l.*, to be degraded from his ministry, to be pilloried, whipt, have an ear cropt off, a nostril slit, and his cheek branded with SS. (Sower of Sedition), at Westminster, and the same to be repeated some days after at

Cheapside. When this barbarous sentence was pronounced Laud pulled off his cap and gave God thanks for it; and it was carried into execution. Prynne, Bastwick, and others, gentlemen and men of education, were treated with similar indignity and cruelty.

Ship-Money.

Among the modes employed by Charles for obtaining supplies, the most remarkable, and the most fatal to himself, was that of demanding ship-money; for from the Anglo-Saxon times it had been usual to require the seaports and maritime counties to furnish shipping for the public service in time of danger, and Charles' lawyers now maintained that this obligation extended to the whole kingdom. Writs for the levy of ship-money were therefore directed to all the sheriffs of counties, and the people were in general obliged to pay the new tax. Some, however, resisted it as illegal. Among others, John Hampden, a gentleman of fortune in Buckinghamshire, refused to pay a demand made on him of twenty shillings ship-money, and the case was argued before the twelve judges, a majority of whom decided in favour of the crown. The people, therefore, paid ship-money, though most reluctantly, and the funds which it produced ill compensated the king for the loss of his subjects' affections.

So gloomy did the aspect of affairs in England appear to many persons, that they deemed an abode in the bleak regions of North America, where they would have to contend with the elements and with the savage tribes of the soil, preferable to one in their native country under a despotic government. Every year, therefore, numbers sailed for the lately-settled colony of New England; and after the decision of the judges in the case of the ship-money, persons of still higher rank, such as the lords Say and Brooke, resolved to quit their enslaved country. It is said that Hampden himself, his kinsman, Oliver Cromwell, and some others, were actually on board of the vessel which was to convey them to the New World, when an order arrived, procured by Laud, forbidding masters of ships to carry out any one who had not a license from the privy-council, and a certificate from the minister of his parish. Little did Laud foresee the mischief he was doing his master and himself by this ill-judged act!

Affairs of Scotland.

It was Laud, in effect, that was the chief means of plunging the king into all his future difficulties. The measure just alluded to proceeded from that prelate's aversion to the puritans, as those persons were named who held the opinions called Calvinistic in religion, and who, as he found to his cost, were a very numerous and very powerful body, whom common prudence would have counselled to treat with tenderness and caution. But Laud was not gifted with prudence, and when he accompanied Charles to his native kingdom of Scotland, he succeeded in inducing him to attempt to change by force the religion of that country, and reduce it to his own notions of perfection.

The Scots, in their hatred of popery, had receded from it as much as possible, and they had adopted the form of church government called Presbyterian, in which there are no bishops. They had, however, been induced by king James to receive bishops with limited powers, and it was now the object of Charles and Laud to place these bishops on a footing with those of the church of England, and also to make the Scottish church adopt a liturgy or fixed form of prayer. The liturgy, accordingly, when approved of by Laud, was sent down to Scotland. The Scottish bishops, who knew the people they had to deal with, recommended great caution in introducing it; but Laud would listen to no suggestion of prudence, and a proclamation was issued enjoining the use of it in every parish-church on a certain day.

On the appointed day the dean of Edinburgh prepared to officiate according to the liturgy in St. Giles's church.

At first the people did not interrupt him; but at length an old woman, filled with zeal, stood up and flung the stool she sat on at the dean's head, crying, "Villain, dost thou say the mass at my lug [ear]?" A tumult arose; the women rushed to seize the dean; the bishop ascended the pulpit to try to appease the people, but sticks and stones were flung at him, and only for the magistrates he would have perished on the spot. The liturgy was resisted all over Scotland; and as the king would make no concession to the prejudices of the people, they at length resolved to assert their right to think and act for themselves in matters of religion by force of arms. A Solemn League and Covenant, or engagement, to that effect, was drawn up, which was signed by almost every person in the kingdom; and as they well knew that the king would endeavour to reduce them by arms, they raised troops, and summoned Lesley and other old soldiers from the continent to command them. Charles soon appeared on the frontiers at the head of twenty-three thousand men, but his troops were ill-inclined to fight against men who only stood up, as it seemed to them, for their religious liberty, and his cavalry turned and fled as soon as they came in view of the Scots. He therefore listened to proposals for an accommodation, and the troops were disbanded on both sides.

The Short Parliament.

It soon, however, appeared, that no accommodation could be effected, unless one party or the other were prepared to give up all the points in dispute. Charles, therefore, whose character it was to yield to nothing but force, resolved on another appeal to arms. But as all his modes of raising money were now exhausted, he found it necessary to summon a parliament; and thus, after an interval of twelve years, the great national council met once more. But it proved to be the same in character as the former parliaments. When the king pressed for an immediate supply of money, the parliament talked of the redress of grievances; and at last, in a fit of anger, he dissolved it, after it had sat only three weeks, whence it was named the Short Parliament. He then obtained what money he could by voluntary loans from the nobility and others, and made the counties supply him with soldiers and horses at their own expense. But the Scots crossed the Tweed, and made themselves masters of the counties of Northumberland and Durham; and Charles, finding that his troops would not fight, was obliged to consent to a treaty and to summon another parliament.

The Long Parliament.—Strafford.

On the 3rd of November, 1640, the new parliament, named from its duration the Long Parliament, met at Westminster. Late experience had shown the real weakness of the king, and the parliament lost no time in displaying its power. Its favourite weapon of impeachment was immediately put in use. Laud was impeached and sent to the Tower, and Leighton and his other victims were set at liberty; other members of the council only escaped a similar treatment by flying to the continent. But the great object of the vengeance of the commons was Wentworth, earl of Strafford.

Sir Thomas Wentworth, a man of large fortune in Yorkshire, had sat in several parliaments, and he had mostly acted as neuter in the disputes between the crown and the commons, till Buckingham, with his usual insolence, deprived him of an office which he held in his county. He then joined the patriots, and was one of the most active and able champions of liberty. As soon, however, as Buckingham was dead, he was easily induced to come over to the court, to which he had been always inclined. He was created earl of Strafford, made president of the council of the north and lord-lieutenant of Ireland; and he was universally regarded as the great supporter of the royal despotism, for in energy and talent he far exceeded any of the king's ministers.

This great man the commons were resolved to strike down. He knew his danger, and wished to remain in the north with the army; but the king, who wanted his aid, insisted on his coming up, assuring him that the parliament should not touch a hair of his head. On the very day after his arrival in London, however, John Pym, a leading man in the house of commons, appeared, followed by three hundred members, at the bar of the house of lords, and impeached the earl of Strafford of high treason in the name of the commons of England.

Trial of Strafford.

Strafford was immediately committed to the Tower. The king, in his anxiety to serve him, proposed to give places at court and in the ministry to Pym, Hampden, and others; but the project was not carried into effect, and the patriots, angered at their disappointment, became only the more inveterate against the earl.

When all the requisite preparations had been made, the trial commenced in Westminster Hall. The peers in their robes sat in the centre of the hall, the commons on scaffolds at each side; at the upper end was a lofty vacant throne, and on each side of it a latticed box for the king and royal family, and at the foot of it was a gallery for ladies of quality. A bar stretched across the hall, leaving about a third of it at the lower end for the public.

The trial commenced at nine o'clock every morning, at which hour the earl entered the hall. He was dressed in black, he wore his George (*i. e.* a medal with a figure of St. George on it), as he was a knight of the garter, hung round his neck by a golden chain. When he had saluted the peers, he took his place at a small desk, the lieutenant of the Tower standing beside him, and his four secretaries at his back. The prosecution on the part of the commons was conducted by Pym and others; and as the charges did not, in reality, amount to treason, and the earl defended himself with great ability, the sentiments of many of the peers were evidently inclining in his favour, and the ladies, who always possess influence, were all captivated by his manly and graceful eloquence. Pym, seeing that his prey was likely to escape him, attempted to produce in evidence some notes of the opinions given at the council-table on the occasion of the Scottish war, taken by sir Henry Vane, the secretary, and which sir Henry's son had stolen out of his closet and given to Pym. Being foiled, however, in this attempt, he made the commons pass a bill of attainder; an odious measure, devised to destroy those for whose real or imputed offences the laws had provided no penalty. When the bill was brought to the lords, the solicitor-general, St. John, argued for two hours in vindication of that mode of proceeding. Among other arguments he used the following: "He that would not have had others to have a law, why should he have any law himself? It is true we give law to hares and deers, because these be beasts of chase; it was never accounted cruelty or foul play to knock foxes or wolves on the head as they can be found, because these be beasts of prey. The warrener sets traps for polecats and other vermin for preservation of the warren." So that, by this reasoning, as Strafford had acted, according to his accusers, contrary to law and justice, he was himself to be destroyed without any law.

The following Saturday the king summoned both houses, and told them he could not give his assent to a bill of attainder, but that he was willing to remove the earl from all employment. As it was irregular for the king thus to interfere with a bill in progress, the commons were loud in their complaints of this breach of privilege, as it was termed; and the next day being Sunday, the puritan clergy in the city made the pulpits resound with declamation on the necessity of executing justice on some great delinquents; and the following morning an armed rabble came to Westminster, crying for justice on the earl of Strafford, and they posted up the names of the members who had voted against the bill of attainder, calling them Straffordians and betrayers of their country.

Execution of Strafford.

The bill finally passed both houses, and with it another pledging the king to allow the parliament to sit as long as it pleased, and to give it authority to raise money if it should deem it necessary. By assenting to the former bill Charles would make himself a party in putting to death a man, who, however guilty he might be toward others, had always been faithful to him; by assenting to the latter, he would in effect divest himself of his regal authority. Yet the infatuated monarch was induced, chiefly it is supposed by the queen, who thought only of her own safety, to give his assent to both the bills.

It is said, that in his mental agony on the subject of Strafford, Charles consulted some of the bishops on the case. Juxon, bishop of London, a plain honest man, advised him to follow the dictates of his conscience regardless of consequences; but Williams, archbishop of York, made a distinction between the public and the private conscience of a king, according to which he might in his public capacity do an act which in his heart he held to be a crime. The conscience of Charles, who was fond of these subtle but dangerous distinctions in morals, may possibly have been satisfied by this reasoning, and a letter from Strafford himself, urging him to pass the bill, helped to decide him. "Sir," said the earl in the letter, "my consent shall more acquit you herein to God than all the world can do besides. To a willing man there is no injury done."

A man of truly noble mind would have perished rather than comply with such a request; but Charles, deeming himself now fully justified, made no further scruple about passing the bill. Strafford, who had probably only intended to awaken his master's better feelings, would not at first believe that the king could have acted as he did; when convinced of the truth, he stood up, raised his eyes to heaven, and, laying his hand on his heart, said, " Put not your trust in princes, nor in the sons of men, for in them is no salvation."

Two days after the earl was conducted to the scaffold on Tower-hill. Laud, at his request, stood at the window of his chamber to give him his blessing as he passed. The feeble old man raised his hands for the purpose, but unable to speak, he fell back into the arms of his attendants. The earl then moved on: when the lieutenant advised him to take coach at the gate, lest the mob should tear him to pieces, he replied that it was equal to him whether he died by the axe or by *their* fury. The people, however, were English, generous even in their enmity. Not a word of insult was heard from the immense multitude that was assembled. The earl took off his hat several times and saluted them; he then addressed them, assuring them that he had never been, as he was accused, an enemy to parliaments. Seeing his brother weeping, he gently reproached him. "Think," said he, "that you are now accompanying me to my marriage bed. That block shall be my pillow, and here I shall rest from all my labours." He then began to undress, saying, "I do as cheerfully put off my doublet this time as ever I did when I went to bed." He knelt and prayed, then laid his head on the block, and it was taken off at a single blow.

The Irish Rebellion.

The earl of Strafford was executed on the 12th of May, and in the following month of August the king set out for Scotland, to try to acquire the means of regaining his authority in England. With this view he lavished the lands of the church, and places and honours, on the men of most influence. Among others, he made old Lesley, who had commanded the Scottish army against him, earl of Leven, and his second in command, Munro, earl of Callender. On this occasion Lesley, it is said, assured him that he would never more serve against him, but that his service should be the king's be the cause what it might. We shall see how he kept this promise.

While Charles was in Scotland a dreadful rebellion broke out in Ireland, and vast numbers of the protestants dwelling in that kingdom were barbarously massacred by the papists. The following was its origin.

In consequence of the rebellions of Tirone and others of the native Irish, large tracts of land had been declared forfeit, and they were granted to English and Scottish settlers. The inferior Irish could not see why *they* were to lose their lands because their chiefs, in pursuit of the objects of their own ambition, had taken arms against the crown, and they hated the new colonists both as being protestants and as being more civilised than themselves. They were, therefore, ready implements in the hands of any one who knew how to use them, and such a person there then was in Ireland. A gentleman of small fortune, named Roger Moore, who had served in the Spanish armies, seeing that the Scots by taking arms had made the king submit to their desires, thought that the same might be effected in Ireland, and that if the catholics were suddenly to rise and seize the forts, and expel the new settlers, they might recover their lands and make their religion triumphant. An extensive conspiracy was speedily organised, in which several of the leading catholics of the English as well as of the Irish race shared.

It was arranged that there should be a simultaneous rising of the catholics on the 23rd of October. As it was a great object of the conspirators to get possession of the castle of Dublin, in which there was a large quantity of arms and ammunition, Moore and other gentlemen came up to that city, each followed by twenty men, in order to make the attack on it with their united force. The government had not the slightest knowledge of the conspiracy till the night of the 22nd, when a man named Owen O'Conolly brought them information. This man, who, as his name indicates, was of Irish origin, had lived chiefly among the English, and he was a protestant in religion. For some reason, which is unknown, one of the conspirators, who was named MacMáhon, wished to engage him in the plot, and therefore wrote to him to come to him at his house in the country. Conolly, therefore, went thither, but found that he was gone up to Dublin. He followed him up and arrived on the evening of Friday the 22nd of October. MacMahon took him to lord MacGuire's, and informed him of what was to take place next day. They then returned to MacMahon's lodgings, where O'Conolly representing to him how little likely the plot was to succeed, urged him to discover it and thus save his estate. But he refused, swearing at the same time that O'Conolly should not quit his lodgings that night. They then sat down to drink, and after some time O'Conolly desired to be let go down to the yard. MacMahon kept his sword, and sent his own man with him, but O'Conolly jumped over the wall and hastened with his information to the government. Next morning lord MacGuire, MacMahon, and some of the others were arrested, but Moore had gotten timely warning, and he effected his escape.

The discovery made in Dublin did not prevent the breaking out of the rebellion. On the morning of the 22nd, which was a Friday, the priests, it is said, in many parts of the province of Ulster, dismissed the people after the mass with directions to go and take possession of their lands. Next morning they assembled, armed with staves sithes, and pitchforks, and drove off the cattle of the English, and turned the owners out of their houses. They stripped them naked, and forbade any one to give them food or shelter. Soon, however, the savage Irish proceeded to greater acts of cruelty. Some they buried alive, others they hung up by the arms and cut at them with their swords till they died. They dashed out the brains of young children, or trampled them to death. Multitudes of the protestants were shut up in houses to which fire was set, and they thus were burnt alive. At some places they were driven by hundreds into rivers, and drowned. Worst of all, wives and children, we are assured, were sometimes induced by a promise of their lives to put their own husbands or parents to death, and when they had thus violated the laws of nature, were themselves slaughtered. In these bloody deeds the women were more forward than the men, and the very children lent their aid to destroy the English heretics. The priests in many cases would give the sacrament to their people only on the condition of their sparing neither man, woman, nor child. The total number massacred, it was believed at the time in England, was two hundred thousand persons, but the account which seems to be best entitled to credit, makes it about forty or fifty thousand. The king was charged by the parliament, but unjustly, with being the author of this bloody massacre, by having, as they asserted, given the Irish catholics authority to arm themselves and expel the English.

The Five Members.

Soon after his return from Scotland the king dined with the city of London at the Guildhall, and the people greeted him so heartily on his way to and from it, and testified so much loyalty, that he thought himself strong enough now to venture to attack the parliament. On the 3rd of January, 1642, he sent the attorney-general to the house of commons to charge Pym, Hampden, and three other members with high treason, and to demand that they should be surrendered. At the same time persons were sent to the lodgings of the five members to seal up their papers.

As the members had not been given up as required, the king himself went to the house of commons next day to demand them. He was attended by his guards and by two or three hundred gentlemen and soldiers, mostly armed. Leaving these in the hall he entered the house with his nephew, the elector palatine; he took off his hat and advanced to the speaker's chair, who quitted it at his approach.

He stood before it, and having looked round for a time he told the house that he would respect their privileges, but that treason had no privilege. He then called two of the five members by name, and no answer being returned, he asked the speaker where they were. The five members, we may here observe, had got notice from a friend at court that the king was coming, and they had left the house and sought refuge in the city. To the king's demand the speaker replied that "he was a servant to the house, and had neither eyes nor tongue to see or speak anything but what they commanded him." The king then said that "he thought his own eyes were as good as his;" he added that he saw that "his birds were flown, but that he did expect that the house would send them to him, and that they should have a fair trial." He then retired, pulling off his hat till he reached the door. Many voices cried "Privilege! privilege!" as he passed along.

It is said that Charles was driven to this most injudicious step by the queen, whom the commons had threatened to impeach; and that when on cooler thoughts he hesitated about going to the house, she cried to him, "Go coward; go pull those rogues out by the ears, or never see me more." It is added, that when the hour for the deed was past she said to one of her friends, "Rejoice, for I hope that the king is now master in his states, and that such and such are in custody."

Next day the king went into the city; but as he passed through it his ears were assailed with cries of "Privilege of parliament!" and one person had the audacity to fling into his coach a pamphlet or sermon, entitled, "To your tents, O Israel!" the words with which the ten tribes abandoned Rehoboam the son of Solomon. Hearing soon after that preparations were being made in the city for bringing the five members back to Westminster in triumph, in order to escape being a witness to the insult he quitted Whitehall, and retired with his queen and children to Hampton-court.

Next day, in the afternoon, the river Thames was

covered with boats, and between two rows of lighters and long boats, carrying artillery, the five members, attended by the sheriffs and a part of the trained-bands or militia of the city, proceeded in barges to Westminster. Another body of the trained-bands marched along the Strand, followed by great numbers of the populace, who, as they passed Whitehall, insolently shouted, "What is become now of the king and his cavaliers?"

Commencement of the Civil War.

Both parties were now resolved on war. The king having sent the queen to Holland with the crown-jewels to purchase arms and ammunition, retired to York. He hoped to make himself master of Hull, where there was a large quantity of ordnance and ammunition, but when he went to that town for the purpose, he found the drawbridges raised, the gates closed and the walls manned, and the governor, sir John Hotham, appeared on the walls, and with the greatest professions of respect and duty refused to admit him, for fear, as he said, of offending the parliament. The king retired after having proclaimed Hotham a traitor, and the ordnance and ammunition were shortly after sent up to London.

It is to be observed that at this time there was no regular standing army in England, and that the only troops were the militia or trained-bands, as they were named, of each county. These were commanded by the lord-lieutenant of the county, and they could not, of right, be marched out of their own county, except in cases of rebellion or invasion. It was about the militia that the king and the parliament finally quarrelled, as they wanted him to give them the power of appointing its commanders, which had always been the right of the crown. Charles knew that by so doing he should part with his royal authority, and sooner than become the slave of his parliament he resolved to try the chance of arms. Most of the nobility and gentry of the kingdom, with their servants and tenants, ranged themselves on his side; the chief support of the parliament were the city of London, and te great towns, and the eastern counties. But every town, village, and almost every family, were split into parties, some being for the king and some for the parliament, and indeed there was so much of right and so much of wrong on each side, that it was not an easy matter for a conscientious man to choose his party. The nickname for the adherents of the king was Cavaliers, that for those of the parliament Roundheads, as the puritans, who were all on this side, wore their hair closely cropt.

On the evening of the 25th of August, 1642, the king set up his standard at Nottingham. The weather, which was gloomy and blustering, gave a melancholy foreboding of the future, and this was augmented by the circumstance of the standard's being blown down in the night. The king went thence to Shrewsbury, and his troops there mustered eighteen thousand men. The chief command was committed to the earl of Lindesey, an experienced old soldier; the cavalry was commanded by the king's nephew, prince Rupert*. The march was directed by Bridgenorth and Birmingham to Kenilworth, with the intention of advancing to London; but at a village named Edgecot, within four miles of Banbury, the king learned that the parliamentary forces were arrived at the village of Keinton, within about seven or eight miles of Edgecot, and it was resolved to turn back and give them battle.

Battle of Edgehill.

The parliament had given the chief command of their forces to the earl of Essex, the son of Elizabeth's favourite, whom we have seen so shamefully treated in the case of his countess and Somerset, in the late reign. He was a

* Elizabeth, the only daughter of James I., had been married to the Elector Palatine in Germany. By accepting the crown of Bohemia this prince lost his patrimonial dominions, and his family were now living in poverty in Holland. The present royal family of England are descended from Sophia, the daughter of this elector.

man of honour, and no enemy to either the church or the monarchy. He had been selected for command on account of the military experience which he had acquired by serving in the Netherlands, and of his influence over the minds of the soldiery. As there was not yet any established uniform in the English army, the troops on both sides wore the colours or liveries of the noblemen or gentlemen who had raised them, and as Essex's colour was what was termed orange-tawny, scarfs of that hue distinguished the soldiers of the parliament.

Early on the morning of Sunday the 23rd of October, the cavalry of the royal army appeared on the summit of Edgehill, which overlooks the Vale of the Red Horse, in which Keinton lies. As most of the infantry were quartered in villages at some distance, it was noon before the royal army began to descend into the vale, where Essex had drawn out his troops in front of Keinton. The day was one of those calm clear days familiar to the month of October. For the first time since the war of the Roses, Englishmen stood opposed to each other in battle array; but each party deemed its cause to be founded in justice, and fearlessly made this ultimate appeal to Heaven. The engagement commenced between two and three o'clock by the firing of cannon on both sides, and the infantry then advanced to the combat with resolution. Rupert, by an impetuous charge, drove the cavalry opposed to him beyond Keinton, but instead of returning to support the infantry he fell to plundering the enemy's baggage. The royal infantry was therefore thrown into confusion, lord Lindesey was mortally wounded, and himself and his son were made prisoners; the standard-bearer, sir Edward Verney, was slain, and the standard taken, but it was afterwards recovered; the king himself and his two sons were at one time in danger of being captured. Night ended the conflict; the royalists retired over the hill; the parliamentarians remained all night on the ground. The number of the slain was probably equal on both sides; most accounts make it amount to five thousand, but there is good reason to suppose that it did not much exceed one fifth of that quantity. The advantage was evidently on the side of the royalists, for Essex fell back to Warwick, and the king took Banbury, and then advanced to Oxford.

Progress of the War.

The parliament, in great consternation, recalled Essex to their defence, and they sent a petition for peace to the king, who had reached Colnbrook. He made a favourable reply, but instead of remaining where he was, at the instance of prince Rupert, who was his evil genius, he advanced to Brentford, and attacked and routed the troops which lay in that town. Next day Essex drew out all his forces, which, when augmented by the trained bands of the city, mustered twenty-four thousand men, on Turnham-green, but the king, aware of his inferiority in strength, declined the combat and retired to Oxford, and the parliament then charged him with perfidy and breach of faith. They, however sent commissioners to Oxford, but nothing could be effected.

The war was not confined to the parts where the king was present. In the west of England the royal cause was supported by sir Bevil Greenvil, sir Ralph Hopton, and other gallant gentlemen, while that of the parliament was upheld by sir William Waller, and various actions were fought, in one of which on Lansdown-hill, near Bath, the brave sir Bevil Greenvil was slain. Waller, shortly after, was totally routed on Roundway-down, near Devizes. In the north the earl of Newcastle headed the royalists, and lord Fairfax and his son sir Thomas, the parliamentarians.

Death of Hampden.

Essex having besieged and taken the town of Reading, advanced to Thame, within ten miles of Oxford. One evening prince Rupert secretly left that city with a part of his cavalry to beat up the enemy's quarters, as it was termed, that is, to fall on them unexpectedly in the towns and villages where they lay, for neither party had camps. The royalists had great success; but as they were returning with their booty and prisoners, they were attacked by a party of the enemy just as they were entering a lane, leading from a plain named Chalgrave-field. After a smart encounter they drove them off, and pursued their route to Oxford. This skirmish was made memorable by the death of the celebrated John Hampden. He had put himself at the head of a troop of horse to join in the pursuit of the prince, and in the action he received two bullets in the shoulder. He was conveyed to Essex's head-quarters at Thame, and after suffering for six days he expired. It was observed by the royalists that Hampden had mustered his tenantry on Chalgrave-field when he prepared to take up arms against the crown, and they regarded his mortal wound received on the same plain as a judgement from Heaven. Such decisions are, however, not to be approved of. Hampden, though he might be mistaken in his views, was a conscientious man, and he believed himself to be acting in the right, and for the true interest of his country.

Siege of Gloucester.

After this success, prince Rupert marched to the west, where he took the city of Bristol. As Gloucester was the only place of importance between that and Lancashire now held by the parliament, the king, instead of marching to London, where he might have concluded the war, resolved to lay siege to that city. When he had raised his standard on a hill within a moderate distance of the town, he sent in a trumpeter to offer pardon without any exception. He gave two hours for a reply, but "within less than that time," says Lord Clarendon, "together with the trumpeter, returned two citizens from the town, with lean, pale, sharp, and bad visages, and in such garb and carriage that at once made the most severe countenances merry, and the most cheerful hearts sad. The men, without any circumstances of duty or good manners, in a pert, shrill, undismayed accent, said they had brought an answer from the godly city of Gloucester to the king." The answer proved to be a refusal to obey him; the siege was therefore urged on, and the town was reduced to extremity, when Essex arrived with his army to its relief. The royal forces withdrew; but as Essex, on his return to London, came near to the town of Newbury in Berkshire, he found it occupied by the king, and saw that he could not, as he had hoped, reach London without fighting.

Battle of Newbury.

At six o'clock on the morning of the 20th of September, 1643, both armies engaged, and the contest lasted till it was terminated by the night. It is difficult to say to which side the victory properly belonged, but the next morning the royal army did not appear to renew the combat, and Essex having buried the dead, pursued his march to London. Rupert followed him with his cavalry, and made some attempts on his rear-guard; and the royalists placed a garrison in Reading as soon as he had left it.

In the battle of Newbury there fell on the side of the king the earls of Sunderland and Carnarvon; but the person whose loss was most felt and lamented was Lucius Cary, viscount Falkland. This nobleman had in the beginning been as zealous as any for the redress of abuses, but when he saw the lengths to which the parliament was going, and that the monarchy was actually in danger, he took the side of the crown. He expected that a decisive victory on the part of the king would have led to an accommodation; but seeing his hopes all baffled, he grew thoughtful and melancholy, and often after sitting long silent among his friends, he would utter the words " Peace, peace," in a sad tone, and declare that the thoughts of the war took his rest from him, and would shortly break his heart. On the morning of the battle he called for a clean shirt, saying, that if he was slain, they should not find his body in foul linen, for he had a strong persuasion that he should not outlive that day. He placed himself in the front rank of a regiment of horse commanded by lord Byron, and he received a wound of which he died.

In the following winter the celebrated John Pym died in London. He was buried with great state in Westminster-abbey, all the members of both houses attending the funeral.

Battle of Marston-Moor.

At the time when, after the battle of Edgehill, the parliament found themselves in danger of being overcome by the king, they sent sir Henry Vane the younger and some others to try to form an alliance with the Scots, and obtain their assistance. The Scots, though Charles had assented to their demands, and they had therefore nothing now to complain of, were so much allured by the prospect held out to them of seeing Presbytery, their favourite form of church government, established in England, that they readily agreed to aid the parliament; and a Scottish army, led by the earl of Leven, crossed the borders. Lord Newcastle, who had retired to York, was besieged in that city by the Scots and by the troops of sir Thomas Fairfax, and soon after the besiegers were joined by fourteen thousand men under the earl of Manchester and his lieutenant Oliver Cromwell.

Newcastle wrote to the king to say that if not relieved he must surrender, and Charles ordered prince Rupert, who was at the head of a large force, to proceed without delay to the relief of York. Rupert moved with his usual rapidity, and he soon appeared within view of that city with twenty thousand men. The besiegers retired at his approach, and he entered the town. Newcastle wished him to be content with this advantage, but Rupert had positive orders from the king to fight; and on the following day, the 2nd of July, 1644, the royal army advanced to where the enemy stood in order of battle on Marston-moor, about five miles from York. The engagement did not commence till seven o'clock in the evening. Rupert charged with his usual impetuosity at the head of his cavalry, and drove those opposed to him off the field; the royalist centre was equally successful; but Cromwell was victorious on the wing where he commanded, and he knew better than Rupert how to use his advantage. The evening, therefore, closed on the total defeat of the royalists, who retired, leaving fifteen hundred prisoners and all their baggage, artillery, and ammunition in the hands of the enemy. The total number of the slain of both parties was four thousand. Next day York surrendered; Newcastle and some others withdrew to the continent, and the royal cause was now hopeless in the north.

Second Battle of Newbury.

Meantime better success attended the army led by the king in person. He defeated sir William Waller at Cropredy Bridge, near Banbury, and he then pursued Essex into Cornwall, where he cooped him up so closely at Lestwithiel that he and his principal officers found it necessary to make their escape in a boat to Plymouth, leaving the army to its fate. The cavalry, by taking advantage of the darkness of the night, contrived to effect its escape, but the infantry was forced to surrender. As the king was on his return to his head quarters at Oxford, he found an army at Newbury prepared to give him battle. The engagement commenced at three o'clock in the afternoon of Sunday the 27th of October, and lasted till ten at night, without any decisive advantage on either side; and this battle ended the campaign.

Trial and Execution of Laud.

In the course of the following winter the trial of archbishop Laud, which had been going on for nearly a year, was brought to a conclusion. He was charged with an attempt to introduce arbitrary power, and to subvert the true religion established by law, and introduce popery and idolatry. Prynne, his inveterate foe, was the solicitor on the part of the commons, and he showed none of the magnanimity of a generous enemy. He seized all the archbishop's papers, even his private diary and his written defence, and he hunted out witnesses against him; and as Laud was informed, drilled them in their evidence. Yet even Prynne acknowledged that the primate "made as full, as gallant and pithy a defence, and spoke as much for himself, as was possible for the wit of man to invent." Finding that they could not convict him by the known law of the land, the party who sought his blood had recourse to a bill of attainder. This measure passed the commons rapidly, but as the lords demurred at it, on Christmas-day, which the puritans, in their enmity to the church, had converted into a day of "fasting and public humiliation," the pulpits in the city were all set at work; and such a fanatic spirit was excited among the people, that the lords gave way and passed the bill. The only favour that the archbishop could obtain was to have his sentence changed from hanging to beheading.

On the 10th of January, William Laud, archbishop of Canterbury, now in the 72nd year of his age, appeared on the scaffold on Tower-hill. His look was serene and cheerful; taking a verse from the epistle to the Hebrews for his text, he made a speech in form of a sermon to the people, explaining and justifying his conduct. The sun, which had been hidden all the morning, shone out and irradiated his placid countenance as he spoke, and the darkness returned when his head was stricken off, and continued for the rest of the day. The shedding of the blood of this now powerless old man was the most barbarous act committed by the parliament, but there is little doubt that it was done solely to gratify the Scots, who were his implacable enemies.

The New Model.

In consequence of the discord which prevailed among the commanding officers, and urged on by the secret machinations of some who were aiming at more extensive changes than had yet been made, the parliament now resolved to put their army on an entirely new footing. As a previous measure they passed what was termed the Self-denying Ordinance, by which all members of either house were required to lay down their civil and military offices. Essex, Manchester, and others therefore resigned their commands, and a New Model, as it was termed (the royalists nick-named it the New Noddle), of the army was formed, the chief command being given to Fairfax, with Cromwell for his lieutenant-general. The church was also new-modelled at the same time; the book of common prayer was abolished, and fines and other penalties were imposed on those who continued to use it. In its place was substituted a Directory for Public Worship. Presbytery took the place of episcopacy, or government by bishops, in the church; about two thousand clergymen were put out of their livings, some for immorality, others for attachment to the old constitution in church and state, and presbyterians were put in their place. A fifth, however, of the income of the parish was reserved for the support of the families of the ejected clergy.

Battle of Naseby.

When the New Model was completed, the war was resumed. The king was the first to take the field; he marched from Oxford at the head of ten thousand men to raise the siege of Chester. The enemy retired at his approach; he then advanced against the town of Leicester, which his troops stormed and pillaged. As he was on his way back to Oxford, the rear of his army was overtaken by the van of Fairfax's near a village named Naseby, which lies between Daventry* and Harborough, in Northamptonshire. On the following morning, the 14th of June, 1645, both sides stood prepared for action. The battle resembled that of Marston-moor in this respect, that prince Rupert, who, as usual, by his impetuous charge, drove those opposed to him off the field, as usual, by his imprudence in continuing the pursuit, lost the advantage of his success; while Cromwell, who commanded the cavalry on the enemy's right wing, when he had routed that on the left wing of the royalists, fell on the rear of their centre. This unexpected charge quite dismayed that body, which had hitherto combated with great steadiness, and they threw down their arms and called for quarter. One regiment, however, though twice charged, still resisted, till Fairfax, making one of his officers attack it in front, fell himself on it in the rear, and it then broke. Fairfax killed the ensign with his own hand, and seized the colours, and when the soldier to whom he gave them in charge afterwards boasted of the deed as his own, Fairfax mildly said, "Let him retain that honour; I have to-day acquired enough beside." As for the king, when he saw his infantry broken, he resolved to make one daring effort for his all; and he cried out to his guard and those horsemen who had gathered about him, " One charge more, and we recover the day;" but they had no heart to renew the combat, and seeing the battle lost beyond recovery, he rode off the field. The royalists had only four or five hundred men slain; but they lost all their artillery and ammunition, and left four thousand five hundred prisoners in the hands of the enemy.

End of the War.

The battle of Naseby, in effect, ended the civil war, which had lasted for three years. Bristol, Exeter, and other towns surrendered; the noblemen and gentlemen,

---

* Usually pronounced Daintry.

who had converted their mansions into fortresses, and maintained them for the king, seeing further resistance useless, opened their gates to the parliamentary commanders. Among these royalists, two catholic noblemen, the marquesses of Winchester and Worcester, and a French lady, the countess of Derby, were the most distinguished. The first held out, in his mansion of Basing-house, near Winchester, all through the war; Ragland-castle, the stately mansion of the second, was one of the very last to surrender. Its noble owner, who had passed his seventieth year, ventured to defend it against Fairfax and five thousand men. The countess of Derby, a daughter of the noble house of La Tremouille, stoutly maintained Latham-house, in Lancashire, against many parliamentary officers. To the credit of the parliament, they used their victory with great moderation, and no superfluous blood was shed. Fairfax was one of the mildest of men, and Cromwell was far from being cruel.

Charles and the Scots.

The unhappy king, after wandering about in various parts with the troops which still remained with him, at length shut himself up in Oxford. When the parliamentary forces began to close in the town, he saw that he had only to choose between surrender and flight, and he finally resolved on the latter. The Scottish army was then lying before the town of Newark-on-Trent; the king had been negotiating with its commanders through the French ambassador, Montreuil, and they had expressed themselves willing to receive him in their camp, providing it could be done without offending the parliament. Charles therefore resolved, as the lesser of evils, to commit himself to them, and on the night of the 27th of April, 1646, he quitted Oxford. In order to disguise himself he cut off his long lock of hair and pointed beard, and rode with a portmanteau behind him as the servant of his faithful follower Ashburnham. A clergyman named Hudson, who was well acquainted with the country, acted as their guide. It would seem that the king had afterwards adopted the judicious course of going to London and throwing himself on the sympathies of the more generous English people, instead of trusting himself to the cold calculating Scots, for he went so near to London as Harrow-on-the-hill; but he then unfortunately resumed his original purpose, and rode to St. Albans, where, finding that his escape in the dress of a servant was known, he assumed that of a clergyman. When he drew near to the Scottish camp he halted, and sent Hudson on to Montreuil, who, though he had now seen reason to distrust the Scots, gave it as his opinion that it were best for the king to put himself into their hands. Charles accordingly came to his residence, and after dinner Montreuil conducted him to Leven's head quarters. Leven, when he saw the king, raised his hands in real or affected surprise, but he treated him with great respect. When, however, Charles, to try if he was really free, went to give the word to the guard, Leven said, "I am the older soldier, sir; your majesty had better leave that office to me," thus giving the king to understand that he was in effect a prisoner.

The Scots resolved to get away with their royal prize as fast as they could, and having prevailed on the king to order the governor of Newark to surrender, they set out homewards. So rapid was their march that on the ninth day the parliament had information of their arrival at Newcastle-on-Tyne. Had the Scots remained in the heart of England, they would probably have been compelled to surrender the king; but as they had gotten so near home, there only remained the way of negotiation. As they claimed a large sum of money as arrears of pay, etc., the present was selected as the best time for settling the account; and they thus obtained a much larger sum than they would have got under other circumstances. The payment of this money being connected with the surrender of the king, the Scots have been charged with the base act of bartering the liberty and life of their sovereign for lucre; but the charge is not just; they had no alternative but war, and they acted under the advice of his friends in the English parliament.

Charles was accordingly delivered up to the parliamentary commissioners, by whom he was conducted to Holdenby, or Holmby-house, near Althorpe, in Northamptonshire. He quitted the Scots without reluctance, for though respectful, they had been harsh, and they wearied him with disputes on the subject of church-government. We are told, that one Sunday, one of their ministers having preached before him in what they termed bold, that is, disrespectful terms, concluded his sermon by calling for the fifty-second psalm, which began thus:

> Why dost thou, tyrant, boast thyself
> Thy wicked works to praise?

The king instantly stood up, and called for the fifty-sixth psalm, beginning with

> Have mercy on me, Lord, I pray,
> For men would me devour.

The people took no heed of the minister, but sang the psalm for which the king had called.

Seizure of the King by the Army.

At Holmby, Charles was treated with respect, but he was not permitted to have any of his episcopal chaplains with him, and his attendants were selected by the parliament. Among other indulgences, he was allowed to ride about the country, and to go over to Althorpe to take the recreation of bowling, an exercise in which he delighted, in the bowling-green of that place. Here, one day, a circumstance occurred which had a most important effect on his future fate. To explain it we must take a slight view of the condition of the parliament and the army.

The presbyterians, in their eagerness to pull down the

episcopal church and to reduce the power of the crown, forgot that, in the license which they claimed for private judgement in religion and politics, others might come to different conclusions from themselves. The consequence was, that while *they* wished a very limited monarchy, with a church governed by synods and assemblies of the clergy, instead of bishops, a very numerous party were for abolishing royalty altogether, and for having every church or congregation perfectly independent of all others, whence they derived their name of Independents. The principal leaders of this party were Oliver Cromwell and his son-in-law Ireton; and in forming the New Model, care had been taken that most of the soldiers should be of it. The parliament saw the danger, and were anxious to disband the army as soon as possible; but neither soldiers nor officers, many of whom had risen from very low stations in society, were willing to return to their former humble occupation, and their leaders had formed the idea of keeping the army up, and governing the country by means of it. The troops, therefore, refused to disband, under the pretext of the arrears of their pay not being discharged; and they constructed a parliament of their own, the superior officers forming a council, with two Agitators, as they were named, chosen by each troop and company to form a lower house and communicate with the privates. The parliament resolved to act with vigour, and orders were sent to the general to disband the troops without further delay. Cromwell and his party then had recourse to a decisive measure.

As the king was one day playing at bowls on the green of Althorpe, a man in the uniform of Fairfax's regiment was observed among the spectators. The replies which he gave to the commander of the king's guard excited suspicion. The king was therefore hurried back to Holmby, and the guards were doubled. About two in the morning the stranger, who proved to be cornet Joice (formerly a tailor), appeared with a party of horse before the gates.

The guards received the new-comers as brethren; they remained all day engaged in consultation, and at ten o'clock at night Joice entered the king's apartment, his hat in one hand, a pistol in the other. He behaved, however, with much civility, and satisfied the king with respect to the purpose for which he had come. He then withdrew.

At six o'clock next morning Joice drew up his men before the door, and required the king to set out with him for the army. Charles, standing on the steps, asked him if he had a written commission for that purpose from the general; Joice pointed to his men, and said, " There is my commission." The king smiled and said, " I never before read such a commission; but it is written in characters fair and legible enough; a company of as handsome, proper gentlemen as I have seen a long while." Joice gave him his choice of residences; he selected Newmarket; and he was allowed the attendance of his own servants. He then mounted his horse with a cheerful air, and rode away with the party.

The King with the Army.

The treatment of the king by the army was widely different from what he had experienced at the hands of either the Scots or the parliament. He received every indulgence; he was allowed the attendance of his episcopal chaplains; his friends had free access to him; as he moved about with the army, their marches were so arranged as to permit of his stopping at the houses of the nobility, by whom he was splendidly entertained. The parliament had always rudely refused to gratify him with the sight of his children, who were kept at Sion-house under the charge of the earl of Northumberland; but now, by a letter from Fairfax, the earl was directed to take them down to Cavesham*-house, near Reading, where the king was then residing, and they remained for two days with their father.

* Pronounced Cassham.

Cromwell, who was a man of kindly feelings, was present at their first meeting, and he wept copiously as he described it, saying it was the tenderest sight that ever his eyes beheld.

In fact, Charles, if content to be a limited and happy monarch, like his successors of the house of Brunswick, had it now in his power to be such. The army required the aid of the royal authority in their present contest with the parliament. The brave but guileless Fairfax was merely a puppet in the hands of Cromwell and Ireton, and there is no reason to doubt of the sincerity of these men in their present dealings with the king. Proposals of a very advantageous nature were now made to him by them in the name of the army, on his acceptance of which he would have been restored to his dignity. But he had got a notion that nothing could be arranged without him, and that whatever side he joined must have the superiority; and he hoped that, by playing the Scots, the parliament and the army against each other, he would be able to regain his despotic power. He therefore positively refused to assent to the proposals. He would fain have afterwards retracted or softened this refusal; but the army, meantime, had reduced the parliament, and stood less in need of the king. He was removed to Oatlands, and thence to Hampton-court, where Cromwell and Ireton still continued in treaty with him, and he was, if possible, treated with more indulgence than ever, being merely required to give a promise that he would not attempt an escape.

Cromwell and Ireton soon, however, found it necessary to change their conduct. The republican party in the parliament had grown suspicious of them, and a new party had sprung up in the army named Levellers, from their principle that all distinctions between man and man should be *levelled*. The idea of a king was of course odious to these men, and they openly menaced Cromwell and Ireton. Perhaps, however, all this would not have turned them from their purpose, had they not ascertained that the king was insincere in his dealings with them. They are said to have discovered this fact in the following manner. While they were in treaty with the king, they learned from one of those about him who was in their pay that their doom was fixed, in a letter to the queen, which was sewed up in the skirt of a saddle that was to be taken to the Blue Boar in Holborn, to be sent to Dover. Cromwell and Ireton then disguised themselves as common troopers, and going to that inn, sat there drinking till the men whom they expected arrived. They then took and ripped up the skirt of the saddle, and they found a letter in which the king said that " he should know in due time how to deal with the rogues, who, instead of a silken garter, should be fitted in due time with a hempen cord." The accuracy of this story has been disputed, but there can be no doubt that Cromwell had sufficient evidence of the king's insincerity.

The King's Flight.

It is also said that Cromwell had pledged his word to the king to give him warning if his life should be in any danger, and that now discovering that the levellers intended seizing him, he wrote to inform colonel Whalley, in whose charge he was at Hampton-court. The colonel showed the letter to the king, who resolved at once on attempting an escape, and that very night he secretly left Hampton-court, accompanied by a gentleman named Legge, having left on his table a letter to the parliament. They crossed the river at Thames-Ditton, where they found Ashburnham and sir John Berkeley waiting with horses. They rode into Hampshire, and stopped at Tichfield-house, a mansion of Lord Southampton's, opposite the Isle of Wight. The king remained there with Legge, while Berkeley and Ashburnham went over to the isle to inform the parliamentary governor, colonel Hammond, who was nephew to one of the royal chaplains, that it was the king's intention to seek his protection. Hammond turned pale at the intelligence, and would pledge himself to nothing more than to act as a man of honour. With this Ashburnham declared himself satisfied. It was then proposed that one of them should remain while the other went to fetch the king, but Hammond determined to go with them himself, and at Cowes, where they embarked, he made an officer named Baskett also get into the boat. When they came to Tichfield Ashburnham went up to apprise the king. "What!" cried Charles, striking his breast, "have you brought Hammond with you? Oh, Jack! you have undone me, for I am by this means made fast from stirring. The governor will keep me a prisoner." He then told him that having changed his mind he had sent to Southampton for a vessel. Ashburnham then offered to *secure,* i. e. murder, Hammond and Baskett. Charles walked up and down the room weighing the proposal. "I understand you well enough," said he; "but the world would not excuse me. Should I follow that counsel it would be believed that Hammond had ventured his life for me, and that I had unworthily taken it from him. It is too late to think of any thing but going through the way you have forced upon me, and so leave the issue to God." Ashburnham burst into tears. Hammond and Baskett were called up and kissed the royal hand, and Charles then passed over to the island, where he took up his abode in Carisbrooke castle. He was treated with respect, and allowed to ride about the island as he pleased.

Second Civil War.

At Carisbrooke the king was waited on by commissioners from the Scots and the parliament, and he formed a secret treaty with the former, by which they engaged to take arms in his cause, and it was arranged that the royalists should, at the same time, rise in various parts to co-operate with them. But nothing could be more unfortunate than the issue of this plan. The bigoted Scottish clergy, when they found that the king would not agree to set up their idol of presbytery, without even toleration for any other form, did all in their power to impede the levies, and the marquess of Hamilton, who commanded the Scottish army which invaded England, though brave, was no general. His troops were therefore put to flight by Cromwell, and himself was made a prisoner. The English royalists were equally unsuccessful. They were everywhere overcome, and a body of them, commanded by lords Norwich, Capel, and others, were closely besieged by Fairfax in the town of Colchester in Essex. Though the town was only defended by a low rampart of earth, they held out gallantly for three months. At length, when they had eaten not merely the horses, but all the dogs and cats in the place, they were forced to surrender at discretion, quarter being secured to the privates. Three of the officers, sir Charles Lucas, sir George Lisle, and sir Bernard Gascoigne, were condemned to instant death. Lucas was the first shot: when he fell Lisle ran up and kissed his dead body; he then desired the soldiers to draw nearer. "I'll warrant you, sir," said one of them, "we'll hit you." "Friends," he replied with a smile, "I have been nearer you when you have missed me." They fired, and he fell dead. Gascoigne was respited, as it appeared that he was an Italian by birth.

Pride's Purge.—Seizure of the King.

The king was meantime in treaty with the commissioners of the parliament. Finding that the army party were getting stronger every day, and that in their petitions to the commons the soldiers now spoke openly of bringing him to trial, he at length submitted to all the demands made on him. But he had delayed too long; when on the return of the commissioners a majority of the commons voted his concessions to be sufficient grounds for settling the peace of the kingdom, the army-party resolved to have recourse to other measures. Next morning two regiments, one of horse and another of foot, came down to the house, and colonel Pride (formerly a drayman) took his station in the lobby with a list of names in his hand, and as the persons who bore those names were pointed out to him, he seized them and sent them away prisoners. By this means the house was reduced to about fifty members, the mere tools of the army. They were nicknamed the Rump, and the process by which the house was reduced was called Pride's Purge.

The army had the king also in their hands. At midnight on the night of the day following that of the departure of the commissioners, a party of horse and foot arrived at Carisbrooke-castle, and at five in the morning the king was awakened by a summons to depart. He was then conveyed to Hurst-castle, which stood on a rock in the sea joined to the coast of Hampshire by a causeway two miles in length. About three weeks after he was awakened by the sound of the falling of the drawbridge, and the trampling of horses. On inquiring the cause he learned that colonel Harrison was arrived. He became disturbed, for he had been told that Harrison had intended to assassinate him, and the present place seemed suited to such a deed of darkness. But he was mistaken, for Harrison, though one of the greatest fanatics of the time, was incapable of baseness or treachery, and when the king saw his fine open countenance and manly soldierly bearing, he became convinced of his error. He was conducted by Harrison to Windsor, where he was to remain till the parliament, or rather the army, should have decided his fate.

Trial of the King.

The decision was soon made; the bold men who now, as the heads of the army, wielded the power of the state, resolved on the unexampled deed of bringing their sovereign to trial as a criminal, and thus to take on themselves at once the office of judge and accuser. The commons, at their mandate, passed an ordinance, as it was termed, for the trial of the king, and when the remnant of the house of lords, which still sat, ventured to reject it, the Rump, having unblushingly voted itself to be the supreme authority of the nation, and that whatever it enacted was law, without the concurrence of king or lords, passed the ordinance and appointed one hundred and thirty-five persons to form a High Court of Justice for the trial of the king. Cromwell and all the principal officers of the army were members of this court; its president was a lawyer of some eminence named Bradshaw.

From the time when the army had resolved to bring the king to trial they ceased to treat him with respect. He no longer saw the customary ceremony observed toward him, even his meat being brought to table uncovered, and by the hands of the rude soldiery. It is surprising how deeply this circumstance mortified him; yet still he was cheerful, for he could not believe what he was told of the intention of the army to bring him to trial. At length he was convinced of his error when he found himself conveyed to London, in order to appear as a criminal before his own subjects.

On Saturday the 20th of January, 1649, commenced in Westminster-hall that solemn mockery of justice called the trial of the king. At the upper end, in a chair covered with crimson velvet, sat John Bradshaw, the president of the court, wearing a broad-brimmed beaver hat, lined for security with plates of iron; before him stood a desk and velvet cushion. At a table below him, covered with a rich Turkey carpet, on which lay the mace and sword of state, sat the two clerks of the court. On side-benches, covered with scarlet cloth, sat the members of the court, about seventy in number, in their best habits, and with their hats on their heads. Within the bar, and opposite to that of the president, was placed a seat, covered with crimson velvet, for the illustrious prisoner. The galleries and the lower part of the hall were filled with spectators.

The king was brought by water from Whitehall, and it is deserving of notice that the watermen insisted on rowing him bareheaded. He was conducted into court by an armed guard, and led to his seat by the sergeant-at-arms. He looked steadily round the court and then sat down; he rose again, and took another view of the court and the spectators. Bradshaw then addressed him, and Cook, one of the counsellors of the court, accused him of high-treason and misdemeanors, and desired the charge to be read out. At the words *tyrant, traitor, murderer*, and such like, with which it was plentifully garnished, the king was observed frequently to smile. Bradshaw then informed him that the court expected him to reply to the charge. Charles asked by what power he was called thither. " I would know," said he, " by what lawful authority—there are many unlawful authorities, thieves and robbers on the highway—I was brought from the Isle of Wight, and carried from place to place." Bradshaw told him that the authority was that of the people of England, of whom he was *elected* king. " I deny that," replied the king; " England never was an elective kingdom." " I see no house of lords here," added he, " that should constitute a parliament; and the king, too, should have been here." " We are satisfied with our authority that are your judges," replied Bradshaw, " and it is upon God's authority and the kingdom's." He then adjourned the court till Monday.

On Monday and Tuesday the king was again brought before the court, but he persisted in his denial of its authority to try him. The three following days were occupied in hearing evidence, in proof of his having been in arms at Edgehill, Naseby, and elsewhere. On Saturday the court held its final sitting. As the king passed up the hall his ears were assailed by a cry of "Justice! justice! Execution! execution!" raised by some soldiers and a part of the rabble. He told the president that he would waive all debate, which he now saw to be useless, as an *ugly* sentence he believed would pass on him; but he desired to be heard by the lords and commons on a matter which concerned the peace of the kingdom. The court retired to consult; in about an hour it returned and gave a refusal. The king then declared that he had nothing more to say, and Bradshaw, as was his custom, having made a long speech, concluded by passing sentence of death. All the members of the court rose to signify their assent. "Will you hear me a word, sir?" said the king. "Sir, you are not to be heard after the sentence," replied Bradshaw. "No, sir." "No, sir, by your favour, sir," said the stern president. "Guards, withdraw your prisoner." "I may speak after the sentence by your favour, sir," said the king, in hurried, agitated accents: "I may speak after sentence is over! By your favour, hold! The sentence, sir! I say, sir! I do—I am not suffered to speak. Expect what justice other people will have." As he was led away he again heard the cry of "Justice! Execution!" and various insults were offered to him. One soldier cried out, "God bless you, sir;" his officer struck him with his cane. "The punishment methinks exceeds the offence," remarked the king. He afterwards asked one of his attendants if he had taken notice of the cry for justice. He replied that he had, and wondered at it. "So did not I," said the king, "for I am well assured the soldiers bear no malice to me. The cry was no doubt given by their officers, for whom the soldiers would do the like were there occasion."

On the first day of the trial, when the name of Fairfax, as a member of the court, was called, a female voice from one of the galleries replied, "He has more wit than to be here." When the charge was made in the name of the commons and people of England, the same voice exclaimed, "It is a lie! not a quarter of the people! Oliver Cromwell is a rogue and traitor." The speaker, who was masked, was the lady Fairfax, a rigid presbyterian. Colonel Axtell ordered his men to fire into the gallery, and the lady then withdrew. The following incident also occurred. As the king was leaning on his cane the silver head fell off it and rolled on the ground, and he was obliged to stoop and pick it up himself. The circumstance seemed ominous, and the king afterwards owned that it made a great impression on him at the time.

Execution of the King.

The king was taken back to Whitehall, where he remained till Monday. As the Independents, who were now the party in power, had none of the narrow bigotry of the Presbyterians, they made no objection to his request of having bishop Juxon to attend him and give him the sacrament. On Monday he was removed to St. James's, from a motive of humanity, as it would appear, that he might not be disturbed by the noise of the workmen employed in setting up the scaffold opposite Whitehall, the place appointed for the execution. His two young children, the duke of Gloucester and the princess Elizabeth, were brought to him from Sion-house, and his interview with them was of the tenderest nature. He gave them a few presents, and charged the princess, who was the elder, to assure her mother of his unceasing affection. When they had remained with him for some time, he dismissed them, and employed himself in his devotions. He declined seeing his nephew and some noblemen who came to take their last leave of him.

He went to bed and slept for four hours. About two hours before dawn he awoke, and drawing the curtains observed by a light which was burning in the room that his attendant Herbert's rest was disturbed. He awoke him, and inquired the cause. Herbert said that he had dreamt that archbishop Laud had entered the room and knelt before the king, that they conversed, the king looked pensive, Laud sighed, and as he retired fell flat on the ground. "It is very remarkable," said Charles; "but he is dead; had we now conferred together, 'tis very likely—albeit I loved him well—I should have said something to him which might have occasioned his sigh." He then said that he would rise, "for he had a great work to do that day."

Herbert could not avoid trembling as he combed his hair. "Though it be not long to stand on my shoulders," said the king, "take the same pains with it as you were wont to do. Herbert, this is my second marriage-day. I would be as trim as may be." He put on a second shirt; "for," said he, "the season is sharp, and probably may make me shake, which some will imagine proceeds from fear. I would have no such imputation. I fear not death. Death is not terrible to me. I bless my God I am prepared; let the rogues come." When dressed he spent an hour alone with the bishop.

At ten o'clock (it was Tuesday the 30th of January) colonel Hacker announced that it was time to set out for Whitehall. Charles made no delay; he went on foot through the park at his usual quick pace, calling out to the guard, "March on apace!" He was conducted to his own bed-chamber at Whitehall. A repast had been prepared, but as he had received the sacrament, he declined taking any more food in this world. At the suggestion of the bishop, however, he ate about noon half a manchet and drank a glass of claret. Soon after Hacker came with the warrant and called for the king. Charles rose and proceeded with the bishop through the long gallery, which was lined with soldiers, whose faces testified their respect and sorrow. Through the central window of the banqueting-house (a building which still remains) he stepped out on the scaffold. It was hung with black; two executioners in masks stood on it; regiments of horse and foot were ranged beneath; the streets were thronged with anxious spectators. Charles looked toward St. James's with a smile; he then gazed earnestly at the block, and asked "if there were no place higher?"

He addressed himself to those about him on the scaffold, proving by reference to dates and documents that it was the parliament and not he that began the war. He concluded by saying that if he would have consented to have everything changed at the will of the army, he needed not to have come thither, and that therefore he was the *martyr of the people.* Seeing some one touch the axe he stopped, and said, "Hurt not the axe, that may hurt me;" and when another approached it he cried, "Take heed of the axe! take heed of the axe!" He said to the executioner, "I shall say but very short prayers, and then thrust out my hands." Taking then a white satin nightcap from the bishop, he put his hair up under it, saying, "I have a good cause and a gracious God on my side." "There is but one stage more," said the prelate; "this stage is turbulent and troublesome; it is a short one; but you may consider it will soon carry you a very great way; it will carry you from earth to heaven, and there you shall find a great deal of cordial joy and comfort." "I go," replied the king, "from a corruptible to an incorruptible crown, where no disturbance can be." "You are exchanged," said the bishop, "from a temporal to an eternal crown, a good exchange." The king gave his cloak and George to the bishop, saying *Remember.* He knelt down, gave the sign, and one blow of the axe terminated his earthly existence. A deep groan arose from the multitude, and many ran to dip their handkerchiefs in his blood; but two troops of horse were set in motion to clear the streets. The royal corpse, after being embalmed, was sent to Windsor, and placed in the vault which contained the remains of Henry VIII. and Jane Seymour.

Thus was perpetrated this judicial murder, for such it must be called, as those who were the agents in it never for a moment entertained the idea of letting the prisoner establish his innocence. Their only object was to put him to death under forms of law. "I tell you," said Cromwell to Algernon Sidney, long before the trial began, "I tell you we will cut off his head with the crown on it." At the same time many of the judges, and perhaps Cromwell himself, were convinced that they were acting right, and that they really possessed the power which they assumed. Thus colonel Hutchinson, who was a most upright and conscientious man, most earnestly, as we are informed by his admirable wife, sought counsel of the Lord in prayer, and finding no check, acted as a judge, condemned his sovereign to death, and signed the warrant for his execution without scruple. We should deal charitably with both the king and the parliament, and believe that, even in the actions which we are most disposed to reprehend, they may have had the sanction of conscience. Instead of becoming partisans of either party, and supposing all to be right on one side, and nothing to be right on the other, we should make allowance for the faults of both, and view in the civil war an event which, under Providence, has been conducive to our obtaining the liberty which we now possess.

CHAPTER III.

THE COMMONWEALTH.

Abolition of the Monarchy.

IMMEDIATELY after the execution of the king the commons voted the house of peers to be useless and dangerous, and the office of king to be unnecessary, burdensome and dangerous to liberty. Both were therefore declared to be abolished, and a council of state was appointed to administer the government. At the same time a high court of justice (for the rulers feared to trust juries) sat upon the duke of Hamilton, lords Capel and Holland, and other royalists, and as a matter of course condemned them to be beheaded. They all met their fate with courage, especially lord Capel, who died, we are told, "like a stout Roman."

But the royal cause was not yet hopeless; the royalists were numerous in England, the presbyterians abhorred the execution of the king, and the Scots were not willing that their ancient line of monarchy should be abolished by the vote of a fragment of the English parliament; as soon, therefore, as they heard of the execution of the king, they proclaimed his eldest son as Charles II., and they sent to invite that prince, who was residing in Holland, to come over to Scotland. But as they insisted on his taking the covenant, that is, condemning episcopacy and swearing to uphold presbytery, he avoided for an entire year to yield to their demands.

The Marquess of Montrose.

Meantime an attempt was made to replace the royal authority on its old footing in Scotland. There was a nobleman, Graham, marquess of Montrose, who in the late reign had headed the royalists in Scotland, where he had gained several surprising victories; but when the king put himself into the hands of the Scots, Montrose, by his orders, laid down his arms, and retired to the continent. He was now in Holland, and he resolved to make another attempt on Scotland. Having collected about six hundred men he sailed from Hamburgh; he stopped at the Orkney isles and forced a part of the inhabitants to join him, and thus landed with about fourteen hundred men on the north coast of Scotland. He advanced into Fifeshire, where he was attacked by a party of three hundred horse; the unwarlike islanders instantly threw down their arms and fled, and Montrose only escaped by swimming across a river in the dress of a peasant. He was, however, betrayed a few days after by a person with whom he had sought refuge, and was conducted to Edinburgh. As he had sullied his former victories with great cruelty, and the Scots are not a very forgiving people, every kind of insult was now heaped upon him. The magistrates met him at the gates and caused him to be placed, bareheaded, with his arms tied behind his back, on a high seat in a cart, which was led by the executioner to the common jail. His officers were made to walk two and two before the cart. Two days after he was brought up to receive sentence of death, and he was condemned to be hung on a gallows thirty feet high; his head to be fixed on a spike in Edinburgh, and his limbs to be set up in Glasgow and other towns. He heard the sentence with an unmoved countenance. He said that he was prouder to have his head on the prison-walls than his picture in the king's bed-chamber, and that he wished he had flesh enough to be dispersed through Christendom to attest his loyalty. He appeared on the scaffold in a splendid dress, and when the executioner, as directed, hung round his neck a book which had been written of his exploits, he smiled at the impotent malice, and said he wore it with more pride than the garter.

Charles in Scotland.—Battle of Dunbar.

When Charles heard of the failure of Montrose, he no longer hesitated to take the covenant, and in little more than a month after the death of that nobleman he landed in Scotland. But he soon found that he was to be a mere pageant of royalty, and to him who was a gay licentious youth, nothing could be less endurable than the long prayers, long sermons, rigid fasts, and strict sabbaths of the despotic clergy, and their invectives against the iniquity of his father's house, and the idolatry of his mother, must have grated on his natural feelings. Within a month, however, the appearance of an English army on the borders, gave all parties more serious matters to think of.

The English parliament were resolved, as they had abolished royalty among themselves, not to permit it to exist in Scotland, and they prepared to march an army into that country. As Fairfax scrupled to draw his sword against presbyterians, the chief command was given to Oliver Cromwell. This able general had been appointed to the government of Ireland, where he had reduced royalists and catholics alike, and had brought nearly the whole of the island under the rule of the parliament, when he was recalled on account of the affairs of Scotland. As soon as he was appointed to the command, he set out for the north, and he crossed the Tweed at the head of a veteran army of sixteen thousand men. He found the country thence to Edinburgh lying waste and deserted, the most monstrous falsehoods respecting his barbarity in Ireland having been circulated by the government, to make the people abandon their dwellings. The Scottish army, commanded by David Lesley, a cautious, prudent officer, was posted behind a strong entrenchment at Edinburgh, and it was his plan, as his troops were only raw levies, to give the invaders no opportunity of fighting, and thus to starve them out of the country. This plan bid fair to succeed, for sickness soon began to spread in the English army, and Cromwell found it necessary to proceed to the coast in order to put the sick on board of his ships. He then moved southwards to Dunbar, still cautiously followed by Lesley, who now occupied the heights of Lammermoor, near that town. His Fabian policy would have proved completely successful were it not for the arrogant presumption of the clergy and the other civilians, who insisted on his giving battle lest the enemy should escape. Cromwell and his officers had been seeking the Lord, as it was termed, in prayer, and as they were walking, after this exercise, in lord Roxburgh's gardens, and viewing the Scottish camp with their glasses, Cromwell observing in it a great motion, cried, "God is delivering them into our hands; they are coming down to us." He was right; the Scots descended during the night, which was rainy and stormy, and in the morning of the 3rd of September, 1650, wet and weary, they were fallen on by the English troops. Their cavalry, after a brief but gallant resistance, were overcome; the foot then threw down their arms and fled, all but two regiments, who bravely perished where they stood. Their loss was three thousand slain and ten thousand prisoners, with all their ammunition and ordnance. Edinburgh opened her gates, and all Scotland south of the Forth submitted to the English.

The Start.

The clergy had not permitted Charles to be with t army, and he therefore had not been present at the battle of Dunbar. Anything was preferable in his eyes to the state of restraint in which he was held, and he planned an escape to the royalists in the Highlands. Accordingly, one afternoon, he rode out of Perth, where he then was, under the pretence of hawking, and never stopped till he reached a lone house in the Highlands, where his friends were to meet him; but only a few came, and he was persuaded to return by the officer sent in pursuit of him. This Start, as it was called, was however of use to him, as it caused him to be treated with more consideration. On the following New-year's day he was solemnly crowned at Scone, after he had sworn on his knees to all that the clergy required of him.

Another army had meantime been collected; the passes of the Forth were secured, and the troops were placed in a strong position near Stirling. But Cromwell having collected a fleet of boats, passed his army over, and reduced the whole of Fifeshire, and cut off the supplies from the Scottish army, which must now either starve, disband or fight, with the certainty of defeat. In this state of things the king resolved on the bold expedient of a march into England, and leaving Stirling at the head of fourteen thousand men, he set out for the borders.

Battle of Worcester.

Charles entered England at Carlisle. He marched rapidly, and in three weeks from the time of his leaving Stirling he reached the city of Worcester. Six days after Cromwell arrived at the head of thirty thousand men, regular troops and militia. On the 3rd of September, the day of the battle of Dunbar, in the preceding year, he made a general attack on the royalists. Having passed a part of his troops over the Severn, on which Worcester stands, he attacked the Scots who were on the right bank of the river, and drove them back into the town. The same was the fate of the Scots who were posted on the other side of the city. Cromwell then stormed a fortress named Fort Royal, put its garrison of fifteen hundred men to the sword, and turned its guns on the town, which the royalists were forced to abandon. The Scots had fought gallantly. "This has been," said Cromwell in his despatch, "a very glorious mercy, and as stiff a contest for four or five hours as ever I have seen." There fell of the royalists three thousand, of the victors only two hundred men; but as their speech betrayed the Scots, and the whole country rose against them, the number of the prisoners amounted to ten thousand; of whom fifteen hundred were given to the Guinea merchants to employ as slaves in the gold mines of Africa, and nearly all the rest were sent as slaves to America and Barbadoes. In this manner did the parliament, treading in the steps of the ancient Greeks and Romans, venture to treat the free-born soldiers of an independent nation. Surely kings are not the only tyrants. Of the noblemen and gentlemen who were made prisoners, the earl of Derby and two others were tried by court-martial and put to death; the others, English and Scots, were kept in prison.

Escape of Charles.

Charles, who had shown no want of courage in the battle, left Worcester with the Scottish horse. During the night he separated from them, and was conducted to Whiteladies, a house belonging to a catholic gentleman of the name of Gifford. He then cut off his hair, and putting on the coarse threadbare clothes of a peasant, went out next morning with a bill in his hand as a wood-cutter, in the company of four brothers, labouring men, named Penderel. While the others remained on the watch one of them conducted the king into the thickest part of the wood, and as the day was wet and stormy, and Charles was fatigued with his exertions on the preceding day, Penderel spread a blanket for him under a tree. Some time after Penderel's sister came with food for the fugitive: Charles was startled at the sight of her, but she assured him that she would die sooner than betray him; and her venerable mother, who came soon after to see him, fell on her knees and blessed God for having chosen *her* sons to save the life of their king.

About nine in the evening, the king, whose intention it was to get into Wales, set out with one of the Penderels for Madeley, the house of another catholic gentleman near the Severn. It was midnight when they reached it; they lay concealed all the next day behind the hay in a barn, while their host sent to examine the river. But all the bridges were guarded, and all the boats secured, so they thought it best to go back to Boscobel, another of Gifford's houses. Here the king met with colonel Careless, a catholic loyalist; and as the soldiers were very numerous about there, they both concealed themselves all the following day in the dense foliage of an oak-tree (afterwards named the Royal Oak), which stood close to the footpath in a meadow in the centre of the wood, whence they could frequently discern the red coats of the soldiers as they passed through the trees. In the night they returned to the house, where they remained all the next day, which was Sunday. Charles there received a message from lord Wilmot, requesting him to meet him at Moseley, the house of a Mr. Whitegrave. As his feet had been cut and blistered by the walk to and from Madeley, he rode to Moseley on horseback, attended by the Penderels, all armed. Here a new plan was devised. The daughter of Mr. Lane of Bentley, a protestant gentleman, had obtained a pass to go and visit her relation, Mrs. Norton, who lived near Bristol, and it was proposed that the king should ride on the horse before her as her servant. To this he readily consented, and equipped in a suit of grey cloth, he mounted before Miss Lane; her cousin, Mr. Lassells, rode beside them, and on the fourth day they reached Mr. Norton's in safety. As for Wilmot, he rode boldly with a hawk on his fist and dogs at his heels, and no one gave him any trouble.

Miss Lane pretending that her servant was unwell, obtained a separate apartment for him, in order that he might not be exposed to the risk of discovery. But the butler, who had lived in the palace at Richmond, knew the king as soon as he saw him. Charles, when informed of this, resolved to confide in him, and the butler proved honest, and also managed to procure him a secret interview with Wilmot, who was in the neighbourhood. As it appeared that no vessel could be procured at Bristol, it was agreed that they should go to colonel Windham's, at Trent in Dorset, and a letter, stating that her father was dangerously ill, was handed to Miss Lane, in order to furnish a pretext for their departure. They therefore left Mr. Norton's the following day, and parting with Miss Lane and her cousin on the road, the king and Wilmot reached Trent in safety.

A vessel was hired at Lyme to carry a gentleman and his servant to France, and in the evening they went down, Charles riding before a young lady to Charmouth, where they were to be taken on board; but no vessel came, for the master's wife suspecting he was on some service of danger, would not let him stir out of his house. While Wilmot went to Lyme to learn the cause of the disappointment, the rest of the party rode to Bridport, which they found full of soldiers. Charles led the horses through them into the inn-yard, rudely pushing them out of his way. But here the hostler claimed acquaintance with him, saying that he knew him in the service of a Mr. Potter at Exeter, in whose house Charles had really at one time lodged. Taking advantage of the confusion in the hostler's memory, he quickly replied, "True, I did live with him; but I have no time now; we will renew our acquaintance over a pot of beer when I return to London."

When Wilmot returned the party rode back to Trent,

where the king remained for a fortnight. He then removed to the house of a lady named Hyde, who lived near Salisbury. He stayed there for five days, during which time one colonel Gunter managed, by means of a merchant named Mansell, to agree with Tattershall, the master of a collier which was lying at Shoreham, in Sussex, to carry two gentlemen to France. Charles accordingly rode over to the adjoining fishing village of Brighthelmstone, (how altered now as Brighton!) where he sat down to supper with his friends, and Mansell and Tattershall. The last, who had seen him before, knew him at once, and taking Mansell aside, complained of the fraud that had been practised on him. The king, when informed, took no notice, but kept them drinking and smoking till four in the morning, when they all set out for Shoreham. When they got on board, Tattershall assured the king of his fidelity, and the ship being got under weigh, the course was directed to Deal, for which place she was bound. Charles then, as had previously been arranged, addressed the crew, and telling them that he and his companion were flying from their creditors, begged them to join with him in persuading the captain to land them in France; at the same time he enforced his entreaties by a gift of twenty shillings for drink, and the sailors, in consequence, became zealous advocates. Tattershall made many objections; at length he affected to yield, and the next morning the two adventurers were put on shore at Fechamp in Normandy. Upwards of forty persons had been privy to the king's escape, and many of them were in humble circumstances; yet, though the parliament had offered a reward of £1000 for his apprehension, not one was base enough to betray him. This surely is creditable to human nature.

Parliament dissolved by Cromwell.

The arms of the parliament speedily reduced both Scotland and Ireland, and a naval war was carried on with success against the Dutch. But the parliament was doomed to fall by the hands of their own servants, and Cromwell, whose influence was unbounded over the army, had resolved to make himself sole ruler. As a means to this he used every effort to force the parliament to vote its own dissolution; but the members had too long known the sweets of power to be willing to part with it, and on their side they were anxious to disband the army.

While matters were in this state word came one day to Cromwell and his friends, as they were in consultation, that the parliament was engaged on the subject of the dissolution. Those who were members of the house hastened thither; but finding that it was not an immediate dissolution, as the army required, that they were about to vote, Harrison "most sweetly and humbly," we are told, urged them to pause, while another officer sped away to Whitehall, to inform Cromwell. Acting with his usual decision, the general ordered a party of soldiers to follow him, and set out for the house. Leaving the soldiers in the lobby, he went in, and taking his seat on one of the outer benches, sat listening to the debate. He was dressed, we may observe, in a plain suit of black, with grey worsted stockings. The speaker was about to put the question, when Cromwell rose, put off his hat, and began to address the house. At first his language was moderate; but as he proceeded and warmed his tone altered, and he told them of their injustice, self-interest, and other faults; "but," said he, "the Lord has done with you, and has chosen other instruments for carrying on his work that are more worthy." A member declared that he never heard such language, and that from their own servant. "Come, come, sir," said Cromwell, putting on his hat and springing forward, "I will put an end to your prating." He paced up and down the floor apparently in great agitation, and then, stamping with his foot, cried, "You are no parliament; I say you are no parliament. Bring them in; bring them in." The door opened, and colonel Worsley entered with more than twenty soldiers. "This is not honest," cried sir Harry

Vane, "yea, it is against morality and common honesty." "Sir Harry Vane, O sir Harry Vane," said Cromwell, "the Lord deliver me from sir Harry Vane! *He* might have prevented this, but he is a juggler, and has not so much as common honesty." Pointing to one member, he said, "There sits a drunkard;" to two others, "There are two whore-masters." He proceeded to charge others with their vices and ill lives, and then, turning to the guard, directed them to clear the house. Harrison advanced and handed the speaker from his chair. As the members retired Cromwell resumed. "It is you," he cried, "that have forced me to do this. I have sought the Lord both day and night, that he would rather slay me than put me on the doing of this work." "It is not too late to undo it," observed alderman Allen. Cromwell charged him with fraud in his office, and gave him into custody; and then, looking at the mace, "What," said he, "shall we do with this fool's bauble*? Here, carry it away." He ordered the doors to be locked, and went back to Whitehall. In the afternoon he visited the Council of State, and told the members to consider it as dissolved. Bradshaw, its president, addressed him in the stern language of a republican; but Cromwell made no reply, and they retired.

CHAPTER IV.

THE PROTECTORATE.

Barebone's Parliament.

Though Cromwell had thus dissolved the Long Parliament, he felt that he could not venture as yet to assume

---

* The bauble was an ornamented piece of wood, which the fools, who were kept in great families, carried as a kind of badge of office. It is often mentioned by Shakspeare.

the sole authority in the state, and as moreover a government without a parliament would be a kind of monster in the eyes of the people of England, his object was to have an assembly which should bear the name of parliament and yet be entirely at his devotion.

Accordingly directions were sent to the ministers of churches in the different counties, directing them to take the sense of their congregations respecting persons "faithful, fearing God, and hating covetousness," and transmit their names to the council. Out of these Cromwell selected one hundred and thirty-nine persons, and when they met at Whitehall he gave them the supreme authority for a term of fifteen months. The members were in general respectable honest men in independent circumstances, but they were narrow-minded and fanatic. As one of them, a leather-seller in London, was named Praise-God Barebone, the assembly, which was commonly called the Little Parliament, also got the nick-name of Barebone's Parliament.

The idea of proceeding cautiously and respecting existing interests and prejudices, never entered the minds of these legislators, and the reforms which they meditated in the church and law and other departments were of such a sweeping, root-and-branch description, that the gentry, the clergy, and the lawyers all grew alarmed; and Cromwell thought he might now safely venture on the measure of dismissing the parliament and governing alone. By his directions, therefore, colonel Sydenham proposed to them one day that they should go in a body and resign their power into the hands of Cromwell. He himself, the speaker, and about fifty others, set out for the purpose; the remainder sat deliberating on what was best to be done, when a party of soldiers arrived and requested them to withdraw, and seeing that resistance was vain they complied. The very next day Cromwell was made king in effect, though not in title.

Cromwell made Protector.

On the following day the streets were lined with soldiery from Whitehall to Westminster-hall. At one o'clock the lord-general entered his coach and came to the hall; he descended at the door, and the procession then was formed. First went the judges and law-officers, the lord-mayor and aldermen, all in their robes; then came the general in a suit and cloak of black velvet, with long boots and a broad gold band round his hat; he was followed by the council of state and the council of the army. They thus proceeded to the court of chancery, where the general took his seat on a chair of state surrounded by the judges; the civilians stood on the right, the military on the left side of the court. General Lambert then came forward, and in the name of the army and the three kingdoms prayed him to accept the office of Protector of the Commonwealth. He gave his consent with feigned reluctance. The oath of office being read out to him, he took and signed it; Lambert then on his knees offered him the civic sword in its scabbard; he took it, and laid aside his own military sword. He sat down and put on his hat; the great seal was presented to him, and the lord-mayor handed him the city sword. He took them and gave them back, and having exercised these acts of sovereignty he returned to Whitehall. Next day the protector was proclaimed with the ceremonies used on the accession of a king.

Pomp of Cromwell.

Cromwell himself cared little for show and state, but he knew their effects on the minds of the people, and he prudently adopted them. When about to open the next parliament which he summoned, he invited the members to meet him in Westminster-abbey, and he proceeded thither in great pomp. First rode two troops of his lifeguards; they were followed by some hundreds of officers and gentlemen all bare-headed; his highness's lackeys and pages in rich liveries walked before his coach; a captain of the guard was on each side of it; his son-in-law Claypole, as master of the horse, followed, leading a charger superbly caparisoned; and last came in coaches the great officers of state and the members of the council.

A short time after Cromwell met with an accident which was near terminating his reign and life. The duke of Oldenburg had sent him a present of six Friesland coach-horses, and one day he drove with his secretary Thurloe and some of his gentlemen to Hyde-park, and dined under the trees. After dinner the fancy took him to drive the coach himself, and he mounted the box, putting Thurloe inside. For some time he went on very well, but when he began to use the whip rather freely, the horses got into a gallop and ran away. The postillion who rode the two foremost horses was thrown; Cromwell himself fell on the pole, his foot got entangled in the harness, and a pistol which he carried in his pocket went off. At length his foot came out of his shoe, and he fell under the body of the coach, and thus escaped. Thurloe, who had leaped out, received some bruises, and they were both confined to their chambers for some weeks. The royalists prophesied on this occasion that Cromwell's next fall would be from a cart, that is, he would be hanged.

Cromwell's vigorous Government.

Cromwell sustained the national honour abroad in a manner such as had not been known since the glorious days of Elizabeth. He made an honourable peace with the Dutch, after giving them two great defeats at sea, and France and Spain and all the continental powers sought his favour. When the brother of the Portuguese ambassador committed a murder, he had him dragged from his brother's house and carried to Newgate; and when a mixed jury of English and foreigners had found him guilty, he had him hanged in spite of the intercession of all the foreign ambassadors. As the piratic states of the north coast of Africa had done much injury to British commerce, the protector sent the famous admiral Blake with a fleet into the Mediterranean-sea. Blake cast anchor before the port of Algiers, and required the Dey or prince to deliver up the English ships and men taken by his subjects. The dey complied, and Blake then sailed to Tunis, where he made a similar demand: but the dey of that place, pointing to two strong castles and his fleet, bade him destroy them if he could. Blake took him at his word, and opened a fire on the castles, which he speedily reduced to silence, and he then entered the harbour and burned nine ships of war. He then directed his course to Tripoli, whose dey did not venture to give a refusal to his demands.

Capture of Jamaica.

Though the court of Spain had given him no just ground of offence, Cromwell resolved to deprive it of some of its possessions in the West Indies. A fleet, therefore, of thirty sail, commanded by admiral Penn, and carrying four thousand land-troops under general Venables, sailed for Barbadoes, and having in that island and in St. Kitt's increased their forces to ten thousand men, they proceeded to the Spanish island of Hispaniόla, with the intention of attacking its chief town, St. Domingo; but instead of entering the port at once, when the town would probably have surrendered, they landed the troops at a distance of forty miles from it. The men marched for three days under a burning sun, and living chiefly on unripe fruit, which caused diseases among them. As they drew near the town they fell into an ambuscade, and though they drove off the enemy, the diseased condition of the troops made it necessary for them to fall back and remain inactive for a week. On their next advance toward the town, they found the road, which lay through a thick wood, commanded by a battery and its sides lined with Spanish marksmen. The advance-guard being thrown into disorder fell back on a regiment of foot, which in its turn fell back on a troop of horse; and all was confusion, till a body of sailors cleared the wood of the marksmen. But by that time night was come on, and they returned to their former station. A council of war having decided that success was hopeless, the commanders reimbarked the troops and departed; but as they feared to face the protector without having accomplished something, they landed in Jamaica, and meeting with no resistance made a conquest of that valuable island. Cromwell, however, was so enraged at the failure of his project, that he committed both the admiral and the general to the Tower.

Victories and Death of Blake.

In order to capture the galleons or large ships which brought the silver from the New World, a fleet was sent out under the admirals Blake and Montague. Leaving captain Stayner with six frigates before the port of Cadiz, the admirals sailed to Lisbon to make the king of Portugal pay a sum of money that he owed the English nation. While they were away, a Spanish fleet of eight ships laden with treasure came in sight. Stayner attacked it, and sunk four and took two of the vessels. On board of one of the ships that was destroyed was the marquess Vaydes, viceroy of Peru, with his wife and seven children. When the ship took fire, the marchioness and her eldest daughter fainted, and the marquess refusing to quit them they all perished. One of the sons shared their fate; the remaining five children were saved and brought to England. The value of the silver taken was two millions sterling; and Cromwell, to make the greater display, had it all conveyed in waggons from Portsmouth to London.

Blake meantime sailed to the Canary isles to intercept another plate-fleet, as those that bore the silver were called. He found it lying in a port of the isle of Teneriffe; the plate-ships, ten in number, were moored in the harbour in the form of a crescent, with seven galleons in a line before them; the entrance of the harbour was commanded by the guns of the fort, and there were seven batteries round it. Blake, notwithstanding the hazard, resolved to attack. He caused a solemn fast to be held on board the fleet, and next morning the British ships entered the harbour under a shower of balls and shells, the brave Stayner leading the way. At two in the afternoon the batteries were silenced, and all the ships were in the hands of the English, who had lost only forty men in this daring action. The gallant Blake breathed his last as he was entering Plymouth-harbour on his return to England, and the protector gave him a magnificent funeral and a tomb in Westminster-abbey. Blake, though he thus fought for Cromwell, was a genuine republican, but his word to the seamen was, "It is our duty to fight for our country, into whatever hands the government may fall."

Last Days of Cromwell.

Cromwell, though thus successful abroad, was disquieted at home by conspiracies and insurrections of the royalists and republicans. By means of spies he discovered, and by his vigour he suppressed them; but their frequent occurrence deprived him of ease and enjoyment. He wore armour under his clothes, and he carried loaded pistols in his pocket. He always drove at full speed, his coach filled with attendants and surrounded by guards, and he never returned by the road he went. He changed his bedchamber frequently; his nights were sleepless or his rest was disturbed. Domestic affliction also came to add to his cares. He was a most affectionate father, and his favourite daughter, Elizabeth Claypole, was now dying of an internal complaint. He abandoned all the cares of state, and went to Hampton-court, where she was residing. He spent much of his time in her apartment, and always left it with an air of the deepest melancholy. Though he had long expected her death, it gave him a great shock when it occurred.

He was himself confined at the time with a fit of the gout, and he was also seized with a tertian ague. From a whisper of one of his physicians, which he overheard one day, he began to suspect that he was in danger, and he took to his bed and executed his will; but next morning, when the physicians came, he took his wife by the hand, and said, "I tell you I shall not die this bout; I am sure of it." Observing their surprise, he added, "Do not think I am mad; I speak the words of truth upon surer ground than your Hippócrates or Galen can furnish. God himself hath given this answer, not to my prayers alone, but to the prayers of those who maintain a stricter correspondence and greater intimacy with him. Go on therefore confidently, banishing all sadness from your looks, and deal with me as with a serving-man." This fanatic confidence of the protector was shared by those about him. "O Lord," said one of his chaplains, "we pray not for his recovery; that thou hast granted already; what we now beg is his *speedy* recovery."

These confident anticipations were not, however, to be verified. The protector daily grew worse; he became delirious, and was at times insensible. In one of his lucid intervals he asked his chaplain, Sterry, if it were possible for a man to fall from the grace of God. Sterry replied, according to the Calvinistic doctrine of election, that it was not. "Then," said he, "I am safe, for I am sure I was once in a state of grace." One night he was heard thus praying to himself:—"Lord, I am a poor foolish creature. This people would fain have me live; they think it best for them, and that it will redound much to thy glory; and all this stir is about this. Others would fain have me die. Lord, pardon them, and pardon thy foolish people; forgive their sins, and do not forsake them," etc. etc. The next day, the 3rd of September, the anniversary of the victories of Dunbar and Worcester, his fortunate day as he esteemed it, he breathed his last at four in the afternoon, in the sixtieth year of his age.

CHAPTER V.

THE COMMONWEALTH RESTORED.

Cromwell's Funeral.

RICHARD, the eldest son of the late protector, was proclaimed immediately on his father's death, and no prince of Wales ever came to the throne with less appearance of opposition. But the calm was a deceitful one, and Richard, who was a quiet, amiable man, had not the energy of character requisite for maintaining himself in the difficult situation in which he was placed, where he had royalists, republicans and officers of the army to contend with.

The funeral of the late protector was celebrated with extraordinary pomp and magnificence. Somerset-house, in which he lay in state, was hung with black; his effigy, clad in royal robes, with the sceptre in one hand and the globe in the other, was placed on a bed of state; a crown was on a cushion behind the head. The only light in the apartment proceeded from waxen tapers. After lying thus for two months, the effigy was removed to the great hall, where it appeared in an erect posture, with the crown on its head and the sceptre and globe in its hands. Hundreds of tapers were so arranged beneath the roof, that their light resembled the rays of a sun. At length the effigy was conveyed in state to the magnificent tomb in the abbey, in which the real body had been long since deposited.

Richard was soon obliged to resign his dignity; and the officers of the army, who had forced him to this step, recalled the Rump parliament which his father had so unceremoniously turned out of doors. But the Rump was resolved to exercise its former authority, and not to be the mere slave of the army; and the disputes between the two parties finally terminated in the restoration of Charles II. The manner in which it was brought about was as follows.

General Monk.

The command of the army in Scotland had been given by Cromwell to general Monk, who had formerly been a royalist. On the present occasion he declared for the parliament, and began to make preparations for marching his troops into England, with the secret design, however, as it would appear, of restoring the king. General Lambert, a leading man in the army, marched to Newcastle to oppose him; but meantime a kind of revolution took place; the troops in London and other places abandoned their officers and submitted to the parliament, and Lambert and the others were obliged to resign their commissions. Monk therefore crossed the Tweed unopposed. Lord Fairfax, who was acting in concert with him, seized the city of York, the gates being opened to him by the royalists; and he was there joined by Monk. It was Fairfax's advice that Monk should remain in the north and proclaim the king; but the latter alleged that it would be dangerous to do so, as he could not yet rely sufficiently on his officers. As the parliament sent, inviting him to come to London, he pursued his march.

The troops which Monk had brought with him did not exceed five thousand men; and as there was more than that number in and about London, he wrote from St. Albans to require that five regiments should be sent away to prevent quarrels or seduction. These regiments at first refused to obey the orders given to that effect, but they soon submitted, and quietly marched away; and Monk arrived next day, and took up his quarters at Whitehall.

The royalists were growing stronger and stronger every day in the city. The common council was almost entirely composed of them, and it set the parliament at nought. In order to check them, the government resolved to arrest some of the most active members, and to take away the posts and chains with which the citizens had secured the streets. Orders to this effect were sent to Monk in the dead of the night, and next morning he executed them, though his officers and men murmured, and the citizens received him with groans and hisses. When he had taken away the posts and chains, he sent to say that he thought enough had been done; but he received orders to destroy the gates also. He obeyed, and then led his men back to Whitehall. But he now began to see that the parliament had only sought to make him unpopular, in order to be able to lay him aside; and the next morning he wrote to the speaker, requiring that instant preparations should be made for summoning a new parliament. He then marched his troops into Finsbury-fields, and assured the citizens that he was come to join them in obtaining a full and free parliament. His speech was received with acclamation; he was entertained at the Guildhall; his soldiers were feasted; the bells of the churches rang forth a merry peal; bonfires were lighted, and the populace amused themselves with roasting rumps of beef and other meat at them, in ridicule of the parliament.

Restoration of the King.

After various delays and negotiations, the Long Parliament was at length dissolved, and a new one was summoned. Monk, who had hitherto kept his intentions closely concealed, seeing that the elections were everywhere running in favour of the royalists, at length took off the mask. He admitted his kinsman, sir John Greenville, who was an agent of the king's, to a private interview, in which he made known to him his intentions of restoring the monarchy. Greenville delivered him a letter from Charles, and

Monk drew up a reply to it, which he read out and then cautiously threw it into the fire, bidding Greenville to remember the contents.

On the 25th of April the new parliament met; the house of lords, which had not met since the execution of the late king, also resumed its sittings without encountering any opposition. On the 1st of May, as had been arranged by Monk, Greenville came to the door of the council-chamber, and required to see the lord-general. Monk then came to the door, and Greenville put a letter into his hands; observing that it was sealed with the royal arms, Monk directed the guards to detain the bearer. He then went in with the letter; shortly after Greenville was called in, and the drama was brought to its conclusion. Greenville delivered letters, with which he was charged, to the lords and commons, the army, navy, and city; and a declaration, containing various promises of pardon and of good government. These were all received with marks of the most lively joy, and addresses to the king were voted unanimously. Sums of money were also voted to him and his brothers, and commissioners were sent to invite him to come and receive his crown.

Charles embarked in one of the ports of Holland in the English fleet, which was sent to receive him. He landed at Dover, where he was met by Monk, at the head of the nobility and gentry of Kent. He kissed and embraced the general, made him walk at his side, and ride in the same coach with himself and his brothers. As he proceeded, the people flocked from all parts to see and welcome him. On the 29th of May, which was his birth-day, he reached the capital. The army was drawn out on Blackheath to receive him, and its joyful cheers arose as he passed. The lord-mayor and aldermen met him in St. George's fields, and invited him to partake of a cold collation. From London-bridge to Whitehall the houses were covered with tapestry; the streets were lined as far as Temple-bar, by the trained bands on one side, and the city companies, in their liveries, on the other; and thence to Whitehall, by trained bands and regiments of the army. Troops of gentlemen, richly clad, with their footmen and trumpeters, the city companies, the lord-mayor, sheriffs, and aldermen, rode along; the lord-general and the duke of Buckingham followed; then came the king, riding between his two brothers. The cavalcade was closed by the general's guards and five regiments of horse, and two troops of noblemen and gentlemen. Such was the general joy displayed, that the king observed, in his usual agreeable manner, "It must surely have been my fault that I did not come before, for I have met with no one to-day who did not protest that he had always wished for my restoration."

CHAPTER VI.

CHARLES II.

Execution of the Regicides.

THE constitution was now replaced on its former footing; but the abuses which had been abolished by the Long Parliament were not in general renewed, and thus far liberty was a gainer by the late political struggles. Monk, and the other agents in the restoration, were rewarded with titles and honours; the general being created duke of Albemarle, the admiral Montague earl of Sandwich, and others in a similar manner.

A great number of the regicides, or those concerned in the death of the late king, were brought to trial, and ten were selected for death. The place of execution was Charing-cross, where a gallows was erected for the purpose. The first who suffered was general Harrison. Supported by that spirit of enthusiasm which had always animated him, he gloried in the act for which he was to die, as performed in the cause of God and his country; and he expressed his confidence that the good cause, as he termed it, would revive in happier times. The others showed equal courage, and all died with the constancy of martyrs.

We cannot blame the king for thus taking vengeance for the death of his father; but the sacred privileges of the tomb should have been respected, and a generous enemy wars not with the dead. It is, therefore, with unmingled disgust, that one reads that the bodies of Cromwell, Ireton, and Bradshaw were taken from their tombs in the Abbey, drawn on hurdles to Tyburn on the anniversary of the death of Charles I., hung there on the gallows till evening, their heads cut off and fixed on Westminster-hall, and their trunks thrown into a pit. The bodies of Blake, and about twenty other persons, were also taken out of the Abbey and buried in the adjoining churchyard.

Trial and Execution of Sir Henry Vane.

Neither sir Henry Vane nor general Lambert had had any share in the late king's death, but they were thought to be persons of too much importance to be allowed to escape. They were, therefore, brought to trial for having served under the republican government. Lambert threw himself on the royal mercy, and he was confined for life in the isle of Guernsey, where he lived for thirty years, forgotten by the world, and employing his time in the cultivation of flowers and the practice of the art of painting. The conduct of Vane, on his trial, differed widely from that of Lambert; he asserted that the decision by the sword was given against the late king by that God, who being the judge of the whole earth, doth right, and cannot do otherwise; that the parliament then became the government, and, by a statute of Henry VII., he was justified in obeying it. Right and law were both on the side of the prisoner, but it had been determined not to let him escape, and sentence of death was passed. He was beheaded on Tower-hill. When he attempted to address the people in vindication of himself and the cause for which he suffered, his note-books were snatched from him, and the trumpeters were ordered to blow in his face. "It is a bad cause," said he, "which cannot bear the words of a dying man." One blow terminated his existence.

Conduct of the King.

The king was a slave to pleasure; he lavished, with the most wreckless profusion, the large revenue granted him by parliament; and, to obtain more funds, he, to the great disgust of the nation, sold to the king of France the port of Dunkirk, which had been acquired by Cromwell; he also, for the sake of her large portion, married the infanta Catherine of Portugal, a virtuous and amiable princess. But he treated her with neglect and insult, even placing his mistresses (of whom he had several) in offices about her person. Of the decorum and propriety which had distinguished his father in private life, Charles seems to have had no conception. But his father was a protestant, and a religious man, and Charles II. had no religion at all to regulate his conduct, though he was secretly attached to the doctrines of the church of Rome.

First Dutch War.

The king's brother, the duke of York, held the office of lord high-admiral. He was a brave man, and was anxious to distinguish himself at sea; and for this purpose he contrived to draw the king, who loved peace, into a war with the Dutch, on the pretext of their having inflicted injuries on the English commerce. As England and Holland were rivals in trade, the parliament was very liberal in its grants of supplies, and the war was very popular with the nation in general.

In the spring of the year 1665, the duke put to sea with a gallant fleet of ninety-eight ships of war. It was divided, in the usual manner, into three squadrons, the red, white, and blue. He himself commanded the first, with admiral Lawson for his vice-admiral; prince Rupert commanded the second, and lord Sandwich the third. The fleet rode in triumph for more than a month off the coast of Holland. At length an easterly wind having driven it away, the Dutch fleet, of one hundred and thirteen sail, commanded by admiral Opdam, came out to engage it. It was off the coast of Suffolk that the fleets encountered on the 3rd of June. The sea was calm, the sky was cloudless; during four hours the fight was maintained with obstinate valour, and the result was dubious. The duke displayed the utmost coolness and courage; one shot killed, at his side, three noblemen who were about him, and covered him with their blood. Observing some confusion on board of admiral Opdam's ship, with which he was engaged, he ordered all his guns to be fired into her one after the other, and she took fire and blew up, and the admiral and five hundred men perished. Dismayed at this calamity, the Dutch turned and fled for their own ports. The English ships followed them through the night; but while the duke was taking some repose, one of his attendants went with pretended orders to the master and desired him to shorten sail. The Dutch, in consequence, got safe into the port of the Texel; they had, however, suffered severely, having lost eighteen ships, four admirals, and seven thousand men taken or slain, while the loss of the English had been only one ship and six hundred men.

On the 1st of June in the following year, as an English fleet of fifty-four sail, under the duke of Albemarle, was on its way to the Gunfleet, it met a Dutch fleet of eighty sail, commanded by De Witt and De Ruyter, off the North Foreland. Though the numbers were so unequal, Albemarle resolved to fight. He bore down without any order, and the consequence was, that most of the ships of the blue squadron, which led the van, were captured. Night ended the combat, which was renewed in the morning; and though the Dutch were joined by sixteen fresh ships, the English continued the engagement once more till the close of day. Albemarle then burnt some of his disabled ships, and directed others to make for the nearest ports. In the morning he had only sixteen ships remaining, and these were hard pressed by the enemy, when prince Rupert came to his aid with a squadron of twenty sail. On the following morning, which was the fourth day, the engagement was renewed; but a fog came on, which separated the hostile fleets. Victory was, on the whole, with the Dutch, but the English lost no honour. " They may be killed," said De Witt, " but they will not be conquered." Three weeks later, another battle was fought, in which the English were the conquerors; their fleet rode in triumph off the coast of Holland, and a squadron of their boats and fire-ships entered the channel where the Baltic traders lay, and burned one hundred and fifty of them, with two ships of war and an adjoining town. De Witt, enraged at the sight, swore that he would never sheath the sword till he had had revenge.

The next year his desire of vengeance was in some measure satisfied. Himself and De Ruyter entered the Thames with seventy ships in two squadrons; and while one sailed up to Gravesend, the other prepared to enter the Medway. At the first alarm, the duke of Albemarle had hastened down and erected batteries, and placed guardships for the defence of the boom or barrier at the mouth of that river, and sunk five ships in the channel before it. While he was thus engaged, the Dutch came in with wind and tide, but they were so much impeded by the sunken ships, that they were obliged to fall back. But the next morning, having discovered another channel, they came up it and silenced the batteries, broke the boom, and burned the guard-ships. They then went on to Upnor, where they burned three first-rate men of war. They retired with the ebb of the tide, and for six weeks De Ruyter continued to insult the English coast. Soon after peace was concluded.

The Great Plague.

During this war with the Dutch, England was afflicted with two great calamities, namely, the great plague in the year 1665, and the fire of London, which occurred in the following year.

In consequence of want of cleanliness, want of sufficient ventilation in the houses and streets, want of proper police regulations and other causes, England had, in common with the rest of Europe, suffered at times severely from visitations of that dreadful scourge of the human race, the plague. Happily the one which we are going to describe, though the greatest, has been its last.

During the winter some cases of plague had occurred; as the season advanced they became more numerous, and about the end of May the disease burst forth with fury from the filthy suburb of St. Giles's, and spread its ravages over London and Westminster. The court, the nobility, the gentry, and the opulent citizens fled to the country. Thousands were about to follow, but the lord-mayor refused to give the requisite certificates of health; and the people of the neighbouring towns actually took up arms to drive off the infected persons. With a view to checking the progress of the disease, the city was divided into districts, with proper officers over them; and, as had been always the custom, a red cross was put over the door of every house in which the plague was, with the words "Lord have mercy upon us!" above it. Carts went round every night, preceded by links and the tinkling of a bell to summon the people to bring forth their dead, which then were cast, without coffins or any religious rite, into a common pit in the nearest churchyard. The men employed in this service, who were taken from the dregs of the people, and were hardened in vice and brutality, were frequently guilty of the most horrible actions; and the hired nurses, it is said, used to murder the sick in order to rob them.

The effect of the common danger on different minds was very remarkable: while some employed themselves in religious exercises, awaiting their doom with pious resignation, others madly plunged into riot and dissipation; and the solemn silence which usually prevailed, was from time to time broken by the sounds of unhallowed merriment, which came from the taverns and the other haunts of vice. The terrors of superstition were also felt; many fancied that they saw in the sky a flaming sword suspended over the devoted city; others would assemble in the churchyards, where, in imagination, they beheld the ghosts of the buried stalking round the pits which contained their bodies. A man was seen to walk naked through the streets with a pan of burning coals on his head denouncing woes on the sinful city; another, in imitation of the prophet Jonah, went about proclaiming aloud, " Yet forty days and London shall be destroyed;" a third might be heard, day and night, crying in sepulchral tones, " Oh, the great and dreadful God!"

The months of July and August were oppressively hot; and though September was less sultry, yet the deaths increased. The plan of burning large fires in the streets to purify the air was then tried. On the third night they were quenched by a copious fall of rain, and the deaths began to decrease. The coming of the equinoctial gales aided to check the disease, and the number of the deaths now rapidly diminished. In December the city was pronounced free from the plague, and trade and business were resumed. The number of deaths in London had exceeded one hundred thousand, and the plague committed similar ravages in the other cities and large towns.

Fire of London.

On the night of Sunday, the 2nd of September, in the

following year, a fire broke out in a bakehouse in Fish-street, near London-bridge. As the houses about there were of wood, with pitched roofs, the flames spread rapidly; the pipes which conveyed water from the New River proved to be empty; the engine on the Thames was burnt, and the wind blew strongly. The owners of houses would not suffer them to be pulled down in order to check the progress of the flames, which therefore advanced unimpeded. The spectacle presented on the night of Monday was awfully magnificent. For ten miles round London it was light as day; a column of fire, a mile in breadth, ascended the sky, the flames being bent and twisted by the fury of the winds. The heat was oppressive, and evermore was heard the crash of falling houses or churches. People might be seen flying in all directions with such portions of their property as they had been able to save.

The king, and his brother, the duke of York, exerted themselves in the most laudable manner. They were present everywhere, encouraging and rewarding the workmen, and employing every precaution to prevent robbery. Provisions were brought from the royal stores for the relief of the houseless people, who, to the number of two hundred thousand, were lying in huts or in the open air in the fields between Islington and Highgate. On Wednesday evening the wind abated, and by blowing up houses, the progress of the fire toward the Temple and the Tower was checked, and it soon went out for want of fuel. Two-thirds of the city, in which were eighty-nine churches, lay in ashes. London, however, was soon rebuilt, handsomer and healthier than ever, for the new streets were wider than the old ones, and the houses were of brick instead of wood. The prejudices of the time caused men to believe that the fire was not accidental; and the guilt of firing the city was laid on the papists, who, in this instance at least, were surely innocent. In the inscription on the beautiful column named the Monument, which was raised on the spot where the fire began, it was asserted that it had been kindled by their malice.* This has, however, been effaced of late years.

Attack on Sir John Coventry.

Among the domestic events which occurred in the succeeding years, the following may serve to illustrate the state of manners at that time in England.

Sir John Coventry, a member of parliament, having said something in the house offensive to the king, Charles resolved on a base and cowardly piece of revenge. His chief agent in it was his natural son the duke of Monmouth, by whose direction two lieutenants of the guards, with thirteen of their men, fell one night on Coventry in the Haymarket as he was returning to his lodgings. Coventry snatched the flambeau from his servant; and with it in one hand and his sword in the other, and his back against the wall, he defended himself stoutly. The cowardly assailants, however, succeeded in throwing him on the ground, and they then slit his nose with a penknife. This base assault gave occasion to the Coventry-act, as it is named, which the parliament passed, making it felony to maim or disfigure the person.

Attempt on the Duke of Ormond.

The duke of Ormond, an Irish nobleman of the highest rank and character, had been strongly attached to the late king, and had been the chief upholder of the royal cause in Ireland. The present king, to whose vices Ormond's virtues were a reproach, though he respected, did not love him; and he was naturally an object of dislike to the profligate courtiers. As this nobleman was returning one night from a dinner given by the city, his coach was stopped in St. James's-street, and he was dragged from it, placed behind a man on horseback, and fastened to him by

---

* Pope, who was a Roman-catholic, says,—
  "Where London's column, pointing to the skies,
  Like a tall bully, lifts its head and lies."

a belt. The man then set spurs to his horse and made for Hyde-park; but on the way the duke contrived to get his foot under the rider's, and then, by leaning to the other side, to cause both to fall to the ground. At the sound of approaching footsteps the assassin loosed the belt and fired two pistols at the duke, but they missed, and he then fled and escaped.

Though a reward of 1000*l*. and a pardon to the informer were offered, no information could be obtained at the time. It afterwards appeared that the intention of those who seized the duke had been to hang him at Tyburn. The profligate and unprincipled duke of Buckingham was very generally regarded as the author of the project; and some time after, Ormond's eldest son, lord O'ssory, coming to court and seeing him standing beside the king, went up and said to him, " My lord, I know well that you are at the bottom of this late attempt upon my father; but I give you warning. If by any means he come to a violent end I shall not be at a loss to know the author: I shall consider *you* as the assassin; I shall treat you as such; and whenever I meet you I will pistol you though you stood behind the king's chair. And I tell you so in his majesty's presence, that you may be sure I shall not fail of performance."

Blood's attempt to steal the Regalia.

Some time after, a person dressed as a clergyman, formed an acquaintance with Edwards, the keeper of the jewel-room in the Tower, and proposed a match between his nephew and Edwards' daughter. He came one morning at seven o'clock with two companions, and asked to see the regalia or royal jewels. Edwards led them in; and when they were in the room they suddenly threw a cloak over his head, and knocked him down and gagged him. The clergyman then put the crown under his cloak, another secured the globe, and the third set to work to file the sceptre in two to put it into a bag. But Edwards' son happening to come by, the alarm was given, and the thieves had to run for it; and they had nearly reached their horses, which were at the gate, when they were taken and secured. The king himself attended their examination, and it appeared that the counterfeit divine was an Irishman of the name of Blood, and that it was he who had seized the duke of Ormond. He said that he was one of a band of three hundred, who were sworn to avenge each other's death, and that he had once lain in wait among the reeds at Báttersea to shoot the king as he was bathing in the Thames, but that the awe of majesty had prevented him. From some motive or another, Charles not only pardoned him, but gave him an estate in Ireland, and kept him at court, where he came to have much influence. He also requested Ormond to pardon him, saying that he had certain reasons for asking it. "Your majesty's command is a sufficient reason," was the duke's reply.

Second Dutch War.

The king, who was a secret Roman-catholic, had formed a treaty with Louis, king of France, by which he bound himself to aid the latter in his views of conquering the Dutch, provided Louis assisted him in his plans of overturning the protestant religion, and establishing a despotic government in England. Suitably to the profligate motive from which it was undertaken, the war against the Dutch was commenced by an act which may be termed piracy. Though there had been no declaration of war, and there was an actual alliance with that people, an English squadron was sent out to intercept the richly-laden Dutch Smyrna fleet on its return from the Mediterranean. But the Dutch had put their commanders on their guard, several of the merchantmen were well armed, and the convoy of seven ships of war was so well managed, that out of a fleet of sixty sail, the English were able to capture only four; and the profitless piece of treachery was universally condemned at home as well as abroad.

War was then formally declared. De Ruyter immediately put to sea with a fleet of seventy-five men-of-war and a number of fire-ships, in order to prevent the junction of the French and English fleets. He, however, found them united, and he fell on them in Southwold-bay as they were engaged in taking in men and provisions. The duke of York got about twenty of his ships in line of battle. Though the disparity of numbers was great, the contest was obstinate; lord Sandwich captured the ship of one of the Dutch admirals, but a fire-ship grappled with his own vessel, and set her in flames, and the earl and all on board perished. The duke himself had to shift his flag from the Prince to the St. Michael, and from that to the London, as they were successively disabled. The English were finally successful; as for the French, they had only played the part of lookers-on.

The next year the French and English fleets sailed over to the coast of Holland. De Ruyter gave them battle twice, but neither side gained any advantage. About two months after, the English and Dutch again engaged (the French, as usual, looking on), but this action, the last of the war, also proved indecisive.

The Prince of Orange.

When, in this war, Louis poured an immense land-army into Holland, the Dutch gave the chief command of their troops to William, prince of Orange, the nephew of king Charles, and the future deliverer of England. William, though only twenty-one years of age, proved himself an able general and a true patriot. When urged by the duke of Buckingham to abandon the cause of the Dutch as their ruin was certain, he replied, " There is one certain means by which I can be sure never to see the ruin of my country; I will die in the last ditch." When peace was concluded, the prince came over to England to seek the hand of his cousin, the lady Mary, daughter of the duke of York. But he was not swayed by mere political views. He had told sir William Temple that nothing would induce him to marry a woman with whom he would not have a fair prospect of domestic happiness; it was the favourable report of that minister that led him to think of his fair cousin; and he deferred his proposal till he had seen the princess and judged of her himself. Their auspicious marriage was celebrated by the bishop of London, on the 4th of November, 1677.

The Popish Plot.

About ten months after the marriage of his niece, as the king was one day walking in St. James's park, a chemist named Kirby, who used to assist him in the chemical operations that he was fond of performing, came up to him and said, "Sir, keep within the company; your enemies have a design on your life, and you may be shot within this very walk." On being questioned, he said that two men, named Grove and Pickering, had engaged to shoot, and sir George Wakeman, the queen's physician, to poison him; and he gave Dr. Tonge, a clergyman in the city, as his authority. Tonge, when examined, produced a written narrative of the plot, with which he had been furnished by one Titus Oates. This man, who was the son of a weaver who had turned preacher in the time of the Commonwealth, had taken orders in the church, but having been indicted for perjury he lost his cure; he then became a chaplain in the navy; he was afterwards one of the duke of Norfolk's chaplains, and he finally became a real or pretended convert to popery. He was altogether a man of the most infamous and profligate character.

According to the narrative of this worthy personage, there was a most formidable plot in existence, in which the great agents were the jesuits. The king was to be assassinated, and the crown was to be offered to the duke of York, on his engaging (like king John of old) to be the vassal of the pope and aid in the destruction of protestantism; if not, *to pot James must go,* was the word. Pickering and Grove were to shoot the king at Windsor with silver bullets, and 15,000*l.* had been offered to Wakeman to poison him, and as Oates believed, he had given his consent. He further said that it was the jesuits who had caused the fire of London in 1666, and that they then intended to murder the king, but relented when they witnessed his great humanity. He added many other circumstances equally incredible. When he said that he had been introduced to Don John of Austria at Madrid, the king asked what kind of a man Don John was. He said he was a tall, thin, dark man; whereas the king knew that he was short, fat and fair. When he said that he had seen father La Chaise, the French king's confessor, giving a large sum of money to forward the plot, he was asked where, and he replied, "In the jesuits' house, close to the palace." "Man," cried the king, "the jesuits have no house within a mile of the palace."

Sir Edmundbury Godfrey.

The king, in fact, knew very well that Oates was a liar, and his whole tale a fiction; but such was the general dread and suspicion of popery throughout the nation, that the truth of the plot was almost universally believed. It received further confirmation ere long by the mysterious death of sir E'dmundbury Godfrey, the magistrate, before whom Oates had made oath of the truth of his information.

This gentleman, who had been of late in a very uneasy state of mind on account of his having taken Oates' deposition, left his house early one Saturday morning in the month of October. He was seen in St. Martin's-lane, in Soho, and in Marybone fields. In the afternoon he was seen in the Strand and Lincoln's-inn-fields, and a person supposed to be him was afterwards seen going toward Primrose-hill. As he did not return home at night his family and friends grew very uneasy, inquiry was made everywhere, and various conjectures were formed as to the cause of his absence. The most prevalent report was that he had been murdered by the papists; but no information could be obtained till the evening of the following Thursday, when as two men were going by Primrose-hill they saw a cane and a pair of gloves lying on a bank by a ditch, and on looking more closely they found in the ditch the dead body of a man, with a sword run through his body. His rings were on his fingers and his money was in his pocket. There was a crease round his neck, which was so limber that the face might be turned round to the shoulder. The body proved to be that of Godfrey, and the verdict of the coroner's jury was that he had been strangled, and that the assassin had run his own sword through the body, that he might be supposed to have done the deed himself. The real fact seems to be that he did put an end to himself; but few at the time would believe that he had not been murdered by the papists. At his funeral, which did not take place till a fortnight after, the coffin was preceded by seventy-two of the London clergy, walking two and two; and it was followed by more than one thousand gentlemen in mourning, walking in the same order. The funeral-sermon was preached by Dr. Lloyd, the rector of the parish. At each side of him stood two tall athletic clergymen for his protection, and in the sermon he endeavoured to show that Godfrey had been murdered by the catholics on account of his activity as a magistrate.

William Bedloe.

The parliament had given full credit to Oates; he was called the saviour of his country, and lodgings, with a pension of 1200*l.* a year, were assigned him at Whitehall. Excited by the hope of being similarly honoured, and by a reward of 500*l.* offered for the discovery of the murderer of Godfrey, a man named William Bedloe, nearly as infamous as Oates, soon came forward as an informer.

This man, who had frequently been the inmate of prisons, and was but lately come out of Newgate, was at his own desire arrested at Bristol. He was examined in the presence of the king, and he deposed that he had seen the body of Godfrey at Somerset-house (the residence of the queen), where he had been smothered between pillows by two jesuits, and that he himself had been offered two thousand guineas to help to remove it. He said at another time that Godfrey had been strangled with a linen cravat at five o'clock in the evening; though at that very hour on that day the king was there visiting the queen, and the place was filled with his guards, and the room in which he said he saw the body was that of the queen's footmen, who were always in it. His whole narrative was full of impossibilities; yet such was the general delusion, that on the evidence of this abandoned wretch, three of the servants of Somerset-house (one of them a protestant) were condemned and executed for the murder of Godfrey.

Executions on account of the Plot.

On the evidence of Oates, Bedloe, one Dugdale and some others, Coleman the duke of York's secretary, Grove, Pickering, six jesuits, and Langham the law-agent of their order, were condemned and executed. They all died protesting their innocence with their last breath, and there cannot be a doubt of their truth. But everything that those wretches chose to swear was believed, and no credit was given to the witnesses for the prisoners.

Oates had even the audacity to accuse the innocent queen, and the house of commons received the absurd charge, but the lords indignantly rejected it. Wakeman and three monks, whom he and Bedloe accused, were acquitted, and the two villains had then the impudence to declare that they would never give evidence in a court where the chief-justice presided, and to accuse him to the council. Their career of blood, however, had reached its close; and when we consider how strong was the delusion under which the nation lay, we shall find reason to admire the freedom from bloodthirst characteristic of the English people.

The Meal-tub Plot.

The Meal-tub plot, as it was named, next succeeded. In the hope of making money by it, a fellow named Dangerfield conceived the idea of fabricating a presbyterian plot. One Mrs. Cellier, a Roman-catholic midwife, procured him an introduction to the duke of York and the king, both of whom gave him money. At his desire revenue-officers were sent to search the lodgings of colonel Mansel, a presbyterian, for smuggled lace, and behind his bed they found a parcel of treasonable papers. These, however, turned out to be palpable forgeries, and Dangerfield was committed to Newgate. He then said that he had been bribed by the papists to forge the plot, and that papers would be found in a *meal-tub* at Mrs. Cellier's which would prove the truth of what he asserted. The papers were found; but the jury who tried Mrs. Cellier gave no credit to either them or Dangerfield, and thus terminated this sham plot.

The Rye-house Plot.

The open popery of the duke of York, and the suspected popery of the king, joined with the alarming advances which he was making toward the possession of absolute power, caused the leaders of the popular party in parliament to begin to arrange the means of resistance. Among them was lord Shaftesbury, a man famous in the annals of this reign as an artful intriguer and a violent politician. He was for actual rebellion; but finding that the others would not consent to such extreme measures, and fearing that the court might be able to lay hold of him, he retired to Holland, where he died. His associates, the lords Essex, Howard, and William Russell, the duke of Monmouth the natural son of the king, A'lgernon Sidney, and others, when freed from his presence, acted with caution, and resolved to watch the course of events, and be prepared to meet the danger when it came.

But Shaftesbury had had other associates of a lower

order, such as colonel Rumsey, West a lawyer, and others. These men used to have meetings of their own, in which they talked familiarly of "lopping the two sparks," as West expressed it, that is, killing the king and his brother. There was among them one Rumbold, an old officer of Cromwell's army, who had married a maltster's widow who lived at a place called the Rye-house, near Hoddesden, in Herts, and he observed how easy it would be to shoot the king from it as he was passing by on his way to Newmarket. West approved of the idea, and hence this plot was named the Rye-house plot. Nothing, however, had been fixed on when the government got information, and offered rewards for the taking of the conspirators. West and Rumsey then surrendered themselves, and on the disclosures which they made lord Russell and Sidney were committed to the Tower. Lord Howard was also taken concealed in a chimney in his own house, and he basely turned approver, and on his information lord Essex and Mr. Hampden, a grandson of the patriot, were arrested.

Trial of Lord Russell.

Lord Russell was tried at the Old Bailey. His admirable wife, the daughter of lord Southampton, acted as his secretary in the public court. The witnesses against him were lord Howard, Rumsey, and a wine-merchant named Shepherd. The two last deposed that he had been at Shepherd's when a conversation took place about a rising in the west, in which he shared. Lord Russell owned that he had been at Shepherd's, but said that he only went there to taste some wines. Howard deposed to two meetings at which the prisoner was present. The judge gave a very fair and moderate charge to the jury (no usual thing in those days); but the jury had been selected by the agents of the court, and they brought in a verdict of guilty. Every exertion was then made to save lord Russell. His father, the earl of Bedford, offered the needy and venal monarch 100,000*l.* for his life; the king was also reminded of the merits of the late earl of Southampton toward the royal family; but gratitude or magnanimity had no seat in the bosom of Charles; he would have the blood of a zealous protestant and enemy to despotism.

Last Days of Lord Russell.

During the last week of his life lord Russell was attended by that excellent man the future bishop Burnet. His piety was serene and cheerful; he spoke of his death as giving him less apprehension than the drawing of a tooth; he dined and supped as cheerfully as ever, and talked of the affairs of Europe in his usual manner. After dinner on the day preceding that of his execution he saw and took leave of his children; he said to his wife, "Stay and sup with me; let us eat our last earthly food together." At supper he was remarkably cheerful. A little before his wife went away he took her by the hand and said, "The flesh you now feel in a few hours must be cold." At ten o'clock she rose to depart; he kissed her four or five times; she controlled her feelings not to add to his distress, and they parted in silence. When she was gone he said, "Now the bitterness of death is past;" and he enlarged for some time on her virtues.

He went to bed at twelve, desiring his servant to call him at four. He was asleep when the servant came, and he fell asleep again while he was preparing the things for him to dress. He wound up his watch, which he gave to Burnet, and said, "I have done with time, now eternity comes." He rode in his own carriage to Lincoln's-inn fields, where he was to die. On the way Burnet observed that he was singing to himself; he said it was a psalm, but he should sing better very soon. He expressed his wonder at seeing so large a crowd assembled; he addressed the sheriff briefly, and gave him a written paper. He then laid down his head, and it was taken off at the second blow.

Death of Lord Essex.

The earl of Essex, the son of that lord Capel, who, after the surrender of Colchester had suffered so heroically in the royal cause, terminated his existence with his own hand on the morning of lord Russell's trial. He was naturally of a melancholy temper, and the thought of its having been him who had been the means of putting it into lord Howard's power to injure lord Russell, had proved too heavy for him to endure. His servant on entering his room on that morning found him lying dead on the ground, with his throat cut, evidently by his own hand. Lord Russell, when speaking of him the day before his own death, said he was "the worthiest, the justest, the sincerest and most concerned for the public of any man he ever knew."

Trial and Execution of Sidney.

Algernon Sidney was brought to trial before judge Jeffreys, a man infamous for his prostitution of legal knowledge and judicial authority in favour of the despotism of the crown. The only witness against him was lord Howard, and in cases of treason the law very properly requires two witnesses. To make a second witness, therefore, a treatise on government, which Sidney had written but never published, and which was found among his papers, was produced. It contained doctrines on the subject of liberty, such as almost every one holds at the present day; yet these were regarded as treasonable, and as Jeffreys pronounced the manuscript to be better than two-and-twenty witnesses, the jury found the prisoner guilty. Sidney was beheaded on Tower-hill. He was not attended by any of his friends, or by any ministers of religion, but he had had the latter with him in prison. When asked if he would not address the people, he replied that "he had made his peace with God, and had nothing to say to man." He handed a written speech to the sheriff, which concluded with thanks to God that "he died for that *good old cause* in which he was engaged from his youth, and for which God has so often and so wonderfully declared himself." He made a short prayer, and laid down his head, which was taken off at a single blow.

Illness and Death of the King.

After the death of Russell and Sidney, and the overthrow of the country-party, as the opposition in parliament was named, the power of the king was nearly despotic. Still, knowing how jealous the people were on the subject of religion, he kept his popery carefully concealed; and, with a view to blind the nation on this subject, he gave his second niece, the princess Anne, in marriage to prince George of Denmark, who was a protestant. Charles being a shrewd, sensible man, knew well what any violent attempt on the national religion would end in; he was therefore very much annoyed at the imprudent conduct of the duke of York, who was a zealot in the cause of popery, and he was overheard saying to him one day, "Brother, you may travel if you will; I am resolved to make myself easy for the rest of my life." Some years before he had said to the prince of Orange that "he was confident, whenever the duke should come to reign, he would be so restless and violent that he could not hold it four years to an end,"— words which proved prophetic.

The king was only in his fifty-fifth year, and seemed likely to enjoy a long life; but one Sunday he felt unwell, and next day he fell down in a fit of apoplexy. On Wednesday his recovery was considered hopeless, and the following morning bishop Ken announced to him his danger. He seemed resigned, the bishop read out the office for the visitation of the sick, and on the sick man's making a kind of general repentance, he also read the form of absolution. He then proposed to administer to him the sacrament, but the king said it was time enough. The elements were brought and laid in readiness on a table; but the only reply that could be obtained from the king was, " I will think of it." The duke of York then motioned the company to retire to the other end of the room, and in a whisper asked if he should send for a catholic priest. "For God's sake, brother, do," replied the king, "and lose no time. But will you not expose yourself too much by doing it?" The duke took no heed, but went away, and meeting with a priest named father Húddleston, who had been chaplain at Moseley when the king was concealed there after the battle of Worcester, he brought him up into the king's closet. All but two persons were then ordered to withdraw from the royal apartment, and the duke introduced the priest, saying, "Sir, this worthy man once saved your body, he now comes to save your soul." The king made his confession, chiefly lamenting his having so long deferred his conversion. He continued uttering sundry pious ejaculations, such as, "Mercy, sweet Jesus, mercy!" till the host or consecrated wafer which had been sent for arrived. The priest, who had meantime given him the sacrament of extreme unction, now administered to him the eucharist, and then withdrew by the way he came. The chamber-door was then opened, and the company admitted. Next day, before noon, the king breathed his last. He had been a bad man and a bad king; yet his gay and affable manners had made him popular.

CHAPTER VII.

JAMES II.

Religion of King James.

As Charles II., though he had abundance of natural children, had no legitimate child, the crown came of course to the duke of York. The new monarch, though he had less good sense, had more principle than his brother. He had already braved the resentment of the nation by an open profession of his conversion to popery, and on the very second Sunday after his accession he caused the folding doors of the queen's private chapel to be thrown open, that every one who wished might see him at mass. On Holy Thursday he was attended to the chapel-door by his guards and the gentlemen-pensioners, and on Easter-day by the knights of the garter. On this occasion he said to the duke of Norfolk when he stopped at the door, " My lord, your father would have gone further." " Sir," replied the duke, "*your* father would not have gone so far."

Monmouth's Invasion.

So many circumstances indicated the king's intention to make an attempt to change the national religion, that the duke of Monmouth, one of the late king's natural sons, and his favourite, who had been living in Holland since the time of the Rye-house plot, resolved to take advantage of the general dread of popery and despotism, and try to acquire the crown of England. He therefore landed on the 11th of June (about four months after the death of his father), at Lyme, in Dorset. He was attended by lord Grey of Werk, and about eighty other exiles. He immediately raised his standard, and put forth a declaration, in which he styled king James a usurper, and charged him with the burning of London, and other atrocities, among which was that of poisoning the late king. This declaration drew so many to his standard, that on the fourth day he marched from Lyme at the head of four thousand men. At Taunton he was received with acclamations, and presented with a splendid stand of colours; and twenty young ladies, in their best attire, came to offer him a naked sword and a pocket-bible. He there caused himself to be proclaimed king. He advanced to Bridgewater; and was on his way to Bristol, when he was informed of the approach of the royal troops under lord Féversham. In a council of war it was then determined to march into Wiltshire, where he was led to hope for powerful assistance. He soon, however, began to despair of his cause, since none of the nobility or gentry had joined his standard. He fell back to Bridgewater, and as the royal troops were reported to be encamped at no great distance on the edge of a moor, named Sedgemoor, it was resolved to try the chance of an attack in the night. The duke himself led the foot, lord Grey the horse, and they reached the moor after midnight, but found themselves stopped by a deep drain in front of the royal camp. Grey, on coming to the drain and perceiving the troops to be on the alert, soon turned and led his men off the field. A firing was kept up till day-break, when Feversham ordered his infantry to cross the drain and attack the insurgents, while he sent his cavalry to take them in flank. The half-armed peasants made a gallant resistance, but they were at length obliged to fly, with a loss of five hundred slain and fifteen hundred prisoners; the victors had three hundred killed and wounded.

The unfortunate Monmouth fled with lord Grey and a German in the direction of the New Forest. Early the next morning Grey was taken, and the same was the fate of the German on the following morning. As he owned that he had parted only four hours before with the duke, an active search was made for that prince, and within a couple of hours he was found in a ditch covered with fern and nettles. He was in the dress of a peasant, and in his pocket were some green peas, which appear to have been his only food. He was conveyed to London, and on the evening of his arrival he was, at his own desire, led into the presence of the king. He threw himself on his knees, confessed his guilt, and sued for mercy in the humblest terms; but James was inexorable, and it must be owned that the prisoner had no just claim on him. He was taken back to the Tower and desired to prepare for death on the second day.

Execution of Monmouth.

King Charles had given Monmouth in marriage the duchess of Buccleugh, the wealthiest heiress in Scotland; but there had been no affection on either side, and he had long left her and had lived with lady Harriet Wentworth. The duchess, however, now came to visit him; their meeting was a cold one, and she soon withdrew. He wrote to the king, queen, and queen-dowager and others, imploring mercy and intercession, but to no purpose. He was then visited by bishops Ken and Turner; they found him in a religious frame of mind in general, but as he would not concede that resistance to authority is in all cases sinful, or allow that the connexion between him and lady Harriet Wentworth was morally wrong, they declined giving him the sacrament. Next morning his duchess and children came to take their last leave of him, and their parting was tender. At ten o'clock he entered the carriage which was to convey him to the scaffold. Tower-hill was covered by an immense multitude, whose sighs and groans were succeeded by a profound silence. On the scaffold the divines continued to urge him on those two points, but to no effect. He gave the sheriff a written paper and then laid down his head, telling the executioner to do his work better than in the case of lord Russell. The charge seems to have unnerved the man, for his first blow was so feeble, that the duke raised himself and turned his head, as if to upbraid him. He struck twice more, and then flung down the axe, swearing that his heart failed him. The sheriff made him resume it, and at the fifth blow the head was at length taken off.

Jeffreys' Campaign.

The royal vengeance was now let loose on the adherents of Monmouth. Feversham hung several of his prisoners without any trial. Colonel Kirke, who succeeded him, was a most brutal man. It is said that he used to order prisoners to be hung while he and his officers drank the king's health, and when their feet quivered in the agonies of death, he would say that he would give them music to their dancing, and order the drums to beat and the trumpets to sound. Kirke's Lambs, as his soldiers were called, from the figure of a lamb on their colours, made their name long famous in the west by their cruelty and barbarity.

But these military executions were nothing in comparison with Jeffreys' Campaign, as the king styled it, that is, the judicial proceedings of that brutal judge, who, with four other judges, was sent to try the rebels.

The Campaign commenced at Winchester with the trial of Mrs. Lisle, the aged widow of one of the regicides. She was charged with having given shelter to two of the fugitives from Monmouth's army. Though she denied all knowledge of their being such, and there was little or no evidence against her, Jeffreys bullied the jury into a verdict of Guilty, and he ordered her to be burnt alive that very afternoon. But the clergy of the cathedral obtained for her a respite of three days, during which application was made to the king for her pardon by lord Feversham, and by some ladies of rank whom she had befriended in the time of the Commonwealth; it was also shown that her son actually served in the army against Monmouth. But James, pleading a promise made to Jeffreys not to spare her, declared he would not give her a reprieve for a single day. The only favour he would grant was to change the sentence of burning to beheading, and the venerable matron perished on the scaffold.

The commission proceeded to Dorchester, and other towns. The total number of the executions was upwards of three hundred. The whole face of the country presented a most horrid appearance. Gibbets, and the mangled limbs of men everywhere met the eye, and the stench that exhaled from them rendered the roads hateful to travellers. Meantime the king was amusing himself with horse-races at Winchester, whither Jeffreys transmitted him regular accounts of the progress of the Campaign.

When it was concluded, James, to prove his satisfaction with his conduct, raised him to the peerage, and made him chancellor. Jeffreys is said to have declared on his death-bed that he had done nothing without orders, and that he had not been half bloody enough for him that sent him. We must therefore regard king James as a cruel unrelenting tyrant.

But blood alone did not suffice, money was to be made of this unfortunate rebellion. Jeffreys received large sums for the sale of pardons. Certain courtiers obtained one thousand, a favourite of the queen's one hundred of the prisoners, on their giving security that they should be sold for ten years as slaves in the West Indies. The young ladies who had shown their protestant zeal at Taunton were assigned to the maids of honour, who proved very hard dealers in the article of mercy.

Efforts of James in favour of Popery.

An unsuccessful rebellion is generally found to strengthen a government, and James, elate with victory, expected now to go on unimpeded in his plan of establishing popery. It was observed by the ancients that Destiny deprives of reason those whom it would destroy, and this was never more verified than in the case of this monarch. Though at first success seemed to crown all his measures for the overthrow of the church, it soon appeared that he had been only rousing the spirit of the people, and imperceptibly preparing the event which was to hurl him from his throne.

By means of what was termed the dispensing power of the crown, James hoped to be able to fill all the offices in the state and army with papists; and he also expected to do the same in the universities, in which he made a commencement by allowing the master and three of the fellows of one of the colleges at Oxford to retain their situations after they had become catholics. He moreover permitted the monastic orders of the church of Rome to have houses in London, and they might be seen walking the streets every day in their religious habits. A papal legate also appeared at the court of England, for the first time since the reign of queen Mary; but it was only at the earnest solicitation of James that he had been sent, for the pope very well knew how wild the project was of converting England, and he cared little for James, whom he regarded as the mere slave of the jesuits and the king of France, both of whom he disliked.

The next step made by the king, was to appoint a Roman-catholic to the deanery of Christchurch at Oxford, and as the university had in the late reign, on the occasion of the Rye-house plot, declared that resistance to the supreme authority was in no case justifiable, it had no pretext for disobedience, and it acquiesced in the appointment. Cambridge, however, was not thus fettered, and when the king wrote to the vice-chancellor, directing him to admit a monk to the degree of master of arts, without his taking the requisite oaths, that officer refused, and the king was obliged to give up his fancied right.

Passive obedience, and such like slavish doctrines, may be very fine things to write or declaim about; but men of sense will very rarely be found to act on them. So it was with the university of Oxford; that learned body soon began to see that there was less sin in resisting a monarch, how legitimate soever, than in surrendering to him religious liberty and everything valuable to man. Accordingly, when on the death of the president of one of the colleges the king wrote, recommending one Farmer, a man of low dissolute habits, but a recent convert to popery, they took no heed of his letters, and they elected another person. In the contest that ensued they acted with the greatest spirit, and though the new president and five-and-twenty of the fellows were expelled, the university would not submit.

Trial of the Bishops.

This resistance of the loyal university of Oxford should have caused the king to pause in his course, but blinded by his bigotry, he hurried on to his ruin. With the hope of gaining over the dissenters, who had been cruelly persecuted by the church in the late reign, he had issued a declaration, granting liberty of conscience; and now urged by his confessor, father Petre, a jesuit, who was to him his evil genius, he gave orders for its being read out in all the churches at the time of divine service. The London clergy met and signed a refusal to comply with the order, which they forwarded to the primate; and that prelate, and six other bishops, signed and presented a petition to the king on the subject. When the day appointed for reading the declaration came, it was read in only seven churches in London, and in a very few in the country. Contrary to the advice of his wisest counsellors, the king resolved to have the bishops prosecuted in the court of king's bench. They were previously summoned before the privy-council, and when they had acknowledged their signatures a warrant was made out for their committal to the Tower. As they proceeded to the barges which were to convey them thither, the people gave vent to their feelings in tears and prayers, and implored their blessing. Both banks of the river were lined with spectators, who fell on their knees and prayed for them. At the Tower, officers and men alike of the guard, asked their blessing, and in spite of the catholic lieutenant, the men every day drank their healths. The nobility resorted daily to the Tower; and one day a deputation of ten dissenting ministers arrived to thank the prelates for their constancy to the protestant religion.

When the day of trial came, the bishops, who had been left at liberty on their engaging to appear, entered the court of king's bench, attended by a numerous troop of the nobility and gentry. Of the four judges, one alone could be regarded as impartial, for one was a catholic, and the other two were the slaves of the court; the jury, also, had been selected, and the king and his friends felt certain of success. The event, however, deceived them; the jury, after being shut up the whole night, in consequence of the obstinacy of the king's brewer, who was one of them, came into court at nine o'clock next morning, and pronounced their verdict, Not Guilty. A shout of joy instantly arose in the court; it was taken up without; it spread over the city; it reached the camp on Hounslow-heath, and was repeated by the soldiers. The king, who was dining with lord Feversham, inquired the cause; he was told it was for the acquittal of the bishops. " So much the worse for them," was his remark.

Landing of the Prince of Orange.

If James had said " So much the worse for me," he would have been nearer the truth, for this very thing hastened his downfall, by assuring the friends of religion and liberty that he had not the support of the people to rely on. They had, in fact, long been in communication with the prince of Orange, whose wife was the next heir to the crown; and it had been resolved to wait quietly for her succession. But now, to James's misfortune, his queen, who had ceased from child-bearing for five years, was delivered of a son— a blessing, as the king believed, bestowed on the prayers which he had made on a pilgrimage to St. Winifred's well in Wales. The event filled him with joy, for he now felt sure that it would not be in the power of his heretical daughters to undo his pious work; and that, under a catholic successor, the whole nation would be brought once more under the degrading yoke of Rome. To his great mortification, he found that not one in a thousand of his protestant subjects believed in the reality of the birth, and that the child was regarded as supposititious. We may here observe that this opinion was totally unfounded, and that there never was a prince of Wales whose legitimacy was more certain than that of this ill-fated prince.

The birth of the prince, moreover, decided the friends of the prince of Orange. An invitation, to come to the relief of the country, signed by the bishop of London, the earls of Shrewsbury, Danby, Devonshire and others, was sent to him; and he immediately commenced making preparations for the invasion of England. James, when informed by the king of France, would not give credit to the account; but when he was at last convinced of its truth, he began to prepare for the defence of his throne. He assembled a fleet, he called out the militia, he gave commissions for raising regiments, he recalled troops from Scotland and Ireland; and the army, under lord Feversham, soon amounted to forty thousand men. At the same time, he tried to ingratiate himself with his protestant subjects by showing favour to the bishops, by restoring the fellows of Magdalen college, and by similar gracious acts; but all to no purpose, for he could obtain no confidence.

The fleet of the prince of Orange consisted of sixty men-of-war and seven hundred transports, carrying upwards of fifteen thousand soldiers. It had been determined to sail early in October, but for the first half of that month the wind blew tempestuously from the west. Public prayers were put up in all the churches in Holland, and when the wind abated, a solemn fast was held, after which the fleet put to sea. But a storm came on in the night and dispersed it, and the ships had to go into different ports to repair. At length the Protestant East-wind, as it was termed, came, and the prince once more put to sea. He first sailed northwards, as if he intended to land in Yorkshire; but then changing his course, he passed between Dover and Calais. The wind and tide combined to prevent James's fleet from attacking: the people of the opposite coast stood gazing at the magnificent spectacle of a fleet extending twenty miles in length, and laden with the fate of empires. On Monday, the 5th of November, 1688, the fleet came to an anchor at Torbay, in Devonshire.

The prince advanced to Exeter, but owing to the terror inspired by Jeffreys' Campaign, few ventured to join him; and suspecting that he had been deceived, he began to think of returning to Holland. At length some of the gentry came to him; their example was speedily followed by others: desertion commenced in the royal army; lord Danby, lord Devonshire and others began to raise men in the north, and the friends of the protestant cause took courage in all parts.

The king hastened down to Salisbury to head his army; but instead of advancing at once against the invaders, he agreed to the opinion of lord Feversham, that it were best to retire behind the Thames, and he himself set out on his return to London. Lord Churchill, the lieutenant-general, the duke of Grafton, a son of the late king, and some others, set out that very night to join the prince, and in the morning several of their officers followed them. At Andover James invited prince George of Denmark to sup with him; after supper, that prince, the duke of Ormond and two others, mounted their horses and rode off to the prince of Orange. When James reached London, the first news he heard, was the flight of his daughter Anne. He burst into tears. "God help me," he cried, "my very children have forsaken me." The princess had left her bed-chamber the night before, with lady Churchill, and entered a carriage, in which the bishop of London was waiting for her; and that prelate had conveyed her to his own house, and thence accompanied her to Northampton.

Flight of James.

Finding that disaffection was spreading rapidly over the whole kingdom, James lost all courage, and resolved to place himself and his family under the protection of the king of France. On a dark and stormy night in the month of December, the queen, with her babe and his nurse, crossed the Thames in an open boat to Lambeth, where a carriage was to meet them and convey them to Gravesend. But when they landed the carriage had not arrived, and they were obliged to stand for some time waiting, having only the shelter of an old wall against the rain, which fell in torrents. At length the coach arrived, and they got aboard a vessel which conveyed them to Calais.

The king had promised the queen to follow her in twenty-four hours. Accordingly he rose after midnight the next night, and charging a son of the late king, who, as chamberlain, lay on a pallet in his chamber, not to open the door till the usual hour in the morning, he went down the back stairs, and getting into a hackney-coach, which was waiting for him, drove to the ferry opposite Vauxhall. He there entered a boat and crossed over; and finding horses standing ready, he mounted and rode to Feversham on the Thames, where he got on board a vessel which had been prepared to carry him to France. But some fishermen having boarded the vessel while she was taking in ballast, and suspecting the king and his companions to be jesuits, seized them and brought them back to Feversham, where the king was soon recognised. He was placed in the house of the mayor, and when he wrote up to London, lord Feversham was sent with two hundred of the guards to protect him. Under their escort he returned to the capital, where he was received with every demonstration of popular joy. The crowds shouted, the bells were rung, and bonfires lighted in the usual manner.

This reception of the king gave some alarm to the prince of Orange, who was now at Windsor, and he and his council resolved that James should not be suffered to remain at Whitehall. On the very evening after the king's return a party of the Dutch guards were sent to replace the English guards at that palace; lord Craven, a veteran of eighty years of age, who commanded the latter, was preparing to resist, but at the command of the king he submitted, and led off his men. James went to rest a little before midnight; but he had not been long asleep when he was waked to receive a message from the prince, requiring that he should leave the palace at ten in the morning (as the prince intended to enter London by noon), and retire to Ham-house, near Richmond in Surrey. James objected to Ham as damp and cold, and proposed Rochester. At nine next morning he received permission to go to that city, and at noon, having taken leave of the nobility who were in town, he entered the royal barge, and went down the river followed by the Dutch guards in boats.

The English, as every one who reads their history must know, are a generous and a forgiving people, and are attached to their monarchs. The assembled crowds, therefore, though James had done all in his power to deprive them of their religion and liberty, could not see him thus quitting the palace of his fathers, a captive, as it were, in the hands of foreigners, without sorrow, which was testified by their looks. The king, however, went on and reached his destination. Here he deliberated on what he should do; his friends urged him not to think of leaving the kingdom, as it was the very thing his enemies wished him to do, as was proved by their leaving the rear of the house he was in unguarded. But James was resolved on flight, in which resolution he was confirmed by a letter from the queen; and on the 22nd of December he got up after midnight, and went out through the garden with his natural son, the duke of Berwick, and three other persons, and got on board a vessel which conveyed him to France.

The prince entered London at two o'clock on the day the king had left it. All classes crowded to do him homage. After long debate in the parliament it was determined that the late king had abdicated the government, and that the throne was vacant; and the prince and princess of Orange were proclaimed king and queen of England.

Such was the GLORIOUS REVOLUTION of 1688, the termination of the long struggle between the crown and the people. It saved the nation from arbitrary power, and in all probability from the galling yoke of popery; for it is impossible to say how long the protestant religion of the people might have been able to resist the power or the blandishments of a race of popish princes wielding the supreme authority of the state, supported by a standing army, and little checked by parliament.

HOUSE OF STUART.—PART II.

CHAPTER I.
WILLIAM III. AND MARY II.

Battle of Killicrankie.

THOUGH James had thus been driven from the throne his cause was not yet hopeless; he had many partisans in England and Scotland, and in Ireland, the great bulk of the people being catholics, were of course on his side.

In the latter years of Charles II. a dreadful persecution had been carried on in Scotland against the Covenanters, as those were called who would not submit to the episcopal form of church-government, which the court was attempting to force on the nation. Among those who most distinguished themselves on this occasion, by the activity and unrelenting cruelty with which they carried the royal will into execution, was Graham of Claverhouse, and for his merits in this way he was created viscount Dundee. This man now resolved to maintain the cause of king James by arms, and, retiring into the Highlands, he drew together a large body of the rude and hardy mountaineers, and made himself master of the castle of Blair, in Athol. Leaving a garrison in that castle, he went into Lochåber, but hearing that Blair was hard pressed by lord Murray, to whose aid general Mackay was advancing, he rapidly returned, drove off Murray, and as Mackay was coming up through the pass of Killicrankie he prepared to give him battle at the head of that pass. Accordingly, as soon as the royal troops had emerged from the pass, and stood on the plain at its summit, they were assailed by the highlanders, who, though greatly inferior in numbers and discipline, feared not the regular troops. Having discharged their muskets, they fell on in their usual manner with broadsword and target, and they routed the royalists with a loss of fifteen hundred slain, and five hundred prisoners. Had Dundee lived to improve this victory, it is hard to say what might have been the consequence; but fortunately for the cause of religion and liberty, he received a wound in the action, of which he died next day, and with him died the cause of James in Scotland.

Siege of Derry.

In Ireland the aspect of affairs was widely different. The chief governor, lord Tyrconnel, and the army were catholics, and James, having obtained money and supplies from the king of France, landed himself at Kinsále in that country, and advanced to Dublin. It was only in the north that the protestants were in any force, and there the towns of Londonderry and Enniskillen refused to admit his troops. Against the former James took the field in person. Though the fortifications were slight, the cannon few and bad, and no engineer in the place, and the stock of provisions small, the brave inhabitants resolved to resist to the last extremity in the cause of their religion and liberty. They appointed as governors, an officer named Major Baker, and a clergyman named George Walker, who had raised a regiment in the protestant cause.

The attacks of the besiegers were gallantly repelled, but provisions soon began to run short in the town. General Kirke arrived with troops and supplies from England, but the enemy had placed a boom across the river on which the city stands, and he was unable to sail up. King James, at the same time left the army and went up to Dublin to hold a parliament, leaving the command with the French marshal Rosen. This officer, who was inured to his master Louis XIV's barbarous mode of dealing with his own protestant subjects, sent out parties of dragoons, and collecting all the protestants, men, women and children, within a circuit of thirty miles, drove them under the walls of Derry, there to perish if the garrison did not surrender. The king, when informed, sent orders to allow them to depart, but the marshal took no heed of the mandate. The threat of the garrison to hang all their prisoners was of more effect, and after three days' starvation the poor people were suffered to return to their homes. Several hundreds of them died of hunger and fatigue.

The famine was now at its height in the town; the horses, dogs, cats, rats, mice, tallow, starch, and salted hides, which had lately been the food of the garrison, were nearly exhausted, when Kirke reappeared. He ordered a frigate and two transports to sail up the river and attempt to break the boom. As they advanced the batteries from each side of the river thundered on them, while the garrison gazed from the walls with the most intense anxiety. The Mountjoy transport ran against the boom and broke it, but the shock drove her aground, and the enemy attempted to board her. She fired a broadside and floated; the three vessels then sailed up to the town, and that very night the siege was raised. The loss of the enemy before this heroic town had been between eight and nine thousand men; the garrison had lost three thousand, nearly half their original number.

James' Parliament.

In the parliament which met in Dublin, and was composed of catholics, the only objects thought of were the modes of robbing the protestants of their properties, and even of their lives. One bill attainted from two to three thousand persons, some, as it said, "on such evidence as satisfied the house, and the rest on common fame." By a clause in this bill the king was even deprived of the power of pardoning. Another bill declared the properties of almost every protestant forfeit. As a further mode of pillaging them a base money was coined of brass, bell-metal, and such like substances, which they were forced to take in payment for their goods. The protestant worship was suppressed, the catholics were ordered to pay their tithes to their own clergy, and the fellows of Trinity College were expelled, and their property was seized.

Battle of the Boyne.

The career of James, however, was soon to be checked. A body of English troops under duke Schomberg was landed in the north, and in the following spring king William himself landed at Carrickfergus. As he was not come, as he expressed it, "to let the grass grow under his feet," he assembled the protestant forces from all parts, and advanced toward Dublin at the head of thirty-six thousand men. James, who had been reinforced by a body of six thousand French, marched from Dublin to oppose him, with an army of nearly equal strength, and took his position near Oldbridge, on the river Boyne, not far from the town of Drógheda.

When the English army reached the opposite bank of that river, William rode out to take a view of the enemy. He was recognised, and two pieces of cannon were secretly brought and placed behind a hedge opposite a bank on which he had sat down to rest. As he was mounting his horse the cannon were discharged, and one of the balls grazed his shoulder. His attendants instantly gathered round him; a cry of joy rose in the Irish camp; a report that he was dead flew to Dublin, and thence to Paris, where Louis and his subjects testified an unmanly exultation, by firing of cannon and lighting of bonfires.

Early next morning, the 1st of July, 1689, the English prepared to pass the river in three divisions. The right forced the passage at the ford of Slane; the centre, led by the old warrior duke Schomberg, passed opposite the Irish camp; it was vigorously opposed, but it finally forced the

Irish to fall back to the village of Donóre, where James stood, viewing the battle. William, meantime, had passed at the head of the third division, composed of cavalry, and driven off the enemy's horse. The French general Lausun immediately urged James to set out with all speed for Dublin, lest he should be surrounded. He forthwith quitted the field; the Irish army poured through the pass of Duleek and formed at the other side, and then retreated in good order. Its loss had been fifteen hundred men, that of the victors was about five hundred, among whom were duke Schomberg and Walker, the brave governor of Derry.

James stopped only one night in Dublin; he then fled southwards, and at length got on board a French vessel and reached France in safety. William, after an ineffectual attempt to take the city of Limerick, returned to England, leaving the chief command with the Dutch general Ginckel.

Siege of Athlone, and Battle of Aghrim.

In the summer of the following year Ginckel opened the campaign with the siege of Athlóne, a strong town on the river Shannon, in the centre of the kingdom. Like many of the towns in Ireland, it consisted of two parts, an English and an Irish town, the latter lying beyond the river, and the Irish army was encamped at hand. At the first assault on the English town the Irish troops abandoned it, retiring over the bridge, of which they broke one of the arches. The attempts of the English to repair this arch being frustrated, they resolved to ford the river. Accordingly a body of two thousand men entered the stream and advanced under the thunder of the enemy's artillery; the English cannon also kept up a heavy fire, and a breach in the wall was effected; the fording corps reached the opposite bank and entered the breach; the rest of the army followed in various ways; the Irish fled to their camp, and the town was won in the short space of half an hour from the time the troops entered the river.

On the 12th of July, 1690, the English found the Irish army posted on Kilcómmoden-hill, with a bog in its front, through which there were only two passes, the slope to the bog being intersected with hedges and ditches. Its number was twenty-five thousand, that of the English about eighteen thousand men. The Irish were commanded by the French general St. Ruth.

The action commenced at noon; the pass on the Irish right was attempted and gained, and about five o'clock an attack was made on the enemy's right wing. St. Ruth having drawn off a part of his cavalry from the left to its support, the English cavalry, under general Tollemache, pressed forward and gained the pass on the left, by the old castle of Aghrim. Meantime a part of the English centre floundered on through the bog, and gained the opposite side; but as they attempted to ascend the hill, St. Ruth sent both horse and foot against them, and they were driven back with loss. "Now," cried he, "now will I drive the English to the very walls of Dublin." But the English came on from both the right and the left, and as St. Ruth was charging down the hill a cannon ball struck and killed him, and soon after the Irish broke and fled. Not less than seven thousand men were slain in the battle and pursuit; the prisoners did not amount to five hundred, so little mercy was shown. Ginckel next formed the siege of Limerick; and that town, after a brave defence, surrendered on favourable terms, and the war in Ireland was thus at length terminated.

Massacre of Glenco.

In the following winter a barbarous massacre took place in the Highlands of Scotland, which reflects disgrace on the government of king William. The Highlanders who had been in arms for James were required to submit to take the oath of allegiance before the first of January; all did so but Macdónald of Glenco, whom the snow and other obstacles prevented from reaching the county town till the last day was past. The sheriff, however, took his oath and gave him a certificate. But Macdonald's enemies suppressed the oath and certificate, and then, assuring the king that he was the chief cause of the turbulence of the Highlands, obtained an order "to extirpate that set of thieves," as he and his clan were styled.

Shortly after a detachment of troops under Campbell of Glenlyon, to whose niece one of Glenco's sons was married, came to the Glen, where they were hospitably received and quartered among the inhabitants. In about a fortnight they received orders to fall on and massacre all the men of the clan on a certain night. Glenlyon spent that evening at cards at his nephew's, and all were to dine at old Glenco's next day. That very night, however, when all were buried in sleep, the massacre began. Glenco's sons, suspecting danger from the discourse of the soldiers, made their escape, but the old man was shot in his bed, and his wife, who was stript naked, died next day of terror. Of the two hundred men of the clan thirty-eight were slaughtered, the rest when they heard the shots fled to the hills; for a storm had come on and prevented the march of the troops who were to have secured the passes to prevent their escape. The houses were all burnt to the ground, the cattle were driven off or destroyed, the women and children were stript naked, and left to perish in the snow.

Battle of La Hogue.

James had not yet given up his hopes of recovering his crown. He was in correspondence with the disaffected in England, who were a very numerous party, and he was able to assemble an army of between fifteen and twenty thousand men, with which he encamped at La Hogue in Normandy, where a large fleet was assembled to convey them to England. The English government ordered admiral Russell to attempt the destruction of this fleet; and when joined by the squadrons of admirals Delaval and Carter, and the Dutch ships, he found himself at the head of ninety-nine sail of the line. The French admiral, the count de Tourville, had only sixty-three ships; but Louis, not expecting the Dutch to join so soon, sent him positive orders to fight. The battle, which was a kind of running fight, lasted for three days; Tourville's own ship and two others were driven ashore and burnt near Cherbourg. Eighteen ran aground at La Hogue by James' camp; vice-admiral Rooke manned his boats to attack them; and though the cannon thundered from all parts, the daring British tars succeeded in burning thirteen sail of the line and a number of the transports. James, who from his camp viewed this destruction of his hopes, could not refrain from crying out repeatedly, "See my brave English!"

Last Days of King William.

The death of his amiable and affectionate queen, who was carried off by the small-pox in the thirty-third year of her age, was a great affliction to king William. His reign was rendered uneasy by constant quarrels with his parliament, and by conspiracies of the Jacobites, as the partisans of James were called; and he was obliged to carry on an expensive war against Louis of France in defence of the protestant religion and the liberties of Europe. The death of king James brought him no ease, for Louis acknowledged that monarch's son (who is hence called the Pretender) as king of England; and he was making vigorous preparations for a new war, when he met with an accident which brought on his dissolution.

King William's constitution was naturally delicate; and though he was now only in the fifty-second year of his age, he felt it to be so broken that he told his friend, lord Portland, in the winter, that he could not expect to live another summer. Toward the end of February, as he was riding through Bushy-park to his favourite palace of Hampton-court, his horse stumbled and fell, and in the fall the king's collar-bone was broken. It was, however, immediately set, and he was brought back to Kensington palace.

He was in no apparent danger, till one day, as he was walking in the gallery, he sat down and fell asleep on a couch. He awoke with a shivering fit, a fever ensued, and five days after he breathed his last. The name of William III. should ever be held in reverence by the friends of civil and religious liberty.

CHAPTER II.

ANNE.

The Duke of Marlborough.

KING William was succeeded on the throne by the princess Anne, second daughter of king James, by his first wife, the daughter of lord Clarendon. She was a weak and obstinate, but well-meaning woman, and she was zealously attached to the protestant religion.

To prevent Louis of France from getting the crown of Spain for his grandson, king William, the emperor of Germany, and the Dutch, had entered into a league, called the Grand Alliance, to procure that crown for the emperor's son, the archduke Charles. Queen Anne, on her accession, declared that she would follow up the measures of the late king, and war was declared against France by the three powers on the same day. The English queen gave the chief command of her forces to John Churchill, earl (afterwards duke) of Marlborough, a name ever memorable in the annals of England and of Europe. Though her troops have always proved themselves to be the best in the world, and may be said never to have sustained a defeat in a regular battle, nature has not destined England to be a great military power. She has therefore only two names to place on a line with the great generals of the continent; but these names, Marlborough and Wellington, will bear a comparison with any of ancient or modern times. Neither of them ever sustained a defeat; each was rewarded by the highest honours his grateful country could bestow.

Victories of Marlborough.

The War of the Succession, as it was called, lasted eleven years. Its chief theatre was the Netherlands, and there most of Marlborough's victories were gained. As it would be tedious to enter into the details of the war, we shall content ourselves with noticing these victories.

On the 13th of August, 1704, was fought the great battle of Blenheim, on the banks of the Danube, in Germany. The emperor being hard pressed by the French and their allies, Marlborough marched to his relief. He was joined by the imperial general, prince Eugene of Savoy; and their united force amounted to about fifty-two thousand men, while that of the enemy, under the elector of Bavaria and the French marshal, Tallard, counted fifty-six thousand. The battle began at one o'clock in the afternoon and lasted till night, when it terminated in the total defeat of the enemy, whose loss in killed (including those drowned in the Danube) and prisoners was forty thousand men. Among those taken were marshal Tallard and one hundred of his officers. The loss of the allies was four thousand five hundred killed, and seven thousand five hundred wounded. For this great victory Marlborough received the thanks of the two houses of parliament; the royal manor of Woodstock was conferred on him and his heirs, and the queen gave orders to erect on it, at the expense of the crown, a splendid mansion to be named Blenheim-castle.

In the campaign of the year 1706, Marlborough was preparing to lay siege to the town of Namur. The court of France sent orders to marshal Villeroy to risk a battle in its defence, and on Whit-sunday, the 23rd of May, he engaged the allies near a village named Ramillies. The armies on both sides were nearly equal, each counting about sixty thousand men. As at Blenheim, the action commenced at one o'clock and lasted till night, and it also terminated in the total defeat of the French, who had thirteen thousand men killed, wounded, and taken, while the allies had only one thousand killed, and two thousand five hundred wounded.

The next victory of Marlborough was in the campaign of 1708. The French army, under one of Louis's grandsons and the duke of Vendome, was besieging the town of Oudenarde. Marlborough marched to its relief; the French raised the siege at his approach; but on the 11th of July he brought them to an engagement near that town. The coming on of night saved them from a total rout; but they lost three thousand men killed, and seven thousand prisoners; the total loss of the allies was about two thousand men.

Marlborough's last victory was in the year 1709. As he and prince Eugene were preparing to lay siege to Mons, the French marshal, Villars, hastened to its relief. He posted his army, of ninety thousand men, between two woods near a place named Malplaquet, and secured his camp with strong entrenchments. Here, however, he was attacked by the allies on the 11th of September. The troops were equal in number, but the advantage in position was greatly on the side of the French; the contest was the most obstinate of any that had occurred during the war; but the honour of the day, with the loss of twenty thousand killed and wounded, remained with the allies, the French retiring with a loss of fourteen thousand men. The siege and capture of Mons terminated the campaign.

Though we have thus only noticed the great battles fought by the duke of Marlborough, they by no means alone contribute to his military reputation. The siege and capture of Dendermond, Ostend, Lisle, Ghent, Mons, and other places, are distinguished in the annals of war; and the skill with which he managed to make the troops and cabinets of so many different states act in concert, are worthy of a Hannibal. Marlborough was a man of humanity; he cared for his soldiers, who, in return, were much attached to him. Their familiar name for him was corporal John.

War in Spain.

The war was not confined to the Netherlands; the cause of the claimants to the Spanish throne was also debated on the soil of Spain, where the English troops were commanded by the earl of Peterborough, a nobleman of daring and romantic valour. His most celebrated exploit was the taking of the city of Barcelóna. He had by a successful act of temerity made himself master of a fort generally deemed impregnable, which commanded the town, and the garrison forced the viceroy, a brave old man, to propose a surrender. The terms were arranged; but meantime a great number of the Miquelets or armed peasantry had stolen into the town, and they and their partisans in the place were about to commence a massacre. When Peterborough heard the tumult he rode to one of the gates and demanded admittance. The gate was opened; he quickly suppressed the riot, his first act being to save a lady of rank from the pursuit of the Miquelets; he enabled the viceroy to make his escape, and then withdrew from the town till the time appointed for the surrender should have arrived.

Two misfortunes befel the British arms in Spain. An army, composed of English and Portuguese, advanced into Murcia to engage a Spanish army under the duke of Berwick. They found him encamped on the plain of Almanza; his troops amounted to twenty-five thousand men, while theirs did not exceed seventeen thousand; he was also greatly superior in cavalry, and his men were fresh, while theirs were fatigued with a long morning's march. The battle commenced at three in the afternoon, and ended in the defeat of the allies, who left four thousand men dead on the field. The remaining infantry were forced to surrender, the cavalry alone escaped.

In the campaign of the year 1710 the troops of the archduke had given those of his rival a great defeat under the walls of Saragossa, and had afterwards entered Madrid. But some time after they found it necessary to quit that capital, and on account of the difficulty of procuring supplies, they were obliged to march in separate divisions. One of these divisions, consisting of five thousand English, under general Stanhope, was surrounded in a town named Brihuéga by the entire army of the enemy, and after a gallant defence it was forced to surrender; and this event ended in effect the war in Spain.

Admiral Benbow.

In the beginning of this war, an English fleet, under sir George Rooke, on its return with land-troops from Barcelona, attacked and captured the strong fortress of Gibraltar, which has ever since remained in the hands of England.

Among the distinguished seamen in the reign of Anne was admiral Benbow, a brave man and a good sailor, but rude and rough in his manners. In an engagement with the French, in the West Indies, some of Benbow's captains would not obey his orders and come into action, and he was obliged to let the French escape, after he had had his right leg broken by a chain-shot. He bore for Kingston in Jamaica, where he brought six of his captains to a court-martial, and two of them were sentenced to be shot. Benbow himself died of his wounds shortly after.

Dr. Sácheverell.

But it was in vain that Marlborough and others gained victories and exalted the British name. Everything was sacrificed to the struggle for place and power between the two political parties named Whigs and Tories, and as the former had beaten the armies and humbled the pride of

Louis, the latter, when by means of a bed-chamber intrigue, they came into power, made the disgraceful peace of Utrecht, which gave him all for which he had been contending, and rendered Marlborough's triumphs useless.

The fall of the Whig ministry was hastened by their imprudence in prosecuting an insignificant individual. A clergyman named Sácheverell, preaching before the lord-mayor and aldermen on the 5th of November, asserted the doctrine of passive obedience in the most absolute terms, and violently attacked all those who held the contrary opinion. As he also assailed the ministry, particularly lord Godolphin, and the sermon was printed and widely circulated by the tories, it was very unwisely resolved to prosecute him. The tories and the clergy made every effort to excite the zeal of the populace for the church, and with such effect that multitudes used to collect each day round the coach in which Sacheverell was conveyed to Westminster-hall, and struggle to kiss his hand. The queen herself attended the trial each day, and the populace would crowd round her sedan, crying, "God bless your majesty and the church; we hope your majesty is for Dr. Sacheverell."

Sacheverell was found guilty, but by so small a majority of the peers by whom he was tried, and his sentence was so light, that the tory party regarded it as a triumph, and bonfires and illuminations testified their joy. Some time after a Mr. Lloyd presented him with a living in Wales. As he went to take possession of it the nobility entertained him sumptuously at their houses; the university of Oxford did the same; the magistrates of towns came forth to meet him with their ensigns of office. The hedges for miles were decked with garlands and lined with spectators, streamers waved from the steeples of the churches, and the air resounded with cries of "The church and Dr. Sacheverell!" A Mr. Cresswell met him at Bridgenorth at the head of four thousand men on horseback, and as many on foot, wearing white knots edged with gold, and leaves of gilt laurel in their hats.

Change of Ministry.—Death of the Queen.

The popular feeling being thus shown, the queen was induced to dismiss the ministry and dissolve the parliament. The new parliament proved almost entirely tory; the prime minister was Harley, afterwards earl of Oxford; and a seat in the cabinet was given to Mr. St. John, afterwards lord Bolingbroke, a young man of great talent, but of no principle. This was the ministry that made the peace of Utrecht. It did not, however, long remain at unity. Bolingbroke intrigued against Harley, and had just succeeded in overthrowing him, when the death of the queen altered the whole political aspect of the country. Queen Anne died of gout in the fiftieth year of her age, and she was succeeded by the elector of Hanover.

Union with Scotland.

One of the most important events in the reign of queen Anne was the union which was effected between England and Scotland in the year 1707. It was opposed by a great majority of the Scottish nation, whose national pride would not let them see the advantages they would derive from it. But by the proper distribution of money and promises among the members of the Scottish parliament, this most desirable measure was at length carried, and the two countries were indissolubly united.

HOUSE OF BRUNSWICK.

CHAPTER L.

GEORGE I.

Accession of George I.

BY an act, called the Act of Settlement, the succession to the throne of England was limited to the princess Sophia (daughter of Elizabeth, daughter of James I.) and her heirs being protestants. The son of that princess was George, of the ducal house of Brunswick, and elector of Hanover in Germany. It had been the plan of Bolingbroke and some of the late queen's ministers to bring in the Pretender; but the friends of the revolution by their activity defeated their schemes, and George I. succeeded without any opposition. Bolingbroke and the duke of Ormond were impeached, and fled to the continent. Oxford, who stood his ground, and who had really no communication with the Pretender, was committed to the Tower, but he was afterwards liberated.

Mar's Rebellion.

The Pretender and his partisans, however, resolved to make an effort for the overthrow of the new government. Their principal reliance was on the clans in the Highlands of Scotland, who were blindly devoted to their chiefs, and were ready to draw their swords in any cause at their call. The earl of Mar, therefore, when he raised the Pretender's standard in the Highlands, was joined by ten thousand men, at the head of whom he advanced to Perth, where he fixed his head quarters, those of the duke of Argyle, who commanded the king's troops, being at Stirling. The Pretender was at the same time proclaimed in the north of England by the earl of Derwentwater and Mr. Forster, who were joined by the Scottish lords, Wintoun, Nithisdale, Carnwarth, and Kenmuir, and Mar sent a body of Highlanders to their support.

Misfortune everywhere attended the jacobite arms. The English and their Scottish auxiliaries resolved to advance into England, and they proceeded as far as Preston in Lancashire. Here, however, they were assailed by the royal troops, and were forced to surrender at discretion. On the very day of their surrender, the 13th of November, a battle was fought between Mar and the duke of Argyle. As the former was preparing to march southwards to join his English friends, the latter, leaving Stirling with four thousand men, encamped by a moor named the Sheriffmuir. Here he was attacked by Mar at the head of nine thousand of his Highlanders. The royal left wing was in the short space of seven minutes routed and driven off the field; but the rebel left wing was defeated in the same manner, and when the right wing of each army returned from the pursuit, it found itself occupying the ground previously held by those who now stood facing it. The combat was not renewed, and in the evening each party retired. Next morning Argyle returned to the field, but the enemy did not appear. The loss had been about five hundred men on each side. Mar returned to Perth, and soon after the Pretender himself landed at Peterhead, whence he proceeded to join the army at Perth. He was proclaimed everywhere as he passed, and the day was fixed for his coronation at Scone. But intelligence of reinforcements having joined Argyle soon convinced him of the hopelessness of his cause, and he himself, Mar, and some others, got on board a French vessel and made their escape to France. The rebel army was disbanded, the common men returned to their homes, and the officers got away to the continent. Of those who surrendered at Preston, and were brought to trial for high treason, Derwentwater, Kenmuir, and Wintoun were beheaded, Nithisdale escaped out of the Tower in women's clothes, brought by his mother the night before the day of his execution; the lives of the rest were spared. Four persons were hanged in London and twenty-two at Preston and Manchester, and thus terminated this first rebellion in favour of the Pretender.

The Quadruple Alliance.

The remainder of the reign of George I. passed away in tranquillity. Toward the end of it England was engaged in a league called the Quadruple Alliance, to repress the ambition of the court of Spain, and sir George Byng was sent with a fleet into the Mediterranean, where he totally destroyed a Spanish fleet of twenty-seven sail of the line, off the coast of Sicily. The following despatch of captain Walton, whom the admiral had sent in pursuit of some of the enemy's ships, is deserving of notice:—"Sir, we have taken and destroyed all the Spanish ships and vessels which were upon the coast; the number as per margin. I am, &c., G. Walton."

The king, who was in the habit of visiting Hanover every year, set out for it as usual in 1727; but on the road to Osnabrück he was seized with paralysis, and he breathed his last in that town, in the sixty-eighth year of his age.

CHAPTER II.
GEORGE II.

King's Accession.— War with Spain.

GEORGE I. was succeeded by his son of the same name. The new king was forty-five years of age, he was a German by birth, and Hanover was of more importance in his eyes than England. His queen, Caroline of Anspach, was a woman of superior mind, and exercised great influence over him. At the head of his ministry was sir Robert Walpole, an able statesman, and a great lover of peace; and as cardinal Fleury, the French minister, was of a similar disposition, external tranquillity prevailed during the early years of the reign of George II.

These years were only distinguished by the ordinary struggles in parliament between the ministry and the opposition. But at length this last party, aided by the trading interest, contrived to force Walpole into a war with Spain: for as the Spanish government did not allow foreigners to carry on a direct trade with its colonies in America, the English merchants, urged by the love of gain, engaged in an extensive smuggling trade. To prevent this the Spaniards had guard-ships on the coast of America, and as some acts of cruelty and injustice were occasionally committed by their commanders on the crews of the English vessels which they searched for prohibited goods, the merchants, who were impeded in their smuggling, raised a great outcry, of which the opposition in parliament, though they knew it to be unfounded, took advantage in order to overthrow the minister. Sooner than lose his place Walpole engaged in a war which he knew to be unjust and impolitic.

Admiral Vernon.

It was resolved to assail Spain in the New World. Admiral Vernon, a brave but self-sufficient officer, having asserted in the house of commons that with only six ships he could take the town of Porto Bello, which admiral Hosier with a large fleet had failed to take in the late reign, the minister allowed him to make the experiment. Success crowned his temerity; he took, plundered, and destroyed that town with scarcely any loss on his part. This conquest was greatly magnified and extolled at home[*], and so high was the opinion entertained of his talents that he was entrusted with the command of a large fleet, carrying a body of land forces under general Wentworth, and destined for the attack of Carthagéna, on the coast of Mexico. But owing to the ignorance of the two commanders, and to their want of harmony, and to the injurious influence of the climate, the attempt proved an utter failure, and the fleet and troops retired with disgrace. Vernon never again made any figure as a commander, which proves that he was more indebted to fortune than merit for his success at Porto Bello.

Anson's Voyage.

While attempts were thus made on the eastern side of Spanish America, another English commander was sent to ravage its western coast. Commodore Anson sailed with a squadron of five sail and some smaller craft for the Pacific Ocean. But the greatest ignorance or negligence was shown by those who had the charge of fitting out this fleet. Almost everything was different from what it should be; the poor old pensioners, for example, were dragged from their retreat at Chelsea to serve as marines, and such was the heartless barbarity shown on this occasion, that among them there was actually a man who had fought at the Boyne fifty years before. The consequence was that when

[*] It was on this occasion that Glover, the author of Leonidas, wrote his beautiful ballad of Hosier's Ghost.

a dreadful scurvy broke out in the fleet these wretched invalids were all swept away: the sailors also suffered severely; a furious tempest assailed the fleet in its passage through the straits of Le Maire, in which one ship was cast away and two were forced to return to the Brazils. Anson therefore appeared in the Pacific with only two ships, the Centurion and the Gloucester. Having stopped some time at the romantic island of Juàn Fernandez to recover his men, he proceeded along the coast of Peru, capturing the Spanish traders, and he took, plundered, and burned a town named Paita. In order to capture one of the large galleons which came annually richly laden from the Philippine Islands to Mexico, he steered across the Pacific, but the ravages of the scurvy had been such that there were not men enough now remaining to navigate the two ships, and he therefore set fire to and burned the Gloucester, having removed her crew into the Centurion. On account of the state of his men's health he stopped for some time at the island of Tinian, whence he proceeded to Canton in China. He once more put to sea in search of the galleon, and he was fortunate enough to meet with and capture it. He returned to England by the Çape of Good Hope, being the first Englishman since Drake who had sailed round the world. He had been absent nearly four years.

Battle of Dettingen.

An attempt of the king of Prussia to rob the empress Maria Terésa of a part of her dominions gave occasion to a war on the continent, in which both France and England shared. A body of English troops was sent to join the Austrians in Flanders, and an army of forty thousand men, which was thus formed, as it was on its march for Germany, found itself, on approaching the village of Déttingen on the river Maine, confronted by a much larger French force, under the marshal Noailles. The French general had taken his measures so well that retreat seemed impossible, and nothing remained but surrender, for he would give no opportunity of fighting. The imprudence of his nephew the duke of Grammont, however, marred his plan, and brought on an engagement on the 26th of June, 1743, and the French were forced to cross the Maine with a loss of from five to six thousand men, that of the allies being only two thousand. The king of England was personally present at this engagement, and though now sixty years of age, he showed all the fire and heroism of youth.

Battle of Fontenoy.

In the spring of the year 1745, a French army, commanded by marshal Saxe, and in which the king and the dauphin were both present, laid siege to the important city of Tournai. The allies, commanded by the duke of Cumberland, son of George II., advanced to its relief. Though his army was much inferior in number, and the French were advantageously posted behind the village of Fontenoy, the duke resolved to attack them. The action commenced at nine in the morning of the 30th of April. The British and Hanoverians advancing under a tremendous fire, drove the enemy beyond his lines, but the Dutch were beaten on the left, and Saxe taking advantage of some errors committed by the English commanders, brought up his reserve, and surrounding the victorious division, poured on it a storm of artillery from all sides. The allies were forced to retire with a loss of upwards of ten thousand men; their victory cost the French a nearly equal number, but they captured Tournai and several other towns.

Scottish Rebellion.

Thirty years had now elapsed since the Pretender had made his futile attempt at gaining the crown of Great Britain. As the English troops were now on the continent, and as jacobitism was thought to be very prevalent in England, the court of France began to think it might make some use of the Pretender, whom it had hitherto treated with neglect. But as he was now grown old and inactive, his son, called the Chevalier St. George, and the Young Pretender, was the person fixed on to head the enterprise. It was resolved to commence, as usual, with the Highlands of Scotland, and the Pretender therefore proceeded thither in a French frigate. Numbers of the clans flocked to his standard; and as sir John Cope, who commanded in Scotland, had marched to secure Inverness, leaving the southern counties defenceless, the Pretender quitted the mountains and entered Perth, where he caused his father to be proclaimed king. He then passed the Forth at Stirling, and entered Edinburgh, where he took up his abode in Holyrood-house, the ancient palace of his fathers.

Cope meantime embarked his troops and landed at Dunbar, where he was joined by two regiments of dragoons which had retired from Edinburgh. He was advancing to attempt the recovery of that city, when at the village of Preston-pans he was suddenly fallen on by the Chevalier at the head of two or three thousand of his highlanders. A sudden panic seized the royal troops, the dragoons fled, the infantry were all killed or taken, and the baggage, ammunition, and artillery became the prize of the victors. The Chevalier, after loitering upwards of a month at Edinburgh, resolved to try his fortune in England. Though he had been joined by the lords Lovat, Balmérino, Nairn, Kilmarnock, and others, none of the men of high rank and importance in the kingdom had declared for him, and the presbyterian population of the Lowlands were steady adherents of the house of Brunswick. He therefore could muster no more than five thousand men for the invasion of England. He entered by the west border. Carlisle surrendered; he pushed on rapidly to Manchester, where he was received with every appearance of joy; he then advanced to Derby, but there his career terminated. He was deceived in his expectations of the landing of a French army in the south; the English jacobites did not stir; two armies, each superior to his own, were in his rear. It was therefore resolved to retreat, and by rapid marches he reached Carlisle, whence he proceeded to Glasgow, and thence to Perth, where he was joined by the earl of Crómarty, with two thousand men. He then laid siege to Stirling-castle, and at Falkirk he defeated general Hawley, who was coming to its relief. But at the approach of the royal army under the duke of Cumberland, he raised the siege and retired northwards. The duke fixed his headquarters at Aberdeen, whence he advanced against the rebels, who were said to be at Inverness. On the 16th of April he found them, to the number of four thousand, at a place named Cullóden, prepared to give battle to his far superior force. The battle commenced at one o'clock, and in the short space of thirty minutes the rebels were totally routed, yet their loss did not exceed twelve hundred men, though orders had been issued to give no quarter. But the victory of the duke was tarnished by his subsequent cruelty. Numbers of innocent people were put to death or exposed to the brutality of the soldiery; and when the duke marched into the Highlands the men were slaughtered, the women violated, the cattle and provisions carried off, the houses burnt, and the country turned into a desert.

The unhappy Chevalier sought refuge in the Highlands. A reward of 30,000*l.* was offered for him, dead or alive. He had to assume every variety of disguise, seek every kind of concealment, trust at different times to the fidelity of not less than fifty persons of different ranks in life; yet not one was found base enough to betray him. At length, after having, for the space of five months, endured privations and encountered dangers without number, he got on board a French privateer, and landed safely in France.

Meantime, the courts of law were punishing the crimes or errors of his adherents. The lords Kilmarnock, Balmerino, Cromarty, and Lovat were found guilty of high-treason; Cromarty was pardoned, the others were beheaded, the last instance of this mode of death in England. About fifty persons were hanged in England, and more than one hundred in Scotland; and a good number of the common men were transported to America. Such was the fatal termination of this last effort in favour of the house of Stuart.

Admiral Byng.

A war, named the Seven Years' War, having broken out in Europe some time after, the French sent a fleet and army to attack the island of Minorca, then belonging to England. A fleet, under admiral Byng, sailed to its relief; but though a part of it engaged the French fleet, the whole, in consequence of the admiral's rigid adherence to rules, did not come into action, and the French were let to escape. Byng then took his ships to Gibraltar to refit, and during his absence the island was taken.

The popular indignation at this loss was great. Byng was burnt in effigy in London and all the great towns, and a mob attacked his seat in Hertfordshire. Addresses were presented to the throne, calling for justice on him; and the ministers, to shift the blame from themselves, augmented the popular ferment. The admiral was brought home a prisoner, and confined in Greenwich hospital, the governor of which had the brutality to shut him up in one of the garrets, whose only furniture were a deal table and a chair; and, as if he feared that the prisoner would attempt to escape, he secured the windows, and even the chimney, with iron bars.

The admiral was brought to trial before a court-martial on board of the St. George, at Portsmouth. He was acquitted of cowardice and disaffection, but the court decided that he had not done his utmost to take or destroy the ships of the enemy, of which neglect, by the articles of war, the penalty was death. The court strongly, however, recommended him to mercy; but the influence of his enemies over the royal mind was too great, and the warrant was signed for his execution. At noon, on the appointed day, Byng, having taken leave of his friends, came from his cabin upon the quarter-deck, sat down on a chair, bandaged his own eyes, gave the signal to the marines, and fell dead, pierced with five bullets. The whole transaction had occupied the space of only three minutes.

Hostilities in America.

It was in the reign of George II. that America first became the scene of hostilities between the French and English. The latter had established their colonies along the east coast of that continent; the former had a colony in Canada, to the north, and in Louisiána, to the south of these colonies; and as the river St. Lawrence and the great lakes were in the former, and the river Mississippi was in the latter, they proposed to connect the two provinces by a chain of forts, and thus prevent the English from extending their possessions into the interior. The English government remonstrated against this; but as the French took no notice, orders were sent out to the colonies to employ force. An expedition, therefore, under major Washington, of Virginia, proceeded to the river Ohío, but it was forced to retire before the French and their Indian allies. In the following year, troops were sent out from England under general Braddock to act against the French. Washington joined him with his provincials; but the general would not listen to his advice as to the proper mode of carrying on war in the woods of America. He moved on with as little caution through the forests as if he were marching over the plains of Germany, till one day, at noon, the Indian war-whoops assailed his ears, and a heavy fire was poured on his troops. The enemy was invisible; instead of trying to dislodge him from his covert, Braddock was only anxious to make his men form according to the rules of the parade. At length he received a mortal wound. The regular troops then turned and fled, and the provincials covered their retreat.

Taking of Quebec.

During the Seven Years' War, hostilities were carried on by the French and English, on the borders of the great lakes. At length an extensive plan for the invasion and conquest of Canada was formed by the English minister, the celebrated Mr. Pitt. It was proposed that three corps of troops should proceed thither from different quarters, and meet under the walls of the city of Quebec. Owing, however, to various circumstances, this plan was not carried into effect; and only one expedition, which went by water, appeared before that town. The fleet was commanded by admiral Saunders; the troops were under the command of general Wolfe, an officer, who, though young, had acquired fame, and who gave promise of proving one day a general of a high order. The discernment of Mr. Pitt had caused him to give Wolfe the preference over those who were his superiors in rank.

The city of Quebec stands on, and at the foot of a lofty rock which runs parallel to the river St. Lawrence. The count Montcalm, the French governor, lay encamped at hand, with a force of ten thousand between two rivers, his rear being defended by dense woods. With Wolfe's inferior force an attack on either the town or camp seemed equally hopeless; yet he would not retire without making some attempt. An attack on the camp was tried, and failed; and Wolfe was beginning to despond, when the idea struck him of scaling the lofty rock and gaining the Heights of Abraham, as the plain on its summit is named. Accordingly, one night, the troops were landed, and by the aid of the projecting rocks and trees they climbed up, and then formed in line of battle on the plain. Montcalm instantly led back his troops to the defence of the town, and a smart action ensued, in which both generals received mortal wounds. As Wolfe lay expiring, he heard a cry of " They fly, they fly!" He asked who fled, and on being told the French, "Then," said he, "I depart content," and breathed his last. Quebec surrendered; and the whole of Canada was reduced in the following year.

Naval victories also augmented the glory of England and of Mr. Pitt in this war. Admiral Boscawen defeated one French fleet off the bay of Lagos, in Spain, and sir Edward Hawke another off Quiberon-bay, in France.

Successes of Clive.

But even the remote East now felt the rivalry of France and England. The French and English had both settled, for the sake of commerce, on the wealthy coasts of India. The English settlements were at Madras, on the Coromandel, or east coast of the Indian peninsula, and at Calcutta, in Bengal; the French were at Pondicherry, on the former coast, and at Chandernagore in the latter. The English, devoted only to trade, abstained from taking any share in the politics of the country and the quarrels of the native princes; but the French, whose character it is to be restless, ambitious, and encroaching, could not long remain at repose. Dupleix, the governor of Pondicherry, thought, by taking advantage of the circumstance of there being a dispute for two of the native thrones, to be able to extend the French influence over the greater part of the peninsula, and to expel the English. He, therefore, took part with the candidates whom he deemed best suited to his purpose, and there remained no choice for the English but to support their rivals, or submit to be driven out of the country.

In the contest which ensued, the great military talents of Robert Clive found a fitting opportunity for their development. He was the son of a respectable attorney in Shropshire, and at the age of nineteen, he had come out to India in the civil service of the East India Company; but not relishing that service, he obtained a commission in their troops, and he soon distinguished himself on various occasions. One of the candidates supported by the Company, being reduced to a low state, and besieged by his rival, Clive suggested, as the only means for his relief, to lay siege in return to Arcot, the capital of the latter. His proposal was accepted, and the task was committed to himself. At the head of a force, consisting of only two hundred Europeans and three hundred sepoys, or native troops, he set out to attack a fort garrisoned by eleven hundred men, and in a city with one hundred thousand inhabitants. The garrison, however, retired at his approach, and the people received him favourably. Here, however, he soon found himself besieged by an army of ten thousand native troops, and one hundred and fifty French, well supplied with artillery, while his own force was reduced to one hundred and twenty Europeans and two hundred sepoys; and the works of the fort, which were a mile in extent, were in a ruinous condition. Yet he gallantly maintained the place for the space of fifty days, repelled every attack, and finally forced the enemy to raise the siege and retire! He afterwards gave the French and their allies two successive defeats; and the French influence and power sank as rapidly as they had risen.

Taking of Calcutta.—The Black Hole.

The English in Bengal had lived on good terms with the native rulers of that province till the throne came to a violent, licentious youth, named Suraj-ud-Dowla, who, jealous of the English, resolved to rob and expel them. He accordingly appeared before Calcutta with a large army. Little or no effort was made at resistance; the governor and most of the persons in the fort got on board what ships were there, and hastened down the river. About one hundred and fifty persons remained behind; and though they might easily have been brought off, not a single effort was made to save them. Mr. Holwell, on whom the command had fallen, then proposed a surrender; but ere he could obtain a reply, the fort was taken by storm. All the persons found in it, one hundred and forty-six in number, were placed in the Black Hole, as a room, twenty feet square, with only two small grated windows, was named, which the English had used as a place of confinement. The dreadful heat, and the want of air speedily deprived some of existence; others lost their reason, and died raving mad; their entreaties and offers of money to their guards for water were mocked at; and when the prison was opened in the morning, only twenty-three persons remained alive. Suraj-ud-Dowla does not appear to have designed their death, but it gave him no concern. Having plundered the town he departed, leaving in it a garrison of three thousand men.

Victories of Clive.

When intelligence of this event reached Madras, it was resolved to send an expedition to Bengal. The command was given to Clive, who had landed, on his return from England, on the very day that Calcutta was taken. The troops sent were nine hundred Europeans and fifteen hundred sepoys; the fleet was commanded by admiral Watson. Calcutta was recovered at once. Suraj-ud-Dowla then advanced toward it with a large army; but while he was trying to amuse Clive by offers of friendship, and promises to restore the property he had seized, the latter, who had discovered that he was insincere, made a sudden attack on his camp before daybreak one morning, which so frightened him, that he agreed at once to all the demands of the English.

Shortly after, Clive ascertained that Suraj-ud-Dowla was preparing to unite his forces with those of the French; and as he had been always of opinion that it was impossible for the French and English to co-exist in India, and that one or other must be expelled, he felt no scruple at taking part in a conspiracy for the dethronement of that prince by some of his principal officers. As he now lay at a place named Plassey, with an army of fifteen thousand horse and thirty-five thousand foot, Clive advanced against him, though his forces did not exceed three thousand men, of whom not quite a third were Europeans. When he approached the enemy's camp, he posted his men in a grove, which was defended by mud-banks. The enemy advanced and cannonaded them till noon, and then retired to their fortified camp. Clive then attacked in his turn; he stormed an angle of the camp, routed the Indian army, and pursued it for a space of six miles. Its loss, however, was only five hundred men. This almost bloodless victory, as we may term it, secured the power of the English in India. Suraj-ud-Dowla was slain as he was flying from his capital. His successor, Meer Jaffier, bestowed immense sums of money and revenues in land on Clive and on the Company; and Clive returned to England at the age of thirty-five, with an income of 40,000l. a-year, fairly and honourably acquired. He is justly regarded as the founder of the British empire in India; for, independent of what he gained for the Company at that time, he afterwards obtained for them, from the emperor of Dehli, a grant of the provinces of Bengal, Bahar, and Orissa.

It is much to be lamented that most of the persons afterwards employed by the Company, thought more of enriching themselves than of obeying the dictates of justice and humanity, and of sustaining the honour of their country. The natives were pillaged in the most merciless manner; and immense fortunes were acquired in a very short space of time by men who had come out to India, in many cases pennyless adventurers. These men, on their return to England, made the most offensive display of their wealth, exhibiting the luxury of the East with all the insolence of upstarts. They were generally called Nabobs, such being an eastern term for a prince. In the novels and dramas of the time they make a conspicuous figure.

While the arms of England were thus triumphant in all parts of the world, king George died suddenly of apoplexy, in the seventy-seventh year of his age. He was succeeded on the throne by his grandson of the same name.

CHAPTER III.
GEORGE III.

Termination of the War.

THE new monarch was in the twenty-third year of his age. He was affable and polished in manners, and extremely correct in conduct; and as he had been born and reared in England, he was the first monarch of his family who could be regarded as English in feeling.

The Whig party had held the reins of power ever since the accession of the house of Brunswick; but high notions of the royal authority had been instilled into the mind of the young monarch by lord Bute, a Scottish nobleman, who had been placed about him by his mother, and his inclinations therefore led him toward the Tory party. This soon appeared by some changes that were made in the ministry. Mr. Pitt, one of the most haughty and high-spirited men in existence, finding himself thwarted in the council on the question of continuing the war, resolved to resign his post of minister. He waited on the king, who expressed his agreement with the sentiments of the majority of the council, accepted Mr. Pitt's resignation, but offered any rewards in the power of the crown to bestow. The minister was affected. "I confess, sir," said he, "I had but too much reason to expect your majesty's displeasure. I did not come prepared for this exceeding goodness. Pardon me, sir, it overpowers—it oppresses me," and he burst into tears. He was some time after created earl of Chatham, with a pension of 3000*l.* a year.

The new ministry, of which lord Bute was the chief, though anxious for peace, carried on the war with spirit. The most brilliant exploit of the British arms at this period was the capture of the town of Havannah, in the Spanish isle of Cuba, in the West Indies. Fourteen sail of the line and merchandise to the value of three millions sterling were taken at that place. Manilla, the capital of the Philippine islands, was also captured by an expedition sent from Madras. Two Spanish ships, richly laden with silver from America, also fell into the hands of the English. Beside Canada, France lost all her West Indian islands. By the peace of Paris, England was allowed to retain the greater part of her conquests, and that peace put an honourable termination to a glorious war.

Voyages of Discovery.

External tranquillity prevailed for the succeeding twelve years of this reign. The king, who had married the princess Charlotte of Mecklenburg, by whom he had a numerous family, set a noble example to his subjects of domestic virtue and propriety, and the tone of the national morals was apparently improved. The king was also a great encourager of voyages of discovery, many of which were undertaken at this period by captains Wallis, Byron, Carteret, and Cook. The fate of this last distinguished navigator, who, after making three successive voyages to the Pacific Ocean, and discovering several clusters of islands, perished in a casual quarrel with the natives of one of the Sandwich islands, is well known, and was the subject of general regret at the time.

American War.

The state of repose which the country had enjoyed was broken by the disputes with the American colonies. As the defence of them had been a source of great expense in the late war, it was asserted to be only reasonable that they should share in the burden of taxation caused by it, and it was proposed to levy stamp-duties and some others in the colonies. The Americans replied that the British parliament, as they were not represented in it, had no right to impose taxes on them, and that the mother-country should be content with having the monopoly of their trade.

Their arguments were unheeded, and a bill was passed for levying the duties. The colonists resolved not to submit, and as tea was one of the articles on which duty was to be paid, when the first ship laden with it entered the port of Boston, a party of men, disguised as Indians, went on board of them, and flung their cargoes into the sea.

The British government resolved to reduce the provincials by force; the latter prepared to resist, and an appeal was speedily made to arms. The American militia, to the number of twenty thousand men, blockaded Boston, and a smart action ensued for the possession of an eminence near that town, called Bunker's-hill, in which the king's troops, though they suffered severely, were finally successful. The Americans gave the chief command of their army to Washington, of whom we have already spoken; but though he was a man of considerable military talent, as his troops were mere militia, success was naturally on the side of the disciplined royal troops; and had the English generals been men of ability, the war might have been brought to a speedy conclusion.

The first misfortune which befel the British arms was in the third year of the war. General Burgoyne advanced from Canada into the province of New York, with a force of ten thousand men. The Americans retired before him, and he reached a place named Saratóga, not far from Albany, on the river Hudson. Here, however, he soon found himself surrounded by an American army, three times as numerous as his own, which kept up an incessant fire of cannon and rifles on his troops, and he had, moreover, no means of obtaining provisions. His army was now reduced to less than six thousand men; resistance was hopeless, and the British troops saw themselves obliged to lay down their arms and become prisoners of war.

Victories of Rodney.

On the intelligence of the surrender of Burgoyne, the court of France resolved to aid the colonists with men and money. Its example was followed by that of Spain, and soon also the Dutch shared in the war against England, who thus had to contend single-handed against all the great maritime powers. But the ocean is the scene of England's glory, and she had now, in sir George Rodney, an admiral who could humble the pride of France and Spain.

When Rodney was called by the king himself to the service of his country, he took the command of a fleet which was to convoy a squadron of transports to Gibraltar, and then proceed to the West Indies. A Spanish fleet, hoping to intercept the transports, lay off the coast of Portugal, in the expectation that Rodney would there leave them to proceed alone to Gibraltar. This, however, was not the intention of the British admiral, and in the evening of the 16th of January, near Cape St. Vincent, he brought the Spaniards to action. The battle commenced in a gale of wind; it was continued all through a stormy night, and terminated in the destruction or capture of the whole Spanish fleet. Rodney then proceeded to the West Indies, where he engaged a French fleet about equal in strength to his own; and he would have gained a complete victory, had not his captains, imitating Benbow's, disobeyed his orders. In the last year of the war Rodney engaged a French fleet, commanded by the count De Grasse, in the West Indies. He captured or destroyed eight of the enemy's ships, and reduced the remainder to the condition of wrecks.

While Rodney thus defeated the French and Spaniards, another of England's naval heroes chastised the Dutch. Admiral Parker engaged off the Dogger-bank a Dutch fleet of nearly twice the strength of his own. The action was long and obstinate, for the Dutch were the only people who were a match for the English on the sea; both fleets were disabled, especially that of the Dutch, who were hardly able to get into their ports.

The war in America had been transferred to the southern provinces, where success was at first mostly on the side of the English. But at length lord Cornwallis, the British commander, with a force of about seven thousand men, was shut up in York-town, on the river Chésapeake, by a combined American and French army of twelve thousand men, while the fleet of count De Grasse took its station in the river. A gallant defence was made; but at length it was found necessary to surrender. This event terminated the war. A peace was concluded soon after, in which Great Britain acknowledged the independence of her colonies, which henceforth are known by the name of the United States.

Major André.

One of the most interesting events of the American war was the fate of major André, the adjutant-general of the British army. The American general Arnold had entered into secret correspondence with sir Henry Clinton, the British commander-in-chief, and proposed betraying to him the strong port of West-point, on the river Hudson, and he desired that some trusty agent might be sent to him. Major André volunteered his services, and he landed in the night from the Vulture sloop-of-war, and conferred with Arnold; but at daybreak, when he would depart, he found it impossible to get on board of the sloop, and being furnished by Arnold with a pass, under the name of Anderson, he attempted to reach New York by land. He was met and detained by three militia-men; he wrote instantly to Arnold to save himself, and that general had just time to get on board the Vulture before Washington's order for his arrest arrived.

André, who no longer concealed his real name and rank, was brought to trial before a court-martial as a spy. He denied that he was such, as he had come on shore under a pass or flag of truce from Arnold. He was, however, found guilty, and sentenced to be hanged. Sir Henry Clinton made every exertion to save him; but Washington's only terms were the surrender of Arnold, and with these he would not comply. André's petition to be shot was rejected, and he underwent his ignominious fate with the constancy of a brave soldier.

Siege of Gibraltar.

The war concluded in Europe with the termination of the siege of Gibraltar. The court of Spain was most anxious to recover this important fortress, which the English had held since the reign of queen Anne, and as soon as it engaged in the war a combined Spanish and French army appeared before Gibraltar. It was bravely defended by the governor, sir Gilbert Elliott, and the besiegers had made no progress, when, in the last year of the war, the command of the combined army was taken by the duke of Crillon, who had lately reduced Minorca. Ten floating batteries, proof against shot and fire, were then constructed; forty-seven sail of the line, beside frigates, were assembled in the bay; on the isthmus connecting the rock with the land were raised batteries, mounting two hundred guns and protected by forty thousand men. A general canonade was then opened on the fortress, which was returned by shells and red-hot balls. The whole peninsula seemed one blaze of fire; the artillery never ceased to roar even for a second. The day closed, the night came on; two of the floating batteries were then seen to burst into flames. Their light enabled the besiegers to direct their guns, and by morning six more of them were on fire. A part of their crews were saved by the humanity of the British, whose gun-boats did not permit the Spaniards to come to their aid. The siege was then raised, and Gibraltar still remains a British possession.

The French War.

After the conclusion of the American war England remained at peace for about ten years, when the breaking out of the French revolution brought on her the longest, the most formidable, and the most expensive war in which she has ever been engaged. In such limited space as ours it would not be possible to relate the events of that revolution, which moreover does not belong to English history. Suffice it to say, that its atrocities were such as the world never before had witnessed. England prudently stood looking on, till the French, by the judicial murder of their most innocent king, and by their declaration that they would aid any people who rebelled against their government, made it manifest that peace was no longer possible. War was then declared, and it is now our task to enumerate the deeds of the navy and army of England.

Naval Victories.

On the 1st of June, 1794, lord Howe, with the channel-fleet of twenty-six sail of the line, engaged the Brest fleet of twenty-seven sail, under admiral Villaret. A fog had prevailed for the two preceding days, but on that day, which was Sunday, the sun shone forth bright and unclouded. No battle, it is said, was ever fought at so great a distance from the land. Victory remained with the English; the French lost six ships taken and one sunk, and eight thousand men taken or killed.

Two victories mark the naval annals of the year 1797. On the 14th of February, sir John Jervis, with fifteen sail of the line, engaged off Cape St. Vincent a Spanish fleet of twenty-seven sail, of which he captured four. For this victory he was created earl St. Vincent. As the Dutch were now the allies, or rather the subjects of the new French republic, their fleet of fifteen sail and frigates put to sea to aid in an invasion of Ireland. The English admiral, Duncan, with the North sea fleet of sixteen sail, engaged them on the 11th of October, off a place named Camperdown, on the coast of Holland. The Dutch fought with their usual obstinate valour for a space of four hours; but they were finally defeated with a loss of nine ships and two frigates. For this brilliant exploit admiral Duncan was justly raised to the peerage.

Mutiny of the Fleet.

While the British navy was thus triumphant over the enemies of England, a mutiny broke out in it, which menaced the country with the greatest danger. The cause of it was the indifference of the government to the wants and the comforts of the sailors. It commenced in the channel-fleet at Portsmouth. When the admiral, lord Bridport, made the signal to prepare for sailing, the crews gave three cheers, and declared that they would not weigh anchor unless the enemy's fleet should put to sea. They took possession of some of the ships, putting the officers ashore; but they behaved themselves well, and when lord Howe came from London, and informed them that an act of parliament had been made to remove the grievances of which they complained, they cheerfully returned to their duty.

This mutiny had hardly been appeased, when a much more serious one broke out in the fleet at the Nore. The sailors took possession of all the ships, giving the chief command to one Richard Parker, a man of resolution and of considerable ability. They blockaded the mouth of the Thames, and allowed no vessels of any kind to pass; and the greatest consternation prevailed in London. The government caused all the buoys in the river to be taken up, the forts of Tilbury, Gravesend, and Sheerness were put into repair, and furnaces for heating shot were set up at them; ships, also, were coming down to attack the mutineers. They now began to lose courage; some of the more desperate proposed to carry the fleet over to the enemy, but the base suggestion was rejected with indignation. The ships gradually deserted; those that remained were forced to submit. Parker and a few others suffered the penalty of death, and the mutiny thus ended.

The Irish Rebellion.

While the mutiny in her fleet was thus menacing Enggland's existence, a dreadful rebellion was in preparation in

Ireland. In this, two parties were engaged, namely, a large portion of the protestant dissenters, who wished to form a republic on the model of that of France, to whose career of bloodshed and atrocity they willingly shut their eyes; and the Roman-catholics, who chiefly looked to the triumph of their religion and the seizure of the estates of the protestants. The two parties were combined in a society, called the United Irishmen; and their efforts had been directed to the organisation of the peasantry, for the purpose of insurrection. They applied to the French government, who readily promised them the aid of a fleet and army.

In the winter of the year 1796, a fleet of seventeen sail of the line, and thirteen frigates, and carrying an army of seventeen thousand men, sailed from Brest for Ireland. Fortunately for England, it was assailed by storms from the very moment it left the port, and only a part of it reached Bantry-bay, in Ireland; and while its commander was hesitating whether he should land or not, a violent gale blew off the shore, and scattered it once more over the ocean.

The rebellion broke out in the summer of the year 1798. The government, having at length obtained information, had arrested some of the principal leaders, among whom was a brother of the duke of Leinster; and in order to make the mine explode, as it were, had recourse to the horrid expedient of goading the people into insurrection by torturing them, and by burning their houses and destroying their property. As in the rebellion of 1641, a simultaneous rising, and an attempt on the castle of Dublin, to take place on the night of the 23rd of May, was projected. But the government got timely information, and the attempt on the castle was frustrated.

The peasantry rose in some of the counties of Leinster, but it was only in the county of Wexford that they offered any effectual resistance to the royal troops. They there took the towns of Wexford, Enniscorthy, and Gorey, and they made a furious attack for a space of ten hours on that of New Ross, whence however they were finally repelled with considerable loss. Their principal station was on Vinegar-hill, near Enniscorthy. Here they were attacked on the 21st of June, by general Lake and an army of thirteen thousand men, and after standing the fire of the royal troops for about an hour and a half they broke and fled. This battle in effect ended the rebellion.

In this civil war atrocities were, as might be expected, committed on both sides. The rebels had confined upwards of two hundred protestants, of all ages and sexes, at a house named Skullabógue, and during the attack on New Ross some ruffians came to the guard with a pretended order for their execution. They shot or killed with their pikes thirty-seven on the steps of the hall-door, and then shutting the remainder, one hundred and eighty-four in number (among whom it is said were some catholics), up in the barn, set fire to it and burned them all. In their camp on Vinegar-hill they butchered, from time to time, about four hundred protestants, and on the day before the battle they piked and threw into the river Slaney at Wexford ninety-seven of their protestant prisoners. On the other hand, the loyalists, though they did not massacre on so large a scale as this, certainly destroyed more in detail; and when we take into account all the tortures they inflicted by floggings, half-hangings, and so forth, we have no hesitation in saying that the balance of cruelty was on their side.

After the rebellion was over a French force of eleven hundred men landed at Killalla, in the west of Ireland. Being joined by some of the misguided peasantry they advanced boldly into the heart of the kingdom; but at a place named Ballinamúck, finding themselves surrounded by an army of twenty thousand men, they laid down their arms and surrendered. The necessity for a closer connection between England and Ireland being now apparent, a Union, similar to that made with Scotland in queen Anne's time, and obtained by the same means, was effected.

French in Egypt.—Battle of the Nile.

A few days before the Irish rebellion broke out, a French fleet of thirteen sail of the line, with frigates and transports, carrying an army of twenty thousand men, sailed from the port of Toulon. This army was commanded by Napoleon Buonaparte, a young man who had already displayed military talents of the highest order. Its destination was Egypt, a country of which the French have always coveted the possession, and having captured the island of Malta on its way it landed safely at Alexandria. Lord St. Vincent, who commanded the British fleet off Cadiz, when he heard that this French fleet had sailed, despatched sir Horatio Nelson with fourteen ships of war in pursuit of it. Nelson having searched all over the Mediterranean, found it at length, on the 1st of August, moored in line of battle, in Aboukir-bay on the coast of Egypt. Though the distance was small between it and the land, on which there were numerous batteries, he ventured to place some of his ships between the French and the shore. The engagement lasted all through the day and the night, and did not cease till two in the afternoon of the following day. Two only of the French ships escaped, two were burnt, and nine taken. Upwards of five thousand Frenchmen perished, including the admiral; the English had only about nine hundred killed and wounded. Nelson was deservedly created a peer for this great victory.

The French army, however, made itself master of Egypt, whence Buonaparte advanced to the conquest of Syria. But the town of Acre was so gallantly defended against him by sir Sidney Smith, an English naval commander, that he was obliged to give up his plans and return to Egypt, whence he soon after stole away to France, where he managed to overthrow the government and make himself the head of the state.

Some time after his departure, an English army, commanded by sir Ralph Abercrombie, landed in Egypt. It defeated the French, but the British general received a mortal wound in the action. Unable to resist the forces brought against them from all quarters, the French found it necessary to submit, and they obtained honourable terms.

Battle of the Baltic.

Nelson meantime achieved another great victory in the Baltic. The English government having determined to send a fleet against the Danes, sir Hyde Parker, with Nelson as his second in command, sailed to the Baltic with eighteen ships of the line and a due number of frigates. On coming before Copenhagen, he found a line of nineteen ships of war, with floating batteries, ready to receive him, and batteries erected on the land. The undaunted Nelson, however, offered to attack them with twelve sail of the line and the frigates. The admiral gave his consent, and at ten o'clock on the morning of the 2nd of April, 1801, the action commenced. As a change in the wind prevented the admiral from coming up with the rest of the ships, he made the signal for recall at one o'clock; but Nelson ventured to disobey it, and at two the firing had ceased along the enemy's line. The slaughter had been immense among the Danes, but they fought like heroes, and Nelson declared that this was the most dreadful battle he had ever witnessed.

Battle of Trafalgar.

A peace was made with France, which lasted only one short year. Buonaparte, who was now emperor of the French, formed a plan for invading England, and for this purpose he wished to assemble all the ships of war of France and Spain. The English on their side were equally anxious to destroy his navy. Nelson went in pursuit of the French admiral Villeneuve, who with the Toulon fleet had gone to Cadiz. He took his station about fifty miles to the west of that port, taking care to conceal his arrival. Villeneuve, not knowing that the English were at hand, put to sea with a French and Spanish fleet of thirty-three sail of the line. Nelson, who had twenty-seven sail of the line, followed and brought them to action off cape Trafalgár, on the 21st of October, 1805. His last signal was "England expects every man to do his duty." He put on him the stars of all the orders with which he had been honoured, and he seemed to have a feeling that this battle would be his last. A more glorious victory than this was never gained; nineteen sail of the line were taken, and one blown up, and the navy of France was annihilated. But England had to lament the loss of her naval hero ; his stars made him a conspicuous object, and he was wounded in the shoulder by a ball from one of the enemy's ships. He breathed his last at the close of the action, saying, " Thank God, I have done my duty."

Peninsular War.— Victories of Wellington.

It only remains for us now to enumerate the victories of our second Marlborough, the illustrious duke of Wellington.

The grasping ambition of the emperor Napoleon urged him to add Spain and Portugal to his dominions. He sent large bodies of troops into the Spanish peninsula, made the king of Spain a prisoner, and forced the court of Portugal to fly to the Brazils. But the people resolved on resistance, and sought aid from England. An English army of sixteen thousand, commanded by sir Arthur Wellesley (afterwards duke of Wellington), landed in Portugal. At a village named Vimiéro it engaged the French army of general Junot, and defeated it, and the French then agreed to evacuate that kingdom.

The command in Portugal being transferred to sir John

Moore, that officer was ordered to advance into Spain to aid the Spaniards. He went as far as Salamanca, where, finding the Spanish armies routed, and an immense French force under Napoleon himself coming against him, he resolved to retreat to the coast. It was the depth of winter, the sufferings of the army were extreme, but it at length reached the port of Corunna, where, as it was preparing to embark, it was furiously attacked by the French under marshal Soult. The assailants were repelled, but the English lost their excellent general; they buried him that night in the citadel, and embarked unmolested by the enemy.

The command of the British and Portuguese armies was now given to sir A. Wellesley. He drove Soult out of Portugal, and then marched to the aid of the Spaniards. On the 27th and 28th of July, 1809, he fought the French marshal Victor, near the city of Talavéra. The troops were about fifty thousand on each side, but the far greater part of those of the allies were Spaniards, who were of little service. Victory, however, was on their side; the French had seven thousand, the English more than five thousand killed and wounded. Sir A. Wellesley was created viscount Wellington for his conduct of this campaign.

In the summer of the year 1810 an army of nearly ninety thousand French, under marshal Mássena, entered Portugal. Wellington, as he was far inferior in force, fell back behind the lines which he had constructed at Torres Vedras, and Massena, after lying for some time before them to no purpose, was obliged to commence his retreat. While Wellington was cautiously pursuing him, marshal Beresford, whom he had directed to besiege the city of Badajóz in Spain, gave battle to marshal Soult at a place named Albuéra, though he had only six thousand British troops, all the rest being Spaniards. Never was British valour more conspicuous than on that dreadful day: only fifteen hundred of them remained unwounded; but the French were defeated with a loss of eight thousand killed and wounded.

In the following year Wellington took Badajoz by storm, and he afterwards engaged marshal Marmont at Salamanca, on the 22nd of June, 1812. The French army counted forty-two thousand men, that of the allies was somewhat more numerous. Their victory, however, was complete; the loss of the French in killed, wounded, and prisoners, was more than twelve thousand men.

In the year 1813, Napoleon, after the loss of the immense army which he had led into Russia, found enemies rising on all sides against him. Wellington, who was in Portugal, re-entered Spain at the head of a splendid army of English and Portuguese, and a Spanish force was also put under his command. The French, led by Joseph the brother of Napoleon and marshal Jourdan, retired toward the Pyrenees, but on the 21st of June the allies brought them to an action near the town of Vittoria. The advantage in numbers was on the side of the allies; the battle lasted all through the day, and ended in the total rout of the French, who fled, leaving all their cannon, treasure, and camp-equipage in the hands of the victors.

Early in the following year, the allied monarchs, who had defeated Napoleon in Germany, crossed the Rhine and advanced toward Paris. Wellington also entered France on the south; at Orthès he engaged and defeated marshal Soult, and he again defeated that able general under the walls of Toulouse. The war, however, was now at an end. Napoleon abdicated the throne, and was assigned the isle of Elba, off the coast of Italy, for his abode, and the brother of the unhappy Louis XVI. was placed by the arms of the allies on the throne of France.

In little more than a year, however, Napoleon landed on the shores of France; the troops everywhere declared for him; his march to Paris, from which the king had fled, was a triumphal progress. But the allied sovereigns were determined that he should not have the power to be, as heretofore, the tyrant and the scourge of Europe, and large armies were immediately marched over the Rhine. At

Waterloo, in the Netherlands, on the 18th of June, Napoleon, with a greatly superior force, attacked the British army under Wellington. The British troops with unwearied courage sustained all through the day the assaults of his veterans. In the evening a Prussian corps came to their aid, and the army of Napoleon was totally routed. The hopes of that upstart despot were now at an end; he fled to the sea-coast to try to effect his escape to America, but he was obliged to surrender himself to the captain of an English man-of-war. The allies fixed on the island of St. Hélena in the Atlantic as his place of confinement, and he ended his days in that lonely isle.

Conclusion.

The victory of Waterloo gave repose to Europe after a war of three and twenty years. During that time England had extended her dominion over the whole of India, and laid the foundation of a new empire in the Southern Ocean. King George III., though afflicted with blindness and bereft of reason, outlived the termination of the war. He was succeeded by his son of the same name, in whose reign a bill was passed for freeing the Roman-catholics from their political disabilities. In the reign of William IV., the brother and successor of this monarch, the reform bill was passed. The present sovereign of the British empire is Victoria, daughter of the duke of Kent, the fourth son of George III. She is married to prince Albert of Saxe-Coburg, and that her reign may be long, happy, and glorious, is the wish of every loyal British heart.

CHRONOLOGICAL TABLE

OF

KINGS AND EVENTS.

ANGLO-SAXON KINGS.

	Began to reign.	Reigned.
EGBERT	A.D. 800	36 years.
ETHELWULF, son of EGBERT	836	22 —
ETHELBALD, ⎫	858	2 —
ETHELBERT, ⎬ sons of	860	6 —
ETHELRED, ⎨ ETHELWULF	866	5 —
ALFRED, ⎭	871	20 —
EDWARD I., son of ALFRED	901	24 —
ATHELSTAN, ⎫	925	16 —
EDMUND, ⎬ sons of EDWARD	941	6 —
EDRED, ⎭	947	8 —
EDWY, ⎱ sons of	955	4 —
EDGAR, ⎰ EDMUND	959	16 —
EDWARD II., ⎱ sons of	975	3 —
ETHELRED, ⎰ EDGAR	978	38 —
CANUTE, the Dane	1016	19 —
HAROLD I., ⎱ sons of	1035	5 —
HARDACNUTE, ⎰ CANUTE	1040	2 —
EDWARD III., son of ETHELRED	1042	24 —
HAROLD II., son of earl Godwin	1066	

EVENTS.

Landing of Julius Cæsar	B.C. 55
Landing of Plautius	A.D. 43
War with Caractacus	51
———— Boadicea	62
———— Galgacus	85
Landing of Hengist and Horsa	449

Christianity preached by Augustine 596
——————————— by Paulinus 626
First landing of the Danes 787
Alfred's victory over Guthrum 878
Battle of Brunanburgh 937
Conquest and death of Macbeth 1054
Battle of Hastings, October 15 1066

ANGLO-NORMAN KINGS.

WILLIAM I. began to reign 1066; reigned 21 years. Children: Robert, *William*, *Henry*, and daughters.
    Devastation of the North 1070
    Overthrow of Hereward 1072
    Quarrel among the princes 1078
    Death of William 1087
WILLIAM II. began to reign 1087; reigned 13 years.
    Attack on prince Henry 1091
    First Crusade 1096
HENRY I. began to reign 1100; reigned 35 years. Married Matilda of Scotland. Children: William and Maud.
    Battle of Tenchebrai, September 28 . . . 1105
    Death of prince William 1120
STEPHEN, son of Adela daughter of the Conqueror, began to reign 1135; reigned 19 years.
    Escape of the empress from Oxford . . . 1142
    Compromise between Stephen and Henry . 1153

HOUSE OF PLANTAGENET.

HENRY II. began to reign 1154; reigned 35 years. Married Eleanor of Guienne. Children: William, Henry, *Richard*, Geoffrey, *John*, Matilda, Eleanor, Joan.
    Becket made archbishop of Canterbury . . 1160
    His quarrel with the king 1163
    His flight 1164
    The English first land in Ireland 1169
    Return and murder of Becket 1170
    Henry in Ireland 1172
    Rebellion of the princes 1173
RICHARD I. began to reign 1189; reigned 10 years. Married Berengara of Navarre. No issue.
    Richard's Crusade 1190
    His captivity 1192
    His release 1194

KINGS AND EVENTS.

JOHN began to reign 1199; reigned 17 years. Married Isabel of Angoulesme. Children: *Henry*, Richard, and three daughters.
    Murder of prince Arthur 1202
    Quarrel with the Pope 1207
    John's submission 1212
    Magna Charta 1215
    War with the barons 1216

HENRY III. began to reign 1216; reigned 56 years. Married Eleanor of Provence. Children: *Edward*, Edmund, Margaret, Beatrix, &c.
    Confirmation of the Great Charter . . . 1253
    Barons' War 1263
    Battle of Lewes, May 14 1264
    Origin of House of Commons . . . . . ⎱ 1265
    Battle of Evesham, August 4 . . . . . ⎰
    Prince Edward's Crusade 1270

EDWARD I. began to reign 1272; reigned 35 years. Married Eleanor of Castille. Children: *Edward*, and three other sons and eleven daughters.
    Conquest of Wales 1283
    ———— of Scotland 1296
    Battle of Cambus-Kenneth, September 11 . 1297
    ———— of Falkirk, July 22 1298
    Execution of Wallace 1304
    Murder of Comyn 1306

EDWARD II. began to reign 1307; reigned 20 years. Married Isabel of France. Children: *Edward*, John, Jane, Eleanor.
    Execution of Gaveston 1312
    Battle of Bannockburn, June 24 1314
    Execution of Lancaster 1322
    ———— of Spenser 1326

EDWARD III. began to reign 1327; reigned 50 years. Married Philippa of Hainault. Children: Edward, Lionel, John, Edmund, Thomas, and four daughters.
    Execution of Mortimer 1330
    Edward claims the crown of France . . . 1337
    Battle of Cressy, August 26 1346
    Surrender of Calais 1347
    Battle of Poitiers, September 19 1356
    Black Prince in Spain 1364
    Death of the Black Prince 1376

RICHARD II. began to reign 1377; reigned 22 years. Married, 1. Anne of Bohemia; 2. Isabel of France. No issue.
    Rising of the peasantry 1381
    Limitation of the king's authority 1386

Murder of Gloucester 1397
Quarrel of Norfolk and Hereford 1398
Landing of Lancaster and deposition of the king 1399

HENRY IV. began to reign 1399; reigned 14 years. Married, 1. Mary Bohun; 2. Jane of Navarre. Children: *Henry*, Thomas, John, Humphrey, and two daughters.

Battle of Shrewsbury, July 21 1403

HENRY V. began to reign 1413; reigned 9 years. Married Catherine of France. One child: *Henry*.

Battle of Agincourt, October 25 1415

HENRY VI. began to reign 1422; reigned 39 years. Married Margaret of Anjou. One child: Edward.

Siege of Orleans 1429
Maid of Orleans burnt 1431
Murder of Gloucester 1447
———— of Suffolk 1450
Jack Cade's rebellion 1450
Battle of St. Albans, May 22 1455
Duke of York claims the crown 1458
Battle of Wakefield, December 30 . . . 1460
Duke of York made king 1461

EDWARD IV. began to reign 1461; reigned 22 years. Married Elizabeth Grey. Children: *Edward*, Richard, George, Elizabeth, and six other daughters.

Battle of Towton, March 29 1461
———— Hedgeley-moor, April 25 . . . } 1464
———— Hexham, May 15 . . . . . . }
———— Barnet, April 14 . . . . . . } 1471
———— Tewkesbury, May 4 . . . . . }
Death of Clarence 1478

EDWARD V. began to reign 1483; reigned 2 months.

RICHARD III. began to reign 1483; reigned 2 years. Married lady Anne Neville. One child: Edward.

Murder of the princes 1483
Battle of Bosworth, August 22 1485

HOUSE OF TUDOR.

HENRY VII. began to reign 1485; reigned 24 years. Married Elizabeth of York. Children: Arthur, *Henry*, Margaret, Mary.

Battle of Stoke, June 16 1487
Perkin Warbeck 1492
His execution 1498
Death of prince Arthur 1502

HENRY VIII. began to reign 1509; reigned 38 years. Married, 1. Catherine of Aragon; 2. Anne Boleyn; 3. Jane Seymour; 4. Anne of Cleves; 5. Catherine Howard; 6. Catherine Parr. Children: *Mary, Elizabeth, Edward.*

 Battle of Spurs, August 16 ⎫
 ―― of Flodden, September 9 ⎬ 1513
 Field of the Cloth of Gold 1520
 Origin of Henry's divorce 1527
 Death of Wolsey 1530
 Marriage of Anne Boleyn 1532
 Execution of More and Fisher 1535
 ―――― of Anne Boleyn 1536
 Suppression of Monasteries 1538
 Execution of Cromwell 1540
 ―――― of Catherine Howard 1541

EDWARD VI. began to reign 1547; reigned 6 years.
 Execution of Lord Seymour 1549
 ―――― of Somerset 1552

MARY began to reign 1553; reigned 5 years. Married Philip of Spain. No issue.
 Execution of lady Jane Grey . . . . . ⎫
 Queen's marriage . . . . ⎬ 1554
 Burning of the bishops 1555
 ―――― of Cranmer 1556
 Taking of Calais 1558

ELIZABETH began to reign 1558; reigned 44 years.
 Return of the queen of Scots 1561
 Her marriage with Darnley 1565
 Murder of Rizzio 1566
 ―――― of Darnley 1567
 Mary's flight into England 1568
 Execution of Norfolk . . . . ⎫
 Massacre of St. Bartholomew . . . . . ⎬ 1572
 Death of Sir P. Sidney 1586
 Execution of queen of Scots 1587
 The Spanish Armada 1588
 Taking of Cadiz 1596
 Execution of Essex 1601

HOUSE OF STUART.—Part I.

James I. began to reign 1603; reigned 22 years. Married Anne of Denmark. Children: Henry, *Charles*, Elizabeth, and two who died infants.

Gunpowder Plot	1605
Fall of Somerset	1615
Execution of Sir W. Raleigh	1617
Prince's expedition to Spain	1623

Charles I. began to reign 1623; reigned 25 years. Married Henrietta Maria of France. Children: *Charles, James*, William, Mary, Elizabeth, Henrietta.

Buckingham's expedition to Rochelle	1627
Murder of Buckingham	1628
Ship-money	1636
War with the Scots	1638
Long Parliament	1640
Trial of Strafford	}1641
Irish Rebellion, October 23	
Commencement of Civil War	}1642
Battle of Edgehill, October 23	
Death of Hampden	}1643
Battle of Newbury, September 20	
Battle of Marston-moor, July 2	}1644
—— of Newbury, October 27	
Execution of Laud	}1645
Battle of Naseby, June 14	
Flight of Charles to the Scots	1646
King seized by the army	1647
Second civil war	1648
Trial and execution of the king	1649

Commonwealth began 1649; lasted 11 years.

Death of Montrose	}1650
Battle of Dunbar, September 3	
—— of Worcester, September 3	1651
Cromwell made Protector	1653
Capture of Jamaica	1656
Death of Blake	1657
—— of Cromwell	1658
Restoration of Charles II.	1660

Charles II. began to reign 1660; reigned 25 years. Married Catharine of Portugal. No issue.

Execution of Sir Henry Vane	1662

KINGS AND EVENTS.

First Dutch war . . . .⎫ 1665
The Great Plague . . . .⎭
Fire of London 1666
Attempt of Blood 1671
Second Dutch war 1672
The Popish Plot 1678
Rye-house Plot 1683

JAMES II. began to reign 1685; reigned 3 years. Married, 1. Anne Hyde; 2. Mary of Modena. Children: 1. *Mary, Anne.* 2. Charles, and a daughter.

Monmouth's invasion 1685
Trial of the bishops . . . .⎫
Birth of prince of Wales . . . .⎬ 1688
The Revolution . . . .⎭

HOUSE OF STUART.—PART II.

WILLIAM III. AND MARY II. began to reign 1689; reigned 12 years. No issue.

Battle of Killicrankie, May 26 . . . . .⎫ 1689
Siege of Derry . . . .⎭
Battle of the Boyne, July 1 1690
——— of Aghrim, July 12 1691
——— of La Hogue, May 19 1692
Death of queen Mary 1694

ANNE began to reign 1701; reigned 13 years. Married prince George of Denmark. One child: William.

Battle of Blenheim, August 13 1704
——— Ramillies, May 23 1706
——— Almanza, April 25 1707
——— Oudenarde, July 11 1708
——— Malplaquet, September 11 . . . 1709
Union with Scotland 1707
Trial of Sacheverell 1709

HOUSE OF BRUNSWICK.

GEORGE I. began to reign 1714; reigned 13 years. Married Sophia of Zell. Children: *George*, Sophia.

Mar's rebellion 1715

GEORGE II. began to reign 1727; reigned 33 years. Married Caroline of Anspach. Children: Frederick, William, George, and five daughters.

War with Spain . . . . ⎱ 1739
Capture of Portobello . . . . ⎰
Anson's voyage 1740
Battle of Dettingen, June 26 1743
—— of Fontenoy, April 30 . . . . ⎱ 1745
Scottish rebellion . . . . ⎰
Clive's defence of Arcot 1751
Taking of Calcutta. 1756
Battle of Plassey, June 23 . . . . . . ⎱ 1757
Admiral Byng shot . . . . ⎰
Taking of Quebec, and death of Wolfe, September 13 1759

GEORGE III. began to reign 1760; reigned 59 years. Married Charlotte of Mecklenburg. Children: *George*, prince of Wales; Frederick, duke of York; *William*, duke of Clarence; Edward, duke of Kent; Ernest, duke of Cumberland; Augustus, duke of Sussex; Adolphus, duke of Cambridge; Charlotte, Augusta, Elizabeth, Mary, Sophia, Amelia.

Peace of Paris 1762
American War 1775
Surrender of Burgoyne 1777
Rodney's victory of Cape St. Vincent, Jan. 16 ⎱ 1780
Fate of André . . . . ⎰
Battle off the Dogger-bank, August 5 . . 1781
Rodney's victory over De Grasse, April 12 . ⎱ 1782
Siege of Gibraltar raised . . . . ⎰
Peace signed with America 1783
French War 1793
Lord Howe's victory, June 1 1794
Battle of Cape St. Vincent, February 14 . . ⎱
—— of Camperdown, October 11 . . . ⎬ 1797
Mutiny in the Fleet . . . . ⎰
Irish rebellion . . . . ⎱ 1798
Battle of the Nile, August 1 . . . . . ⎰
—— the Baltic, April 2 1801
—— Trafalgar, October 21 1805
—— Vimiero, August 21 1808
—— Corunna, January 16 . . . . . ⎱ 1809
—— Talavera, July 27 . . . . . . ⎰
—— Albuera, May 16 1811
—— Salamanca, June 22 1812
—— Vittoria, June 21 1813
—— Orthès, February 27 . . . . . ⎱ 1814
—— Toulouse, April 10 . . . . . . ⎰
—— Waterloo, June 18 1815

GEORGE IV. began to reign 1820; reigned 10 years. Married Caroline of Brunswick. One child: Charlotte.

  Catholic emancipation 1829

WILLIAM IV. began to reign 1830; reigned 7 years. Married Adelaide of Saxe Meiningen. No issue.

  Reform bill 1832

VICTORIA began to reign June 20, 1837. Married Albert of Saxe Coburg.

  Queen Victoria married, February 10 . . ⎫
  Princess-royal born, November 21 . . . ⎬ 1840

THE END.

CPSIA information can be obtained
at www.ICGtesting.com
Printed in the USA
LVHW051053270821
696246LV00001B/11